A NAOMI SCHNEIDER BOOK

Highlighting the lives and experiences of marginalized communities, the select titles of this imprint draw from sociology, anthropology, law, and history, as well as from the traditions of journalism and advocacy, to reassess mainstream history and promote unconventional thinking about contemporary social and political issues. Their authors share the passion, commitment, and creativity of Executive Editor Naomi Schneider.

The Way Out

The Way Out

JUSTICE IN THE QUEER
SEARCH FOR REFUGE

Rebecca Buxton
and Samuel Ritholtz

UNIVERSITY OF CALIFORNIA PRESS

University of California Press
Oakland, California

© 2026 by Samuel Ritholtz and Rebecca Buxton

Cataloging-in-Publication data is on file at the Library of Congress.

ISBN 978-0-520-39175-8 (cloth)
ISBN 978-0-520-39176-5 (pbk.)
ISBN 978- 0-520-39177-2(ebook)

GPSR Authorized Representative: Easy Access System Europe,
Mustamäe tee 50, 10621 Tallinn, Estonia, gpsr.requests@easproject.com

35   34   33   32   31   30   29   28   27   26
10   9   8   7   6   5   4   3   2   1

We dedicate this book to every queer and trans person who has left home in search of refuge. And to those who will have to leave soon.

For those we have lost in the process,
for Nawar Jiménez,

may their memories be a revolution.

Contents

Preface   ix

Introduction   1

1. Home   22

2. Persecution   42

3. Flight   62

4. Assessment   79

5. Containment   87

6. Reunion   104

7. Sanctuary   121

Conclusion   136

Acknowledgments   145

About the Cover   147

Notes   149

Works Cited   199

Index   231

Preface

This book offers a new way of thinking about the search for refuge. It does so by centering the lives of queer and trans people seeking safety across the world. But it also brings together different ways of thinking about what justice might require for the global displaced.

These different ways of thinking reflect the respective expertise of the manuscript's authors. Rebecca, a political philosopher, has written extensively about the duties owed to refugee populations. Samuel, a scholar of theoretical and empirical politics, has studied LGBTIQ experiences of conflict, crisis, and displacement in Colombia. Together, we share a belief in the central role of theory in the pursuit of justice. By taking the limitations of our current ways of thinking seriously, it becomes possible to articulate new claims about how the world could be better.

A book written by two people together will always involve a kind of encounter, and the work that follows is no different. We are pulled in different directions—one of us towards abstraction and questions of justice and the other towards understanding what the real world can tell us about violence and exclusion. As we learned through writing this book, we require *both* approaches to properly understand the predicament of displacement and the search for sanctuary. We cannot understand what justice requires without attending to the lives of displaced people and the challenges they pose to our abstract thinking. But we also cannot see the larger failures and injustices of the refugee protection regime without considering what these lives tell us about something bigger.

The political theory and philosophy of refuge often take place without paying attention to the lives and experiences of displaced people. Scholars have focused instead on abstract debates about freedom of movement, the state's right to exclude outsiders, or idealized accounts of justice for refugees. But, as this book hopes to show, the political theory of refuge has much to learn from turning back to the "real world," such that this act of shifting our attention can show a new set of problems, debates, and paths forward.

The ever-growing empirical literature on queer and trans displacement has meticulously documented the experiences of these populations on the move, as they seek asylum and in their new host states. The scholarship is notable in its breadth, covering everything from the ways that the existing global refugee regime fails these populations to how people resist these countervailing forces. In this research, scholars have revealed the tensions, contradictions, and surprises that define queer and trans experience. They speak the language of injustice with specificity and magnify the voices of those on the move. Scholars who focus on the real world are often, perhaps rightly, skeptical of what the abstract debates of political theory can achieve. But we cannot have a larger account of the requirements of justice without them.

As coauthors, Rebecca with a mind for political philosophy and Samuel with a mind for empirical politics, we build on the strengths of our respective disciplines to substantiate the claims for recognition and justice that undergird a new approach to refuge for the queer and trans displaced.

This book therefore hopes to speak to many people all at once—academics, policymakers, lawyers, activists, and the broader public—in dialogue with displaced people themselves. This breadth is important, in part, because of what we must learn from one another—but more importantly, what we all must learn from the lives of people who are forced to flee their land and seek refuge elsewhere.

We write this preface in a period of great disquiet. But in this moment, perhaps more so than any other, the efforts of the LGBTIQ displaced to organize for their rights around the world can teach us what it means to turn towards justice. As Hannah Arendt reminds us:

> Even in the darkest of times we have the right to expect some illumination, and that such illumination may well come less from theories and concepts than from the uncertain, flickering, and often weak light that some men and women, in their lives and their works, will kindle under almost all circumstances and shed over the time span that was given them on earth. . . . Eyes so used to darkness as ours will hardly be able to tell whether their light was the light of a candle or that of a blazing sun.[1]

United Kingdom, 2025

Introduction

The hearing was set to begin, and I (Samuel) was calling in from far away.[1] My computer screen turned on, and I found myself hovering over a traditional courtroom scene in the United States. The claimant, Darío, a young gay man from Colombia, sat with his lawyer at the respondent table. Darío fled Colombia after being targeted, in multiple acts of homophobic violence, by a relative of his former boyfriend in different cities around the country. His numerous attempts to report these acts of violence to the police were dismissed and followed by reprisals.

Across from Darío was the judge's bench. The judge was new to the asylum courts and appeared eager to make his mark. But there was an additional complication: located on the United States' Southern border, this court district was overwhelmed with asylum cases and had a reputation for approaching such cases with skepticism.

Once logged in, the judge, working through my qualifications and assessing the extent of my expertise, addressed me almost immediately. I was used to this dance of sorts. As a scholar of violence against queer and trans people perpetuated during the Colombian internal armed conflict, I often participate in asylum cases for queer and trans Colombians seeking safety abroad. In these hearings, I am asked to put individual acts of homophobic and transphobic violence in a broader context and articulate how these acts might demonstrate a "well-founded fear of persecution," which is central to the determination of refugee status.

The judge's voice was sharp and deliberate, each word carefully weighed. He was doubtful yet engaged. After accepting me as an expert witness to the court, the judge turned to the case. "This individual," he began, peering down at the case file, "lived in Colombia for the first thirty years of his life. In that time, he had same-sex relationships and seemed to be thriving until the incident in question. Help me understand how you reconcile that with your claim that LGBTIQ people in Colombia are uniquely vulnerable to violence."

The question seemed laced with the skepticism of someone faced with an apparent contradiction. I responded, "Your Honor, my claim relates precisely to this point about vulnerability. Life can seem stable, even safe, for an LGBTIQ person in Colombia—until it isn't. What this case demonstrates is that safety for queer individuals in Colombia is conditional and precarious. The claimant's years of relative calm do not erase the fact that, when violence struck, the state failed him."

The judge countered, "But Colombia has advanced the rights of LGBTIQ people—marriage equality, anti-discrimination laws, the claimant even went to Pride parades in Bogotá. How do you square that with your claims of state acquiescence to violence?"

My response came from the years of research I have done in the country, during which time I saw the limits and hopes of inclusion at both the local and national levels, as well as in rural and urban society. When I had first started researching in Colombia in the wake of the 2016 peace deal, the steady march toward progress at the national level was just beginning to be challenged by growing "anti–gender ideology" movements. Eight years later, progress was still being made, but it was haphazard and retreating in many places. I replied: "Your Honor, those laws and public celebrations are real, but to many, they represent more a promise than a reality. Many rights on paper have not translated into protection in practice. When this claimant sought help from the police after being attacked, they dismissed him, even mocked him. These moments are not exceptions; they are part of a broader pattern. The claimant's queer identity placed him in a space where state recognition of his rights did not extend to state protection of his life."

The judge scribbled a note and looked up again. "But if the state is not actively persecuting him—it's not like this violence is sanctioned—how can I accept that this qualifies as asylum-worthy?"

I nodded, prepared for this line of questioning. "The absence of active persecution does not absolve the state of responsibility. It's not that the state participates in this violence, but it is either unable or unwilling to prevent it. The refusal to act effectively, to adequately protect, is just as telling. It's about the relationship between vulnerability and exposure. For queer Colombians, life can feel like balancing on a knife's edge. Things are fine—until they are not. And when they fall apart, as they did for the claimant, the institutional response reveals the limits of their safety. This isn't a failure of the state to act in an isolated case; it's a systemic pattern that renders LGBTIQ people unprotected. It is a vulnerability to violence and its effects."

With that, I was thanked; my participation in the case was over. It was not until a few weeks later that I learned that the applicant received asylum. In that time, and in conversation with Rebecca, I realized that this exchange was not just about one person's asylum claim; it was about framing displacement itself in ways that existing paradigms fail to capture. It was about recognizing the particularities of queer and trans lives, lives often rendered invisible in legal and academic frameworks that treat vulnerability and violence as static concepts.

Samuel's encounter with the asylum judge serves as our entry point for this book, as it compels us to grapple with what justice for queer and trans people seeking refuge means in theory and how it might be realized in practice. Darío's case underscores a central theme explored throughout the book: despite strides in legal recognition and acceptance, LGBTIQ people worldwide continue to endure profound violence and discrimination, which upends their lives and drives multiple cycles of displacement. By centering the experiences of the queer and trans displaced, we can illuminate the complexities and contradictions of seeking sanctuary in a persistently exclusionary global refugee regime. And we might also see how to change it for the better.

Throughout history, the queer and trans displaced have been excluded from seeking refuge. In 1981, The Netherlands became the first country to recognize sexual orientation as a grounds for international protection.[2] In 1990, Fidel Armando Toboso-Alfonso was the first gay man in the United States to successfully fight deportation because of the grave danger he would face if returned to his home country of Cuba.[3] It was not until 1994 that the attorney general of the United States issued an order that would allow homosexual men to seek asylum if they were persecuted *because of their sexuality*.[4] The United States later recognized homosexual women and transgender people as eligible for asylum because of their sexual orientation and gender identity, respectively, in 1997 and 2000.[5] Elsewhere in the established "host" nations of the anglophone world, Australia and Canada first permitted LGBTIQ asylum applicants in 1991, with New Zealand following in 1995 and South Africa in 1998.[6] The United Kingdom only officially followed suit in 1999.[7]

The refugee regime has shifted under our feet. Over the last thirty years, the international system of extending protection to noncitizens by offering asylum has shown its capacity to expand. Progress for LGBTIQ refugees at the end of the twentieth century was slow, with very few states offering formal protection. This is perhaps unsurprising, as queer and trans people are still fighting a long history of exclusion and unfreedom. In many countries, LGBTIQ people were actively excluded at the border through legislation that prevented those displaying "psychopathic personality" and "sexual deviance" from moving across legal boundaries.[8] Even when homosexuality was no longer considered a mental illness, immigration authorities continued to actively exclude those who were openly gay.[9]

Today, the world for LGBTIQ asylum seekers and refugees looks somewhat different. At least thirty-seven states explicitly accept LGBTIQ refugees on the basis of sexual orientation or gender identity.[10] Some states now even have specific pathways to assist LGBTIQ people on the move, as well as providing special integration networks, housing, and support.[11] This shift occurred in many places without the passage of any new domestic laws or international treaties. Instead, courts and governments *queered* their interpretations of existing law in the service of inclusion.[12] Despite little change in the legal background of the refugee regime, queer and trans people are now included more than ever in its history. And so, things have certainly improved for the queer and trans displaced. LGBTIQ people who face persecution because of their sexual orientation or gender identity now qualify for asylum, at least in principle. Without these expansions in our thinking about who deserves asylum, the queer and trans displaced would have remained trapped outside the boundaries of international protection.

Even with this international protection, LGBTIQ refugees and asylum seekers—most of them outside these thirty-seven states—still face hostile institutions and social practices throughout their experience of displacement. Beyond the question of legal admission, much of the LGBTIQ refugee's journey in search of international protection remains exclusionary and dangerous. Homophobia and transphobia (homo/transphobia) define the experiences of the LGBTIQ displaced, with this related violence often coming from multiple sources, from border guards to family members to host communities. The pervasiveness and persistence of this prejudice drives multiple cycles of displacement, as LGBTIQ people are uprooted and forced to search for safety elsewhere. As such, this piecemeal increased legal recognition is only part of the equation. Most policies and practices at the international, national, and local levels still fail to address the complex harms that drive queer and trans displacement, well before they can even seek admission to the legal refugee regime.[13] So, while the framework for international protection has expanded somewhat, given that there is now the possibility in some states to apply for asylum on the grounds of sexual orientation and gender identity, the system of global refugee protection remains deeply exclusionary.

Unfortunately, these limited gains have never felt more fragile. In an era of growing authoritarianism and illiberalism, both the rights of migrants and LGBTIQ people are the targets of right-wing populist movements. In September 2023, the then–home secretary for the United Kingdom, Suella Braverman, gave a speech to the American Enterprise Institute. She announced that the 1951 Geneva Convention on Refugees, created in the aftermath of the Second World War, was no longer fit for purpose. Now, she argued, we live in another reality. World leaders, she continued, "will not be able to sustain an asylum system if, in effect, *simply being gay, or a woman,* and fearful of discrimination in your country of origin, is sufficient to qualify for protection."[14] Her words were quickly rebuked by refugee activists, NGOs, and international organizations throughout the world, who pointed out that countless LGBTIQ people and women face extreme forms of harm, violence, and criminalization. Nevertheless, the right wing of the

British Conservative Party supported her resoundingly. Similarly, in the 2024 American presidential election, Republicans spent over $200 million on anti-trans TV advertisements, some of which took aim at Kamala Harris for supporting gender-affirming care for people in immigration detention, even though this medical access policy existed for undocumented people in federal prisons under the first Trump presidency.[15] One advert ended with the line "Kamala is for they/them. President Trump is for you."

While we may have felt that we were participating in the all-too-slow march of progress, many people believe that our systems have become *too inclusive* of queer and trans people across the world. This slow march has now come to an abrupt halt, with President Trump de facto ending the right to seek asylum or resettlement in the United States.[16] The Trump administration is also actively deporting many LGBTIQ asylum seekers under the guise that they are violent criminals.[17]

In one case, Andry José Hernández Romero, a gay Venezuelan man seeking asylum in the United States, was detained after crossing the Southern border for a prearranged asylum appointment in August 2024.[18] After demonstrating a credible fear of persecution in this initial interview, he was detained to await the next part of the asylum process. But in March 2025, with no warning, Andry was forcibly removed to a maximum-security megaprison in El Salvador known as the Terrorism Confinement Center.[19] His own lawyers were only made aware that he had been deported at the very removal hearing that was meant to decide whether he had grounds to remain in the US.[20] The government alleged that his crown tattoos (which said "mom" and "dad" and were reflective of a religious custom in his hometown of Capacho, Venezuela) "proved" that he was a gang member. No one heard from Andry while he was in detention. He was effectively disappeared. The only report from El Salvador that appeared to confirm that Andry was alive, came from a photojournalist who allegedly heard a young man say, "I'm not a gang member. I'm gay. I'm a stylist." The photojournalist added that this young man then "cried out for his mother, was slapped and had his head shaved."[21]

After 125 days without any contact and amidst concerns for his life, Andry was released from prison and deported back to Venezuela, the very place from which he fled persecution. In interviews since his release, he has alleged that he was physically and sexually abused by guards in El Salvador. He said to one interviewer, "It was an encounter with torture and death."[22] Remarking on the dismantling of US asylum policy during Trump's second term, Steve Roth, Executive Director of the Organization for Refuge, Asylum and Migration (ORAM) said "LGBTQI+ refugees are being abandoned to violence, detention, even death—simply for being who they are. This isn't just a policy failure. It's a moral collapse."[23]

LGBTIQ displaced people sit at the intersection of a double backlash, against migration on the one hand and against the rights of queer and trans people on the other.

First, these concerns about "over-inclusion" exist amidst an increasingly violent system of border management. Despite living in an age of mass movement fueled by war, climate change, and political oppression, displaced people face extreme barriers to their mobility. Thousands die attempting to flee their homes, cross international borders, and survive in detention centers—or even after they have secured refuge.[24] Although most displaced people remain within the Global South, powerful states in the North have driven a new wave of attacks against the rights of refugees, with Australia, the European Union, the United Kingdom, and the United States (among others) pursuing violent deportation and externalization regimes.[25] These states maintain that asylum seekers should enter "legally" while at the same time quietly shutting down the legal pathways almost completely, forcing them to use irregular routes or apply from hostile locations in third countries. Most states continue to cut back their offers of resettlement and financial assistance, making smaller and smaller promises each year or, in the case of the United States, declaring that refugee resettlement is contrary to the interests of American citizens. The number of individuals offered resettlement annually has rarely reached above one percent of the total number of the global displaced population.[26]

When asylum seekers do manage to enter the territories of powerful states in the Global North, they may face hostile local populations and violent unrest. In the summer of 2024, many cities in the United Kingdom saw antimigrant rioters attack hotels housing asylum seekers, with some attempting to set them on fire. Since 2025, scores of asylum seekers in the US have been swept up in Immigration and Customs Enforcement (ICE) raids and deported without due consideration of their asylum claims, with hundreds sent to the same maximum-security prison in El Salvador as Andry. The "prosperous West" is not, then, a mythical haven for the displaced. And so, the experience of LGBTIQ refugees sits within this hostile broader environment of border management.

Second, a newly mobilized wave of anti-queer and anti-trans politics is regaining popularity across the world. This social conservativism seeks to roll back the freshly won rights of queer and trans people, seeing their entitlements as having gone "too far."[27] Phillip Ayoub and Kristina Stoeckl have documented the growing interconnectedness and transnational nature of these movements, with religious-nationalist civil society organizations and conservative governments forming globally networked resistances to the rights of LGBTIQ people.[28] In Europe, these policies have proven popular with electorates, who seem open to the curtailing of the rights of LGBTIQ people as a "solution" to contemporary disorder. As one example, the far-right Giorgia Meloni government in Italy campaigned on the promise to remove the nongenetic parent from the birth certificate of the children of same-sex couples. The consequences of such actions are grave, for if only the nongenetic parent holds Italian citizenship, these children become stateless in their native country.[29]

This backsliding has dovetailed with rising authoritarian movements, whose leaders have recognized the efficacy of scapegoating queer and trans people to consolidate political power. In his speech announcing the 2022 invasion of Ukraine, Vladimir Putin cited the need to protect "traditional values" in Russia as a justification for the aggressive action, thereby framing LGBTIQ people as a direct threat to the Russian State.[30] As documented by the United Nations Independent Expert on Sexual Orientation and Gender Identity, these machinated efforts to allegedly protect "traditional values" are unfortunately a global phenomenon.[31] These frames are used to justify repressive policies against LGBTIQ populations, as evidenced through the passage of laws banning pride marches, "homosexual propaganda," and same-sex relationships. Often, this scapegoating occurs during crises and other forms of political breakdown, allowing leaders to diffuse blame and deflect attention from their own shortcomings.

While much of this mobilization has come from the political right, there has been growing recognition of a socially conservative left taking hold in the Americas, which espouses progressive economic ideals but does not advocate LGBTIQ-inclusive social policy.[32] The rise of this socially conservative left has been seen as a response to the powerful anti-rights movements in the region, who are formed by a unique coalition of Catholic and Evangelical advocacy groups that have been so effective in their organizing that they sunk the 2016 Colombian peace accord plebiscite on the basis of the accord's proposed LGBTIQ (and broader gender) inclusion.[33] As such, while key parts of global society seem to be growing in tolerance to LGBTIQ people and our institutions appear more inclusive than ever before, there remains widespread social unease with our presence. Hate crimes against trans people in the United Kingdom increased by 186 percent between 2018 and 2023, with several organizations arguing that the country is becoming more prejudiced rather than less.[34]

And so, we are being pulled in different directions. In one sense, the story of LGBTIQ asylum is surely one of progress; from a global refugee regime that was explicitly exclusionary to one that is now far more inclusive. But in another, backlash against both migrants and LGBTIQ people across the world fundamentally undermines many established practices of inclusion, revealing the stakes of what might be lost and what might never be gained. It is thus more important than ever to cement the progress that has been made. Perhaps, then, this backlash also reveals the possibility of a new kind of world, one that we can imagine for ourselves. It is time to secure our position, but it is also time to build upon it.

The principal aim of this book is to shift our understanding of the queer search for refuge, moving from a model that overly focuses on states and political institutions to one that also includes social relations and structural forces. The need for this shift is made evident by the focus on the experiences of the queer and trans displaced themselves. This is not to ignore states as a central and dominant feature of our political lives, but instead to highlight the importance of other, sometimes more subtle, forces that drive displacement and its connected injustices. This focus highlights how the harms that undergird displacement, and particularly persecution as the central theoretical pillar of the refugee regime, are *relational* phenomena that are therefore *socially situated, structurally (re)produced*, and *highly mobile*. In other words, the harms that the queer and trans displaced flee often follow them across borders throughout their search for refuge, driving multiple cycles of displacement and complicating the meaning of protection. Relational harms fueled by homo/transphobia follow the displaced throughout their journey—often beginning in the home, rupturing their lives through persecution, immobilizing them during flight, and compounding the suffering of containment. In each of these contexts, the harms faced by the queer and trans displaced transform to reflect their social and political reality. In conceptualizing the harms that drive LGBTIQ displacement and deny queer and trans people protection as relational, more adept solutions can be considered. This might include allowing the displaced to resettle with their chosen family or enabling new communities of solidarity to blossom after asylum has been secured.

In what follows, we identify the ways that the standard conceptualizations of displacement, or hegemonic understandings of displacement tied to an imagined cisgender, heterosexual refugee, can obscure dynamics experienced by the queer and trans displaced. We build on existing social, political, and queer theory to propose more inclusive ways of conceptualizing displacement. If the global refugee regime is already willing to expand its conception of displacement by accepting that LGBTIQ refugees can qualify for asylum (despite no formal change in international law), then it should also seek an account of justice that incorporates and redresses the specific harms experienced by queer and trans people during displacement. Doing so, we argue, would not only make the asylum system more inclusive for LGBTIQ people, but it would also lead to a more just protection regime for everyone.

Each chapter of this book focuses on a different stage in the process of seeking sanctuary. We trace an imagined displacement journey starting with *home* and continuing through *persecution, flight, assessment, containment, reunion,* and *sanctuary.* Of course, most queer and trans people do not experience displacement in such a linear fashion, instead undergoing multiple cycles of displacement. But we adopt this staged approach in order to focus our insights and build theory from the lives of the LGBTIQ displaced themselves. The book therefore draws heavily on both recent work in the study of queer and trans displacement and on the lives of queer and trans migrants and activists around the world. Our contribution is to offer a normative reconstruction of this experience and advocacy to highlight the potential for a more just system of protection. Importantly, we do not advocate for piecemeal changes that might make the institutions of refugee protection more minimally inclusive. Instead, by focusing on the experiences of LGBTIQ refugees and the relational dynamics of harm across different contexts, we hope to throw into question many of the organizing principles of the global refugee regime.

In this spirit of interrogation, we position this text in dialogue with the scholarship of critical refugee studies, which has sought to redefine the field by centering refugees as producers of knowledge. In challenging reductive narratives that portray refugees as passive subjects of humanitarian aid, scholars of critical refugee studies have emphasized interdisciplinary approaches, intersectionality, and the structural forces that shape displacement.[35] This book builds upon the experiences of LGBTIQ refugees to theorize the limitations in our existing conceptualization of displacement, as well as to identify potential forms of redress made evident by their thoughts, actions, and articulations. This work furthers the ambitions of critical refugee studies to integrate theory and policy to advocate for a justice-oriented outcome for the global displaced.

This is a work of political theory that develops insight from the experiences of LGBTIQ people in search of refuge to explore the stakes of inclusion in displacement justice. By turning our theoretical attention to the queer and trans displaced, we aim to reveal, rearticulate, and reimagine different aspects of the global border regime. First, attending to the lives of displaced populations can straightforwardly reveal cracks and imperfections within global migration governance. These might be small and practical, still, they are fundamental. In this sense, the revelations offered by looking to queer experience can teach us something important about the failures of the refugee protection regime as a whole. However, queer experience cannot simply be lifted and transmuted onto different, already existing theoretical disputes. Instead, queer experience helps to rearticulate core concepts within our understanding of borders, territory, and mobility. Often this rearticulation is offered by queer subjects themselves in their attempts to overcome obstructions within the framework of international protection. For instance, in the first chapter, we will see that the concept of home shifts from an origin to a destination through which the queer displaced seek new forms of belonging and community. This rearticulation allows us to push against a path that might simply advocate for queer assimilation into an otherwise hetero-normative regime.

Queer theorists have often highlighted that marginalization can induce suffering, but it can also be a provocation for a new way of imagining freedom, particularly when the oppressed refuse to be absorbed into the world as it is structured. As Rahul Rao puts it, there is always the possibility that "denial might be transmuted into refusal."[36] These processes of revealing and rearticulating help us to reimagine how the international protection regime might be organized for the future. This is not to claim that the future is some far-off promised land, easily separable from either the past or the present. Instead, the future affects our understanding of the past, and the past constrains the practice of liberatory imagination. In our attempt to offer some path forward for the global refugee regime, we hope, at points, to imagine what the world might look like if it were to respond to the calls of the queer and trans displaced and the social structures of exclusion that they face.

Throughout this book, we draw on the analytical approach of queering. But what exactly does it mean *to queer*? In practice, the term is used often to imply the inclusion of a queer perspective, but queer theorists argue that such a definition is insufficient, as it fails to properly recognize the radical potential of queering.[37] Browne and Nash note that "to queer" something is to "challenge the normative social ordering of identities and subjectivi-ties along the heterosexual/homosexual binary as well as the privileging of heterosexuality as 'natural' and homosexuality as its deviant and abhorrent 'other.'"[38] Indeed, many queer theorists intend to identify, challenge, and disturb latent forms of oppression in modern society. In her work, Eve Ko-sofsky Sedgwick identifies queering as a form of deconstruction that seeks to identify "sites that are peculiarly densely charged with lasting potentials for powerful manipulation."[39]

In this manner, queering becomes a form of inquiry that takes on the structures of sexuality and gender as they loom large in society. But an account of justice for the queer and trans displaced—a queering rather of the standard considerations of the rights and obligations owed to this population—cannot just focus on structures of sexuality and gen-der. It must consider the various intersections of their identity that de-fine their experience.[40] We thus adopt Kimberlé Crenshaw's definition of intersectionality as "a lens through which you can see where power comes and collides, where it interlocks and intersects,"[41] and take further inspiration from Patricia Hill Collins's conceptualization of oppression as multidimensional.[42] Further, as articulated by Momin Rahman, we recognize the power of "queer theory ... [to] help us to think about these issues of researching intersectionality precisely because it is focused on the uncertainties of identity categories.[43]

In this book, we queer different aspects of the global refugee regime, as we follow the imagined journey of the queer search for refuge. In doing so, we seek to challenge structural cisheteronormative values that continuously undermine the rights and safety of the queer and trans displaced. The refugee regime is ripe for this form of interrogation: binaries and hard distinctions persist between subjects and how they are categorized (refugee/economic migrant, criminal/vulnerable, Global South/Global North). In leaning into the disruption of categories, then, this approach allows us to not only apply the lens of LGBTIQ inclusion but also to push aside these categorizations as aspects of a contingent legal order.[44] They are chosen and can be chosen anew and for the better.

This text is a labor of love for our community. Though we have not experienced anything close to what those in the stories that line our pages have, we recognize the wisdom in their words and the theory in their actions. We follow a prominent framing of the famed global grassroots movement against AIDS, ACT UP: When you lead with action, the theory comes naturally.[45] Thus, through this approach, we take the lives of queer and trans displaced people as our starting point and build from their interventions and experiences. We begin each chapter with the experience of an individual brave enough to share their story in the public sphere, not to say that their experience is universal but to learn about how their own queer search for refuge can be read as their version of what Saidiya Hartman calls a "revolution in a minor key."[46] These stories of survival, new futures, and new imaginaries demonstrate the power of queer thought and action.

We selected these opening anecdotes with the goal of identifying a range of experiences that illuminate the limits of our current understanding of displacement. These stories at the intersection of sexual orientation, gender identity, and forced migration offer a foundation for theorizing the queer search for refuge as a phenomenon best understood through the experience of the LGBTIQ displaced.[47] We did not seek "representative-ness" in our cases, as this would assume a universality of experience that we do not believe exists. LGBTIQ people are not a homogenous group, and any discussion of the queer and trans displaced must take seriously the varying effects of different policies and practices, as well as intersectional forms of oppression. For discussions of the asylum regime, this is even more important, as most of those displaced across the world are racialized as people of color. LGBTIQ refugees therefore face compounded forms of injustice.

We must also recognize the imbalances in knowledge production as it relates to different groups within the broader community. Regrettably, there is less research and fewer success stories relating to lesbian, bisexual, and queer (LBQ) women as well as nonbinary and intersex individuals.[48] We attend to this heterogeneity throughout the book and avoid making sweeping statements about the experiences of *all* queer and trans displaced people. We aim to highlight the experiences of different sets of LGBTIQ displaced people, as well as identify places in which their experiences diverge: there are moments when those of varying gender identities and sexual orientations will encounter the refugee regime in different ways. Therefore, we incorporate cases that challenge our understanding by presenting some typical and some extreme experiences that push the boundaries of existing frameworks and encourage critical reflection on the assumptions underpinning the global refugee regime.[49] Our approach incorporates purposeful variability by selecting cases across diverse contexts—in relation to both geographic location and intersectional identities—ensuring an exploration of patterns that can inform more inclusive theories of displacement justice.[50] Together, these cases not only highlight gaps in existing conceptualizations but also serve as fertile ground for theorizing transformative approaches to protecting displaced LGBTIQ individuals.

The method of queering therefore shares important features of intersectional feminist and decolonial analysis, which challenge the aftershocks and realities of a global system constructed by imperialism and patriarchy.[51] Any criticism of the refugee regime that fails to take account of its colonial history would be flawed.[52] The history of the Geneva Convention itself is deeply intertwined with the European colonial project, and the contemporary approach to global movement management still depends on an imperial logic of who "deserves" to be saved.[53] Throughout the book we therefore not only highlight the exclusion of queer and trans people on the move, but all those who face injustices while seeking protection and sanctuary.

Part of this book's novel approach results from our effort to bring queer perspectives and normative political theory into conversation. There is an ever-growing literature on the ethics of migration.[54] At the same time, there is a booming literature on queer and trans displacement, with many scholars detailing the struggles, triumphs, and injustices of LGBTIQ inclusion in the global refugee regime. Taking both forms of theorization into account, we can analyze the practices of the queer and trans displaced to identify the source of injustice and then envision a more just outcome for all. We hope this book shows that a queer perspective is not just an important addition to this debate but is in fact necessary for its completion.

A NOTE ON TERMINOLOGY

Throughout this book, we use both "queer and trans" as well as "LGBTIQ" (lesbian, gay, bisexual, trans, intersex, and queer) to describe people with diverse sexual orientations, gender identities, and sex characteristics. Sometimes, when used in a quote, the acronym might appear in a different order or with a "+" (which is an inclusive effort to represent specific identities that may fall within the acronym that are not directly mentioned). Out of respect for the authors, we do not modify their usage.

We take *cishetero* to be the opposite of queer and trans. *Cis* is short for cisgender, when one's gender identity matches the gender assigned at birth. *Hetero* is short for heterosexual, when one is attracted to someone of the opposite gender. *Cisheteronormativity* is a social system of power relations that constructs cishetero identity as the "norm," thereby subordinating queer and trans people.[55] Gender identity is understood, in line with the Yogyakarta Principles, to refer to "each person's deeply felt internal and individual experience of gender, which may or may not correspond with the sex assigned at birth, including the personal sense of the body (which may involve, if freely chosen, modification of bodily appearance or function by medical, surgical or other means) and other expressions of gender, including dress, speech, and mannerisms."[56] We are aware that the term queer comes with a certain set of political connotations that people may reject. For many years, the term queer was a pejorative, used as a slur against LGBTIQ people. But in the years since, the community has reclaimed the concept and rearticulated it as an inclusive phrase that avoids the silos of an ever-expanding acronym. Judith Butler finds that the "term 'queer' is a site of collective contestation, the point of departure for a set of historical reflections and futural imagining."[57] However, many people on the move that we will discuss do not think about themselves as queer or even LGBTIQ in terms of an identity category.[58] In line with broader practices, we use *queer* to be inclusive of trans people. We accept this trans-inclusive use of queer in most settings, especially as a verb, but when speaking of groups of people, we separate the two concepts in recognition of the work of trans studies scholars who have argued that the phenomenological associations of sexual orientation and gender identity differ.[59]

When we use the terms *LGBTIQ refugees* or *queer and trans refugees*, we might be referring to two different groups: individuals who are displaced *because of* their sexual orientation or gender identity or refugees who are displaced by other things (war, climate change, humanitarian crisis, political persecution) but are also LGBTIQ.[60] These groups face different challenges, but also at many times intersect in their experiences. Throughout the book, we have tried to make it clear when we are speaking only about LGBTIQ-related persecution and when we are speaking about the experiences of LGBTIQ displaced people more generally.

Within the ethics of migration literature, there is a well-established debate on "who counts" as a refugee.[61] This is something that we do not engage with in this book. Indeed, many of the dominant accounts of who qualifies for asylum would easily include LGBTIQ refugees.[62] In many cases, the harms, or physical and psychosocial injuries, faced by refugees and other people on the move intersect with one another, particularly when those harms are created by a violent border apparatus that does not care for such distinctions. Moreover, as postcolonial scholars have noted, these distinctions are often shaped by questions of who has a claim to equality, both moral and political, and whether particular subjects are viewed as deserving protection.[63] So, while focusing our analysis on those experiencing displacement, much of what we discuss will apply to a broader category of migrants or undocumented people. While not aiming to explicitly argue for a new understanding of refugeehood, we nevertheless do put pressure on the boundary points in this debate throughout the book.[64]

We also do not claim that LGBTIQ refugees are necessarily (by virtue of being LGBTIQ) the "worst off" or the "most harmed" by the refugee protection regime. As will become clear throughout the book, queer and trans refugees do suffer extreme harm, in ways that are often more serious than the harms that cishetero people on the move suffer. For instance, LGBTIQ people in detention are ninety-seven times more likely to be subject to abuse than their cishetero counterparts.[65] In some cases, however, they might be perceived as "better off," when, for example, they receive specific assistance and resettlement pathways to some states. Nevertheless, such discussions of prioritization often assume that LGBTIQ refugees are "innately" vulnerable. This is echoed in discussions of refugee women. As Heaven Crawley puts it, "Women are thus categorized as 'vulnerable' *a priori*, without real consideration of the structural and contextual causes of this vulnerability."[66] We therefore must not assume that LGBTIQ people are inherently vulnerable but instead that they are made vulnerable by the contexts and institutions within which they are situated. There may be cases where non-LGBTIQ people on the move are more impacted by certain policies. But this comparison—determining who is the "worst off"—is not intellectually nor politically worthwhile.

THE STRUCTURE OF THE BOOK

This book follows the imagined path of an LGBTIQ person seeking refuge. We recognize that most queer and trans people seeking safety do not experience displacement in such a linear fashion. Rather, as will become clear through our argument, harms persist throughout what we refer to as the queer search for refuge, causing itinerant stops and starts, temporary moments of safety, and multiple cycles of displacement. Still, we adopt this staged structure in order to highlight the normative stakes of certain moments throughout the displacement process. Furthermore, our argument on the relational nature of harm and its manifestation through the search for safety is not necessarily causal but, rather, dynamic. It is with the conceptualization produced by this argument that we can identify multiple sites of persecution, irrespective of the order of the stages of displacement, that a queer or trans person might face in their state of origin, their state of transit, and even in their state of asylum.

In chapter 1, we start at the beginning of the displacement journey: *home*. An unfortunate reality for the queer and trans displaced is that home is often the first locus of prejudice-based harm. Queer and trans refugees detail intrafamilial violence, including forced marriage, conversion therapy, and physical abuse. Here, we begin the project of showing the relational nature of harm by demonstrating that persecution often comes from the people who are closest to us. In turning our attention to the social environment more broadly, we begin to develop an account of relational harm that is not necessarily contingent on political and legal repression, such as criminalization, but rather on a set of homo/transphobic social relations that reinforce the dominant ideology of cisheternormativity. Building on queer and trans experiences of intrafamilial violence, we develop a queer theoretical intervention to reconceptualize home from an origin to a destination free from persecution.

In chapter 2, we turn to the concept of *persecution*, which is central to the institutions of international asylum. However, assumptions about what kinds of violence count as persecution still shape the exclusion of queer and trans refugees. This chapter argues that traditional applications of persecution fail to recognize the unique violence and prejudice faced by queer and trans refugees. We therefore outline the contours of the current legal definitions of persecution, showing how adjudicators often fail to consider specific forms of prejudice-based violence against LGBTIQ people. Here we extend our theory of relational harm to reconceptualize persecution, emphasizing its *socially situated* nature. Focusing on the case of Black LBQ women, we demonstrate how persecution relates to the individual's social position.

In chapter 3, we consider the harms that LGBTIQ displaced people face while in *flight*. Queer and trans refugees often speak of the violence they experience during their journey. Given the relational and social nature of anti-LGBTIQ violence, this harm can follow displaced people while they are on the move. This chapter outlines the concept of *induced immobility*, which occurs when displaced queer and trans people face constraints on their movement while attempting to seek protection as a result of both discrimination and structural conditions. Many of these conditions are put in place by the "refugee prevention regime," the Global North states and supranational political bodies working to limit migration flows. We build this account by focusing on three trans women who are trapped in Ukraine during the 2022 Russian invasion. For LGBTIQ refugees, mobility is constrained not only by border guards or facts of geography but also often by forms of social oppression and persecution. In adopting both group mobility and visibility as political acts, refugees are self-organizing to protect and provide for themselves. Queer-led organizations, like the Rainbow Railroad and the *Red Regional por la Movilidad Humana LGBTIQ+*, have recognized this agency and sought to facilitate it by operating safe houses around the world and enabling the movement of queer and trans refugees from hostile places.

In chapter 4, the halfway point of the book, we make a different kind of intervention relating to *assessment*. Much of the literature on LGBTIQ refugees focuses on the asylum interview as part of the refugee status determination (RSD) process. Many queer and trans asylum seekers face extreme barriers to accessing protection at this stage. They are often not believed about their sexuality or gender identities, with interview questions unsuccessfully relying on Westernized conceptions of homosexuality and coming out stories to render refugees' experiences intelligible. Building on the existing scholarship on the asylum interview and its many flaws, we confront the reader with the kind of interrogation that many LGBTIQ refugees face when they are interviewed for asylum. This chapter foregrounds the actual questions that queer and trans refugees have been asked when attempting to seek asylum to underscore how the state of asylum or transit—the supposed source of protection for displaced people—can also be a site of relational harm.

In chapter 5, we discuss two forms of *containment*: encampment and detention. In March 2021, two LGBTIQ refugees living in Kakuma camp suffered severe burns after being attacked by fellow camp residents. A month later, one of these individuals died from their injuries. These events have only amplified existing concerns about the safety of queer and trans people living in camps and reinforced the calls from the queer and trans displaced to have more agency in relation to their mobility. Similar conditions are faced in immigration detention. Human rights groups have shown that violent practices such as physical and sexual abuse, perpetrated by fellow detainees as well as prison guards, as well as solitary confinement, are routinely deployed against LGBTIQ people in detention centers. In the wake of these practices, advocates have started calling for an end to detention for queer and trans asylum seekers. Encampment and detention are two containment practices that, we argue, can be analyzed in similar ways. Containment policies compound the vulnerability of LGBTIQ people to relational harms because of the mobility restriction imposed by state policies. As a result, the state becomes complicit in new forms of harm (and persecution) experienced by this population. This argument, rather than offering justification for segregation or prioritization, helps to show why containment practices ought to be avoided altogether. In other words, it establishes a normative argument in favor of camp and detention abolition.

Chapter 6 focuses on the idea of the family in refugee protection, particularly through the right to *reunion*.[67] In October 2018, a group of migrants began their journey from San Pedro Sula, Honduras, to the Southern border of the United States. Among those walking the four-thousand-kilometer distance were eighty LGBTIQ migrants from across Central America. Included in this "rainbow caravan," as it came to be called, was a group of thirty trans women who presented themselves at the border as a unit. Rather than being treated as a group, these women were separated from one another and forced to seek asylum alone. We make the normative argument that queer and trans family units ought to qualify for refugee reunion and group status determination. We do so by considering the concept of queer and trans "chosen families," arguing that these queer rearticulations of kinship are functionally and morally comparable to cis-heteronormative conceptions of the family. This chapter thus presents a relational solution to relational harm. In incorporating these rearticulations of the family into reunion policy, we can begin to reimagine a social world free from the harms faced by the queer and trans displaced.

In the final substantive contribution of the book, chapter 7 considers the harms that persist after asylum has been offered in supposed *sanctuary*.[68] For LGBTIQ refugees, many of the relational harms they flee persist in the state of asylum. This chapter targets the dynamics of postasylum protection in current theorizations of refuge and the duties of the host state. We challenge the assumption that once a refugee receives protection in the Global North, their security is guaranteed. Given the prevalence of racism, xenophobia, and homophobia in the Global North, this protection is not secured upon admission. This chapter uses the case of an LGBTIQ asylum seeker in the United Kingdom to underscore the analytical weakness of this assumption; it argues that considering the experience of queer and trans refugees could lead to more inclusive and just policies in states of asylum. Taking the relational nature of harm seriously requires a conceptualization of sanctuary after asylum that accurately reflects the diverse experiences of the displaced and underscores the role of solidarity networks in advocating for both sanctuary and justice.

1 Home

Victor, a gay man from Nigeria, fled to the United Kingdom after experiencing various efforts to "change" his sexual orientation.[1] These attempts at conversion involved prayer with his mother, confession, starvation, exorcism, degrading treatment from religious leaders, threats of violence from schoolmates—anything his mother and community could do to "fix" him. With limited options for protection in a country that criminalizes homosexuality, Victor left home. Life in Nigeria had become untenable.

Unfortunately, Victor's story is not unique. Around the world, many queer and trans people experience attempts by their family and close relations to "correct" their sexuality, through violent practices of attempted "conversion," which can incorporate a range of abuses, including torture and rape.[2] These acts of violence are often branded "conversion therapy," a discredited practice that attempts to alter the sexual orientation or gender identity of its subject. Conversion therapy relies on a cisheteronormative ideology of "sexual brokenness," whereby heterosexuality and gender conformity are understood as the only "healthy" or "natural" options.[3] While there is no evidence that sexual orientation or gender identity can be changed by conversion therapy, it is a still popular practice and is often initiated by those closest to its victim.[4]

Despite the harms he experienced in conversion therapy and the resultant trauma and mental health struggles, Victor still loves his mother. With time and space to reflect in the United Kingdom after receiving asylum, Victor recognizes that these efforts at conversion began with the hope of "saving" him. The two of them now live in different countries. In an interview, he said, "We're still working on it. It's been very difficult, but one thing I know is that she did everything she did out of love."

Like Victor, many LGBTIQ people flee home because discrimination makes life unbearable. But Victor's statement demonstrates an important fact about the harms faced by many LGBTIQ people: they need not always come from hatred or a desire to injure. Here, a central tension of queer and trans displacement becomes clear: the prejudice, violence, and harm that often precede displacement can come from the people who love us the most. It can come from *home*. For the queer and trans displaced, home is often the first site of prejudice-based harm, which can include conversion therapy, forced marriage, and physical abuse.[5] The NGO, Rainbow Railroad, which helps queer and trans people to escape persecution in their countries of origin, has expressed grave concern for the "epidemic levels of family-based rejection and violence" that it has documented around the world.[6]

These private harms often occur in dialogue with more public forms of persecution. State repression and criminalization drive the displacement of queer and trans people globally. Currently, sixty-five countries criminalize same-sex relations and fourteen criminalize non-hegemonic gender expression.[7] In twelve of these countries, the penalty is death.[8] In contexts without criminalization, state repression can still exist through anti-LGBTIQ policies and rhetoric. These efforts are often framed in defense against "LGBTIQ propaganda" (particularly common in Central and Eastern Europe as well as Central Asia) and in support of "moral values" and the "family" (particularly common in the Americas and Western Europe). In these contexts, hostile rhetoric can lead to state-led crackdowns against LGBTIQ civil society organizations and activists and to intercommunal violence from the general population toward LGBTIQ people.[9]

These public harms are perhaps the drivers of queer and trans displacement that are most intelligible to the scholars, aid workers, lawyers, and judges who act as the adjudicators and enforcers of the international refugee protection regime. This is because in cases of criminalization and political repression there is obvious state-led targeting of the individual due to their sexual orientation and gender identity. Further, these practices generate many severe injuries: death, torture, arbitrary detention, and enforced disappearance are all practices associated with state-led repression and criminalization.[10]

But state repression and criminalization are only part of what drives LGBTIQ displacement.[11] As detailed in Victor's story, many harms are perpetrated by individuals in his social network: family members, religious leaders, schoolmates. Nearly absent in Victor's public recounting is the state, even though Nigeria is a country where same-sex relations are criminalized (as well as punishable by death in the northeast provinces).[12] Many of the harms experienced by Victor were only made possible by the way in which the government's criminalization reifies such anti-LGBTIQ beliefs and emboldens such action. The state may not be the direct perpetrator of violence, but it is an ever-present abettor.[13]

While the state was unwilling to protect Victor from the violence he faced, thus qualifying him for international protection, we still require an analytical account of the harms that drive queer and trans individuals to flee that recognizes the importance of the political and legal context, while still capturing social and cultural practices.[14] Without such an account it is much more difficult to understand how private and public forms of harm concurrently drive displacement.

When we turn to consider broader social forces as opposed to active criminalization by the state, we might be tempted to imagine homophobia as a "reactive attitude" within the minds of individuals rather than as a feature of the social world.[15] But Victor's case shows us that attempts to discipline, correct, and convert can be fueled by a desire to rescue a loved one from some imagined evil. In these cases, the violence that results from prejudice is not necessarily meant to injure or eliminate but instead to reform or diminish a behavior. In her ameliorative account of misogyny, Kate Manne argues that we should locate the ideological hatred of women in the social environment rather than in the individual. Seeing misogyny as a feature of the world rather than as a characteristic of agents allows us to move beyond what she calls the "naïve" account, which focuses on the beliefs or attitudes of particular people. Instead, misogyny is the policing arm of patriarchy: A set of punitive social mechanisms that enforce hostile gender norms.[16]

A similarly naïve account of homo/transphobia, especially in our context, might focus on the attitudes and hostility presented in states with active systems of anti-LGBTIQ criminalization. However, an ameliorative account of homo/transphobia would reframe our attention towards its presence in features of the social world more broadly. These features are the policing arm of the cisheteronormative order, which functionally enforces a dominant ideology of gender and sexuality. In this context, stateled criminalization is just one extreme symptom of a much broader set of social practices in a world in which queer and trans people are forced to flee for their lives. Instead of focusing on the belief or attitude of the perpetrator or locating homo/transphobia exclusively in states that actively and explicitly criminalize, we should ask what social environment queer and trans people are asked to inhabit and how that environment might force them to flee in search of something safer.[17] Our turn to the social, then, asks what kind of social order is created and upheld through our shared practices, norms, and systems of enforcement.

And so, while criminalization and state repression remain important drivers of LGBTIQ displacement, we offer a more expansive account of harm as relational in order to more fully grasp other drivers. Relational harm, a concept used throughout the book, seeks to capture the deeply social nature of oppression and prejudice, experienced through our interactions with other people and structured by dominant normative ordering principles. In being relational, the form of harm experienced by LGBTIQ people and other marginalized groups is highly adaptive; it remolds itself in response to the position of the individual and their social environment.

This approach recognizes that queer and trans people often flee harms that are pervasive in an oppressive social environment and often develop out of social exclusion. Harms thus exist in contexts of criminalization as well as in more apparently progressive states. Our analysis therefore complicates the role of the state in displacing queer and trans people. In addition to state practices, LGBTIQ displaced people are forced to flee violence perpetuated by loved ones, their communities, their neighbors, and their acquaintances, as well as the injury that results from their exclusion from broader society. In decentering the state as the sole cause of LGBTIQ displacement, we turn to one of the most traditionally depoliticized spaces within the global refugee regime: the home itself.

As a space of intimate relations and networks, the home becomes a foundational site for our relational account of harm. Home is not a building but a rich set of experiences. It is "the accumulation of many relationships and much history."[18] As a central idea in the theorization of displacement, the home is also vital to understanding queer experience. Building on queer and trans experiences of intrafamilial violence, we first consider how home can be reconceptualized from a place of refuge to a site of persecution. Inherent in this conception of home is a tension: home can be both a place of love and danger. We then consider the implications of this reconceptualization by focusing on the experiences of queer and trans populations, who ultimately transform the concept of home from an origin to a destination. Many displaced people are seeking to reimagine forms of belonging, identity, and home in the process of exile.

First, we begin by outlining the relationship between the refugee and queer perspectives. Here we articulate a key idea of this book: that the queer person and the refugee occupy a similar position in that their existence disturbs the hegemonic way of ordering the world. Second, we turn to feminist literature on the idea of home and homemaking, drawing out the tensions between home as a place of safety, danger, and resistance. Finally, we turn to queer articulations of the concept of home. While the physical home is often the first locus of prejudice-based harm, it is also a theoretical destination. A queer rearticulation of home transforms it into something that we escape from and also something that we search for. This rearticulation is importantly dependent upon a better understanding of the kinds of relational harm that LGBTIQ people flee. In recognizing a more expansive account of what drives displacement, we can begin to see the relational solutions that can only be reimagined by creating a new social world for the better.

LOSING HOME: THE QUEER PERSON AND THE REFUGEE

As Liisa Malkki observes, when people think about displacement, they often attend to the people in motion, fleeing from their homes. But she also contends that while "there are innumerable good reasons to focus analytical attention on refugees . . . it is also useful to look back at the scene of violence to discover what in it has not been foregrounded."[19] Definitionally speaking, every forced migrant must leave *somewhere*, but not everyone flees violence that begins within the home itself.

Refugees could be defined by their loss of home.[20] Whether they are described as displaced, exiled, or uprooted, people who are forced to move begin their journeys by being pushed from their homes. This upheaval can be precipitated by any number of events: war, climate disaster, or targeted persecution. But forced migration definitionally involves beginning in one place and being compelled to go to another. For many, it is the loss of home that they find the most distressing about displacement—not to mention the subsequent losses of temporary homes that make up the cycles of displacement that refugees face.[21]

Refugees and the internally displaced might express a longing to return home or an extreme form of homesickness.[22] Of course, this is not a universal fact of displacement (as indeed nothing is). Some will instead find a new and better life in their destination states. But nevertheless, feelings about one's previous home are likely to remain complicated and unsettled during the process of displacement. The loss of home and making home anew therefore seem central to the experience of refugeehood. That the displaced have a complicated relationship—of the type articulated by Victor in the beginning of this chapter—with the concept of home should not surprise us. Just because one leaves for safety does not necessarily mean they leave everything emotionally behind.

Much scholarship has focused on how displaced populations consider the idea and value of home and how it evolves as their journey continues.[23] The costs associated with losing one's home are most powerfully shared in the opening line of Warsan Shire's poem, "Home":

no one leaves home unless
home is the mouth of a shark.[24]

For many, home is a place of safety and comfort. To lose it feels like losing oneself. As Shire reveals with her evocative metaphor, it is never an easy decision to leave.

In being pushed from their old life, refugees might seek and imagine home in new ways. Against the usual assumptions of homemaking and sedentarism, migrants and refugees show us that homes can be multiple.

Helen Taylor writes, "refugees might maintain a deep, emotional attachment to the lost home, while at the same time making a new home in the country of exile, or indeed in another country altogether."[25] Homes are also made on the move in camps, settlements, or contexts of protracted displacement. This not only demonstrates the malleability and flexibility of homemaking but also enables us to see that home need not be tied to a particular place.[26] The idea of home as grounded in a particular place may represent an oversimplified, Global North perspective.[27]

Given that home is central to our understanding of displacement, it is perhaps unsurprising that it also appears in the context of the international community's preferred durable solutions: local integration, resettlement, and return. These traditional durable solutions imply that refugee status can only be resolved with *settlement*.[28] The final destination of the refugee should thus be sedentary; they should attempt to reestablish roots either in their country of origin or elsewhere. As the traditionally preferred solution, specifically during the Sadako Ogata period of the Office of the United Nations High Commissioner for Refugees in the 1990s, repatriation solidifies this underpinning; "an eventual 'return' 'home' to an individual's own 'roots' is seen as the 'naturally' most desirable solution, and as being in both the refugees' and the hosts' best interests."[29] This sedentary underpinning seems to be based on the assumption that all human beings belong to a certain place. This foundation ultimately pushes theorists to conceptualize transnationalism and mobility as temporary rather than long-term durable solutions, as a mobility-oriented framework would undermine our belief that people, especially refugees, belong somewhere.[30]

For Katy Long, the sedentary bias within traditional solutions stems from our framing the refugee problem as one of physical exile, rather than the loss of political and social rights.[31] For Long, the reconstitution of political and legal rights can be accomplished while refugees remain in exile; the fundamental issue here is therefore not one that depends on homecoming or the creation of a new home. Moreover, when policies overtly focus on this idealized notion of homecoming, they fail to consider the realities of return. Returnee experiences in Bosnia and Herzegovina show that the idea of a natural homecoming is largely chimerical. Instead, home must be (re)negotiated upon return, just as it would be in a new community.[32] Thus, according to Long, the sedentary bias must be overcome and replaced with a focus on the reconstruction of de jure rights. Indeed, Barry Stein and Frederick Cuny suggest that, in many cases, repatriation is the wrong term, as "there has been no restoration of the bond between citizen and homeland. Return is a better term, because it describes the fact of going home without judging the circumstance."[33] Similarly, Megan Bradley has argued that a dignified return in line with international protections only becomes possible when the initial injustices that drove the displacement are redressed.[34] Redress, then, is complicated for a solution premised on location. In some cases, there is no home to go back to.

While we share Long's commitment to the reconstitution of political and legal rights and Bradley's commitment to redress, we also see the redevelopment of home and belonging as central to the end of refugeehood. This is not the same as conceptualizing refugeehood as a problem solely of exile. Instead, home seems to be tied to the notion of identity; as Madan Sarup writes, it is "the story we tell ourselves and . . . also the story others tell to us."[35] Instead of conceptualizing refugeehood as simply a loss of place, the concept may also invoke a dislocation in terms of *identity*, as well as the undermining of the protection of basic rights and interests. The reconstitution of de jure rights may not alone signal the end of refugee status when someone is still trying to reconstruct a home for themselves in the wake of social prejudice.

Despite the importance of home, this theoretical framing is often used by states to keep refugees and migrants "where they belong." States use the centrality of home to dictate a durable solutions regime focused not on refugees' but on their own interests. Indeed, in encouraging refugees to "go home," governments often evoke an overly naturalized and exoticized notion of a people's connection to their land; this exoticism on the part of Western governments cannot escape its entanglements with race and empire.[36] This disparity becomes even starker when we consider the double standard of transnationalism applied to Western states. Those from the Global North exercise much greater mobility and are more likely to have a transnational identity accepted. The West exoticizes the Global South by claiming that their identities are constituted by their relationship to their land, and this conceptualization underpins their discriminatory practices. To avoid such tendencies, home must be conceptualized subjectively: whether someone is "home" must not depend on this exoticized notion of being rooted to a certain place. Instead, home is the deeply personal development of this sense of rootedness: no one belongs to one place inherently. Homes are constantly built, negotiated, and renegotiated through time. Settlement-based solutions to displacement mirror the international regime's desire for order. Thus, as Malkki states, they "reflect their own political interests in retaining a 'national order of things,' rather than a concern with refugees' welfare."[37]

This challenge to the national order of things demonstrates the refugee's capacity to disturb. In sitting outside of the usual structures of citizenship, territory, and belonging, the experience of displacement challenges the standard ways of viewing the world.[38] As Malkki has pointed out in the case of Burundi, the production of refugees is also often seen to disturb the natural order of the world, as the "territorializing metaphors of identity—roots, soils, trees, seeds—are washed away."[39] This ability to disturb is precisely what draws queer theory and refugee studies into close quarters. In their shared capacity to challenge and upend the usual order of business, the figures of the queer person and the refugee can think in solidarity. Many queer people (not just queer refugees) experience a loss of home and must push to find new ways of imagining a future one. Similar to many displaced populations, queer people must imagine a new idea of a safe home free from harm. Given that their existence challenges established expectations, the queer person and the refugee are routinely forced back into "order," so that the disturbance they might cause does not harm or affect others. Queer conceptions of home can thus help reveal the precarity of a seemingly ordered world.

COMPLICATING THE CONCEPT OF HOME IN FEMINIST POLITICAL THOUGHT

There is a duality to the concept of home. For many, the home can be a place of comfort, protection, and support. For others, it can be a site of harm, insecurity, and grief.

Many foundational critiques of "home as safety" came from feminist theorists, who argued that the home can become a gilded cage for women. Betty Friedan famously articulated the idea of "the feminine mystique" as an idealized domestic bliss that white women in North America aspired to achieve.[40] But Friedan, and many others, showed that the obligations of unpaid domestic labor weighed women down and denied them agency and the right to produce a sense of themselves that was not in service to others.[41] Luce Irigaray claimed that the ideals of the home resulted from the projection and desires of men, who were nostalgic or longed for their mothers.[42] As such, the confinement of women in the domestic sphere had less to do with their own desires and more to do with protecting and reinforcing a man's sense of self. The home has long been a space to contain and control women by putting constraints on their bodies, freedom, and labor.[43] In an adherence to invented ideas of feminine domesticity and submission, women were routinely denied the ability to own property for themselves. While some of these features of homemaking as subservience are now rejected by women, many still find themselves in the position of supporting their partners because of the institutionalized assumption that women will provide care for "their men."

Later feminist scholarship expanded this critique further by conceptualizing home as a space of privilege that provides safety only by denying such comforts to others. Biddy Martin and Chandra Mohanty argue that the safety of the home resulted from exclusive policies that prevented difference and reinforced oppression.[44] "Home as safety" emerged out of an idealized version of the heterosexual white home. Lesbianism, in its disruption of the cisheteronormative ideal, made this vision of "home as safety" supposedly impossible, removing any protections that could be afforded by race or class. Blackness, in this framing, only exists as a threat "used to establish and enforce unity among whites" by emphasizing their vulnerability to "outsiders."[45]

While home may be a site of submission or domination, it can also be a space in which we recover and organize. bell hooks argued that the home, or the homeplace, was an essential site of resistance for Black women in the United States:

> Despite the brutal reality of racial apartheid, of domination, one's homeplace was the one site where one could freely confront the issue of humanization, where one could resist. Black women resisted by making homes where all black people could strive to be subjects, not objects, where we could be affirmed in our minds and hearts despite poverty, hardship, and

deprivation, where we could restore to ourselves the dignity denied us on the outside in the public world.[46]

For many Black women, the home becomes a place where they can build a family and culture removed from the harms of white supremacy. It is in that homeplace that Black women can build and reinforce Black culture while performing acts of care for members of the family. Though the importance of the home remains gendered here, in the sense that Black women take on a service role, it is also a space of agency and, thus, an important site of resistance. Home, then, for Black Americans becomes more than merely a shelter, it is a place of renewal in an anti-Black world.

It is in these intersecting conceptions of home as a physical, structural, and metaphoric shelter that competing ideas can be found. Iris Marion Young's work has explored these different political meanings of home and identifies it as a place of dignity and resistance.[47] While she recognizes that the gendered and racial associations of the home can lead to multiple outcomes, for Young, home has a unique capacity to help individuals make meaning. She writes:

> A home, on the other hand, is personal in a visible, spatial sense. No matter how small a room or apartment, the home displays the things among which a person lives, that support his or her life activities and reflect in matter the events and values of his or her life. There are two levels in the process of the materialization of identity in the home: (1) my belongings are arranged in space as an extension of my bodily habits and as support for my routines, and (2) many of the things in the home, as well as the space itself, carry sedimented personal meaning as retainers of personal narrative.[48]

As such, beyond the importance of the home as a cultural space for community building, Young identifies a materiality in the importance of home as a site of personal constitution. For Young, home becomes a physical representation of one's past and present. Its power comes from how, through daily practices of routine, it reflects one's internal world.

Young identifies four values of the home to an individual's life: safety, individuation, privacy, preservation. Rather than accepting the safety of the home as a result of problematic privileged thinking, she argues for a change in perspective according to which we understand safety as a basic entitlement associated with a dignified life: "We must be ashamed of a world in which safety at home is a privilege, and express outrage at any stated or implied suggestion that such a need and liberty is too expensive for any society to meet."[49] As such, safety becomes a value that all human beings deserve. She further contends that home allows for individuation, for people to recognize who they are through the process of reflecting on home or making it their own. Speaking about her mother's experience, Young argues that there is an important form of agency that comes from establishing one's home. Vital to this capacity is privacy. Young explains, "A person does not have a place of her own and things of her own if anyone can have access to them. To own a space is to have autonomy over admission to the space and its contents."[50] And it is in this act of designing one's own space, that one can begin to curate the parts of their life that are dear: the photos in the frame, the gifts on the mantel. Young describes this action as a form of preservation, where the "home is the site of the construction and reconstruction of oneself. Crucial to that process is the activity of safeguarding the meaningful."[51]

Young thus adds something important to our conceptualization of the home, underscoring its centrality to identity formation, a process with both social and political dimensions. She troubles both the idea of the home as a prison for women, as well as an idealized site of safety for the privileged. She concludes that "despite the real dangers of romanticizing home, I think that there are also dangers in turning our backs on home."[52]

Home, notwithstanding its sensitivities and complications, remains an important concept in feminist thought because of how it connects the personal and the political. Recognizing its capacity to both stifle and support opens up the possibility of further exploring its complicated role in the lives of the queer and trans displaced.

QUEER AND TRANS COMPLICATIONS OF HOME

The first site of prejudice-based violence or persecution based on one's sexuality and gender identity can occur in the home. Victor's personal story of conversion therapy, familial rejection, and associated violence highlights the ways in which one's family can shift from protector to persecutor.[53] As such, the complicated and multiple understandings of home theorized by feminist scholars relate to queer and trans experiences as well.[54] Because of the intimate relations within the private sphere of the home, families can transmit cultural homo/transphobia in unique ways. Familial homo/transphobia can cause parents to reject their children, either excluding them from family functions or expelling them from the home altogether. Family members can also use humiliation, verbal abuse, and physical violence to try to change or "convert" queer and trans children.[55] In the face of this rejection and harm, a home is no longer a place of safety but becomes a site of insecurity.

Familial homo/transphobia take on both obvious and subtle forms. Nicole Asquith and Christopher Fox find that violence against queer and trans individuals is more likely to be perpetrated by immediate family members than other forms of hate crime.[56] This violence results from a desire to punish the victim for transgressing norms associated with sexuality and gender, reinforce a heteronormative order in the home, and publicly protect the esteem of the family. In this context, violence resulting from familial homo/transphobia relates to honor-based killings as the families who commit these crimes often justify their behavior by appealing to a moral framing focused on the collective good.[57] These effects "are enhanced by the proximity of the relationships, and by the fact that they are committed on the threshold between the intimate haven and the public gaze. In this sense, for gay men and lesbians, there is no place like home."[58] Thus, when considering intrafamilial prejudice-based violence, home becomes a hostile environment, devoid of safety, where the risks come from within the shelter.

This rejection is not only expressed in violence. For gender-expansive family members, who transgress expectations of sexuality and gender, the home can be a place of subtle interactions that attempt to "correct" them into acting appropriately. A doll gets taken away from a young boy's hands. A non-binary child is told that their actions are "not ladylike." Through the disciplining of gender norms, queer and trans young people are taught to conform. Through this discipline, home can transform from a place of protection into a site of oppression. The home is perhaps the most intimate unit in which gender norms are disciplined. Under pressure from the conventions around gender roles and sexuality, the general perception of home as a haven and as the only place where one can be their real self is often inconsistent with the domestic situation of those who have gender identities and sexual orientations that are not compliant with the heteronormative gender binary system. For LGBTIQ youth, home can be a place of oppression.[59] It is in these interactions that Gloria González-López highlights what she calls "heteronormative compliance," the policing of queer and trans children's behavior in order to correct it.[60] These subtle interactions, which cause shame and other harms, relate to Judith Butler's conceptualization of gender as a disciplinary cultural agent; those who step out are often pushed back in line by social norms that punish transgression.[61] For queer and trans people, then, the home can be a place of constant discomfort because of the way their expressions of gender are policed.

The characteristics of this intimate familial violence relate to a particularity of sexuality and gender identity. Sexuality, understood as the orientation of one's sexual desire, and gender identity, understood as one's inner sense of gender, are fluid, culturally specific concepts with no obvious "visible," "physical," or "material" characteristics. In their attachment to social practices, they reject fixed constructions and thus require a cultural context to be legible.[62] Young notes the impact of this fluidity. Writing on sexuality specifically, she states that "homophobia is one of the deepest fears of difference precisely because the border between gay and straight is constructed as the most permeable; anyone at all can become gay, especially me, so the only way to defend my identity is to turn away with irrational disgust."[63] María Mercedes Gómez extends this point to argue that acts of violence are exclusionary because they attempt to subordinate the target and reaffirm both their difference and the perpetrator's normalcy. Thus, sexuality and gender often are not only perceived as fluid but also recognized as intersubjective.

This intersubjectivity is best articulated by Eve Kosofsky Sedgwick in *Epistemology of the Closet.*[64] Sedgwick uses the Torah story of Purim— when Queen Esther comes out as Jewish to her husband, King Ahasuerus, as a means to prevent an anti-Semitic pogrom—to compare the difference between racial/religious identities and sexual/gender identities. According to Sedgwick, there are five ways that Esther's "coming out" as a Jew differs from "coming out" as a lesbian. First, Esther's identity as a Jew is not viewed as debatable or as a mutable fact, compared to LGBTIQ people, who must often defend their identities. Second, Esther expects Ahasuerus to be surprised by her self-disclosure, and he is. In other words, she has a confident sense of control over other people's knowledge about her in contrast to the radical uncertainty felt by closeted LGBTIQ people. Third, Esther worries that coming out will damage her but not that it will damage Ahasuerus. In comparison, when an LGBTIQ person comes out, there is a chance of harming the reputation of other people, especially their family. Fourth, Ahasuerus has no involvement with Esther's religion/ethnic identity. In comparison, when someone comes out as LGBTIQ there is a definitional impact on their relations with others. For a parent, it can mean deciding whether to condone or condemn their child's identity. For a friend, it means potentially being implicated by this "outing" and having their own identity questioned. And finally, Esther knows who her people are and is part of a community and culture by birth. LGBTIQ youth are often not born to LGBTIQ families or into an established or clear community. Thus, these tensions reveal how nonhegemonic sexual orientations and gender identities become contentious in a site of an assumed collective identity: the homeplace.

This assumed collective identity can then turn against the individual, as in the case of Ben. Home for Ben is not in his hometown where he grew up in the United Kingdom. Nor is it with his biological family. The reality is that encounters with his family are difficult. As a bisexual trans man, Ben's family treats every interaction as an opportunity for an intervention into what they consider his lifestyle "choices." Ben explains this in an interview in *The Guardian*: "both . . . [my mom] and my dad spent more or less every waking hour trying to convince me to 'desist.' Essentially, they were doing DIY conversion therapy every time they so much as spoke to me."[65] For Ben, each interaction repeats a pattern of rejection and denial that undermines his humanity. So he left home, finding temporary shelter with a family friend, before seeking family elsewhere, a chosen family among friends who recognize and see him for who he is. Ben's story highlights the tension of familial prejudice in the home. As a bisexual trans man, Ben's gender identity is disbelieved by his family. They attempt to convince him to "desist," a coded term used by a transphobic movement in the United Kingdom to combat what they perceive as "gender radicalization." According to his testimony, his sexuality is either ignored or not taken seriously, a form of prejudice commonly associated with biphobia.[66]

The relational, intrafamilial harm against LGBTIQ populations that complicates their relationships to their home is not specific to any part of the world. As evident in Ben's story in the United Kingdom, many queer and trans youth expelled from their homes subsequently experience a form of homelessness and must seek temporary shelter elsewhere. In the UK, three in ten queer and trans people reported experiencing abuse from their family; the ratio is four in ten for trans populations.[67] In addition, in both the United States and the United Kingdom, LGBTIQ people represent a disproportionate number of youths experiencing homelessness. Many of these queer and trans young people leave because their families cannot or will not provide the unique care they need.[68] In other work, Samuel has argued that these queer and trans youth experiences of homelessness should be considered a form of displacement as it is intrafamilial persecution that caused their situation and a broader societal prejudice that prevents any substantive redress.[69] Cheshire Calhoun further recognizes this forced migration of queer and trans subjects out of the private sphere as a form of displacement that serves as the basis for the subordination of queer and trans populations.[70] Thus, in the wake of intrafamilial harm, many queer and trans people leave their old homes in search of a new one.

In queering home, the boundary between homelessness and displacement blurs even more. For the queer and trans who leave, fleeing extreme rejection, violence, and attempted conversion, the starting place was never really a home; the search for housing and safety therefore becomes a search for home. Politicizing home and the violence that these families inflict makes it more difficult to accept that homelessness that results from sexuality or gender identity could be anything other than displacement. As such, it is evident, if still problematic, that Western democracies such as the United Kingdom can *produce* displacement.

Elsewhere in his interview, Ben talks about crafting new traditions in the wake of this family rejection—for example, celebrating holidays with his chosen family. Chosen family is a queer kinship practice in which those not biologically related engage in regular acts of care often associated with the family. Thus, even coming from a hostile home environment, Ben still works to create a new home with its own intimacy and joy. His experiences reflect the ambivalence of home that feminist scholars have identified and reinforce the critique put forward by hooks and Young that home for queer and trans people can also be a site of resistance when it is made anew.

Much scholarship discussing queer perspectives on home recognizes that queer and trans people use their homes as a private sphere in which they can explore themselves and their identities.[71] In the privacy of a home, a lesbian couple can kiss without fear of violent reprisal. A young trans woman can experiment with various ways to show her desired form of femininity. A group of queer and trans people can come together to celebrate Christmas without fear of an uncomfortable interaction with a prejudicial housemate. Scholars of queer and trans home practices have documented how the home can become a place for identity formation and meaning making. As Youngsook Choi summarizes: "A home can be a closet space for expressing and liberating transgender subjectivities under certain conditions."[72] In creating a "home of one's own" or embracing the privacy afforded in one's home, both queer and trans people can explore the different facets of their sexuality and gender identities.

In addition to the home serving as an important space for identity affirmation, it can also serve as a place of protection from a hostile homo/transphobic world.[73] A home provides a shelter to secure an individual from the outside world. The individual then fills the space with their items and shapes it around their routine, producing a mutually reinforcing dynamic between personal space and personal identity. The home then becomes a place of autonomy for queer and trans people in a world that so often seems out of their control.

Ben's case shows the remarkable resilience of the queer and trans community. In the face of a home that harmed, Ben worked to create his own home. Jason Bryant calls for a queering of the concept of home that better reflects the queer and trans experience. Bryant explains that queering in this context means both "deconstructing home ideology as a set of particular, heteronormative social constructs that disallow wider conceptual possibilities for spaces and sexualities" and "guaranteeing that queers have access to real-world spaces of shelter and comfort."[74] In exploring the queering of home in Audre Lorde's *Zami: A New Spelling of My Name* (1982) and Leslie Feinberg's *Stone Butch Blues* (1993), Byrant identifies two meanings of home: "a material site of shelter and an imaginative set of feelings related to belonging."[75] Taken together, these meanings allow for various sites to be considered a home. Bryant further explains that "queering the home stretches and scrambles the home category ('dyke bar as home,' 'Black lesbian sisterhood as home,' 'body as home')."[76] Queer conceptions of home, thus, become not only a material reality but also a community ideal.

This expansion of home to include a community ideal provides a conceptual shift in home's meaning. Rather than a place one leaves, for the queer and trans displaced, home is something to *search for*. In exploring the meaning of home in queer migrant populations, Anne-Marie Fortier identifies how many queer and trans populations migrate to "terrains of belonging."[77] In this search for community, home becomes a destination as opposed to an origin.[78] Other scholars of queer migration have proposed similar conceptualizations. David Eng describes queer migration as the "traumatic displacement from the lost heterosexual 'origin,'" thus a displacement not of location but of social position.[79] And Kath Weston has discussed the movement of queer and trans people to cities as motivated by the "sexual imaginary" of a welcoming community.[80] Thus a queer concept of home becomes not an idealized lost or never-had past but an envisioned potential future. It is in this framing that homemaking becomes a liberatory practice where queer and trans people can leave one site of discomfort in the hope of arriving at a place of dignity. If the displaced "vote with their feet," then in this sense, the queer and trans displaced who leave their home of origin are choosing themselves.

Leaving one's home of origin does not necessarily always mean leaving the past behind. Home may be rearticulated into a destination, but one's origins might still remain important. The complications of one's original home, the need to leave it for safety, does not necessarily mean that all past relationships end. Victor left home but maintains a relationship with his mother because of what she means to him, because he loves her. The reality of this analysis is that to make things clear or binary would be to oversimplify. No two LGBTIQ people have exactly the same experience of home. And so, while many queer and trans people face family rejection, this experience is not universal; home and family mean many things to many people. Moreover, while intrafamilial violence is a grave harm, it is not the only reason why people chose to leave. In fact, family sometimes help their LGBTIQ kin find a way out. A friend of Samuel is a gay man who fled home after being forcibly conscripted into the army in a country with a documented history of persecuting queer and trans populations. Who helped him leave? His father, a senior figure in the army. In Samuel's interviews with Venezuelan queer and trans asylum seekers in Colombia, many documented the harms they experienced at home in one sentence, before then speaking fondly of the relationship they share with their mothers. A queer rearticulation of home does not demonstrate that home is only ever one kind of thing. Instead, we should see the ambivalence of a complicated concept as a way to recognize the messiness of our realities and the infinite possibilities available to us in responding to it.

A queer rearticulation of home changes home from a reality associated with harm toward a future ideal associated with safety and belonging. A rearticulation recognizes the world as it *should* be for a queer or trans person, not necessarily as it is. This future imagining, present in the rearticulation of home, centers a justification for queer action based on a movement or effort toward that community ideal. José Esteban Muñoz discussed the importance of futurity in queer and trans populations, identifying this push toward utopia as an essential way for queer and trans people to move through the world. Queer utopianism became a way to build the community as well as to mobilize it toward acts of resistance.[81] To fight a world that's built against them, intentionally or not, queer and trans people need to know what they are fighting *for*.

As such, queer and trans people have learned how to dream of a future that is not yet available to them. They need to see the world for what it is—what it has not and will not give them—and recognize what they will need to build for themselves. In this way, queer rearticulations are not constrained by facts about the real world. The point is to challenge, deconstruct, and upend the things that we take for granted.

What then is the global refugee regime to do in the wake of these rearticulations? What is the role of the state in the queer search for refuge? In our introduction, we posited that if the state has shown a capacity to queer its conception of international refugee law to incorporate queer and trans populations, then it has the duty to think through the limitations of how these core concepts are applied to queer and trans people. LGBTIQ people rearticulate concepts that do not serve them or reflect their reality. In fleeing the harms of home, in reimagining home as a destination free of harm instead of a reality of what was left behind, queer and trans people are highlighting that the harms that drive their displacement are intimate and result from social forces; they are not necessarily state-perpetrated, though they are perhaps state-abetted.[82] In doing so, queer and trans people are presenting a more sophisticated approach to understanding the drivers of displacement. Driving their displacement are the relational harms that reflect a broader social environment underpinned by cisheteronormativity: contexts of criminalization, broader state repression, intrafamilial violence, social exclusion, and intracommunal hate crimes collapse into a world that makes life untenable. In cases in which the state is not the clear persecuting agent, established practices of refugee status determination question whether the state is unwilling or unable to protect queer and trans people. But a more foundational question is whether the state of asylum recognizes these varied forms of intimate, socially situated harm as persecution at all. To answer such a question, let us turn to the foundational concept of persecution.

2 Persecution

At thirteen years old, Anu began a relationship with another girl in Nigeria.[1] She described it as the happiest time of her life. But one day her mother caught them together. "She was so angry. She started shouting, calling me an abomination. I felt so exposed. The violence started that day, and it grew." Anu's mother began to physically attack her. This continued throughout the weeks that followed. Soon after, her mother brought two men into their house, who forcibly subjected Anu to female genital cutting. Discussing the effects of this violence, Anu recounted the following:

> After that, I became something else. I didn't know about depression. I just knew I was not myself. My parents thought that the circumcision had worked, that "the devil" was taken out of me. But, of course, nothing had changed about my sexuality, and I was terrified that people would find out.

Following this encounter, Anu hid her sexuality for many years. After traveling to the United Kingdom for her education in 2012, she was pressured by her parents to marry a man. The marriage did not last, and after their separation, Anu's parents refused to pay for her studies. Unable to fulfill the conditions of her visa, she was detained in the infamous British immigration center, Yarl's Wood. She continued to hide her sexuality, including from a Nigerian immigration lawyer who was recommended to her by someone from her community. Throughout this period, she became seriously unwell.

Anu was denied refugee protection twice on two separate grounds. First, immigration officials did not accept that the violence she experienced amounted to persecution. After this initial rejection, Anu was offered support by a charity who found her a legal aid solicitor. It was only then that she felt safe enough to disclose her sexuality to the Home Office. But then, Anu was *again* denied refugee protection because the Home Office did not believe that she was a lesbian, in part due to her previous marriage. After five years in and out of detention and many appeals, Anu eventually received refugee protection, but only after her experience of persecution was denied repeatedly.

In the previous chapter, we discussed the relational nature of harm against the queer and trans displaced. Home, often the first locus of harm for LGBTIQ people, shifts from a place of safety to a site of persecution. Anu's experience attests to this—it was the people closest to her that committed these extreme acts of violence. As a result, homemaking for queer and trans people often changes from an origin to a destination: in searching for a new home, the queer and trans displaced must leave their old one behind. But even with this expanded account of harm—one that does not focus exclusively on state-led criminalization but also the broader cisheteronormative social environment—we might ask whether such acts are properly recognized *as persecution.*

To qualify for international protection, refugees must demonstrate *a well-founded fear of persecution* on the basis of race, religion, nationality, membership of a particular social group, or political opinion. They must, therefore, demonstrate a forward-looking claim: that, if returned, they would experience severe harm.[2] Interpretations of the 1951 Refugee Convention have expanded since its conception, with attempts to make it more sensitive to questions of sexuality and gender identity. The convention does not include a specific category on gender identity or sexuality, and so cishetero women and LGBTIQ people are instead understood as a potential "particular social group."[3] Violence against cishetero women and LGBTIQ people by non-state actors is now also recognized as a possible ground for asylum.[4] Without these expansions in our thinking about the convention, cishetero women and LGBTIQ people would not be able to seek asylum at all.

In making an asylum application on the basis of their sexuality or gender identity, queer and trans people must demonstrate two things. First, they must show that they "really" are of the sexual orientation or gender identity that they claim. In other words, they must prove that they are not faking it. Second, they must then show that the violence they would face upon return, or have faced in the past, amounts to persecution. Only when these two questions are satisfied will they have shown that they have a "well-founded fear of persecution." In reality, asylum adjudicators and case workers often fixate on the first question of sexuality or gender identity. Instead of attending to what *kind* of violence LGBTIQ people are fleeing from, they question whether the person before them is "really" queer at all.[5] In the case of lesbian women fleeing gender-based violence, as articulated in Anu's story, Moira Dustin argues that the credibility question often shrouds any attempt to consider the nature of persecution. Speaking of a woman in a situation similar to Anu, Dustin writes, "The violence the woman experienced took second place to the question of whether she 'really' was a lesbian."[6]

Instead of attending to the question of credibility, we want to turn our attention to the intelligibility of queer persecution. How, if at all, is the experience of persecution as an LGBTIQ person conceptualized differently from other forms of persecution, as imagined by the refugee regime? In this chapter, we build on the idea of relational harm developed in the previous chapter to better theorize how the concept of persecution relates to LGBTIQ people, particularly for those who experience challenges in having their persecution recognized *as persecution*: lesbian, bisexual, and queer (LBQ) women and gender-diverse people. We first explore the concept through existing work in refugee law, which often relies on an unrealistic and idealized version of the queer refugee experience, to recognize how its current conceptualization fails certain populations. Then, we analyze how queer and trans theories of violence might expand or improve those existing concepts. In doing so, we build a case for a new conceptualization of the existing definition of persecution, which recognizes the phenomenon as *socially situated*. We thus argue that persecution transforms depending on the identities of the person being targeted. As a result, when analyzing the persecution claims of an individual, care must be taken to consider how this violence intersects with their identity. We conclude with an analysis of the case of lesbian, bisexual, and queer women racialized as Black to show how their experiences of persecution differ from the imagined experiences of the asylum regime's idealized queer refugee, which results in their being overlooked by mainstream theorists and jurists of asylum.

PERSECUTION AND QUEER SUBJECTS

The concept of persecution is central to the legal definition of the refugee in the 1951 Geneva Convention. Refugees must show "a well-founded fear of persecution" related to several different potential factors: race, religion, nationality, membership of a particular social group, or political opinion.[7] But the convention itself gives no definition of persecution, and there is no agreed upon meaning in the legal jurisprudence or academic scholarship.[8] While this ambiguity may seem unwise, it leaves space for reworking the concept of persecution and for expanding or reshaping our ideas of who is entitled to international protection.[9] This ambiguity therefore presents us with an opportunity.

There are two broad ways of thinking about persecution that have been adopted on the question of entitlement to asylum. Some have adopted "ordinary meaning" approaches and have therefore relied on dictionary definitions of persecution. British courts historically understood persecution according to the following definition given by the House of Lords: it as an effort "to pursue with malignancy or injurious action, especially to oppress for holding a heretical belief."[10] Interpretations of the ordinary meaning of persecution have therefore coalesced around several features. First, persecution must be inflicted by a human persecutor, which need not be the state. De facto state authorities—for instance, a militia or paramilitary group—can commit persecution. Claimants in such cases must nevertheless demonstrate that the state was unwilling or unable to prevent the persecution, which makes non-state actor cases more challenging.[11] Second, persecution picks out individuals for harm based on some immutable characteristic. Third, persecution must be "cruel" or "serious." Most jurisdictions therefore agree that persecution is distinct from "mere" discrimination or harassment. The Australian Migration Act of 1958, which offers a general characterization of persecution, states that instances of serious harm might include a threat to the person's life or liberty, significant physical harassment, significant physical ill-treatment, significant economic hardship, denial of access to basic services, and the denial of capacity to earn a livelihood of any kind.[12] The British Home Office also argues that discrimination can amount to persecution if it results in "sufficiently serious consequences for the person concerned."[13] Of course, the line between discrimination and persecution remains blurred and complicated—as well as politically loaded. Importantly, the severity of some episodic harms—for instance, a single instance of torture—is often thought to be sufficient to constitute persecution. The British Home Office also accepts this. In the case of *Mustafa Doymus v. Secretary of State for the Home Department*, it was decided that "persistency is a usual but not a universal criterion of persecution."[14] However, a claim to asylum can also be comprised of "lesser" harms that aggregate or grow worse over time, demonstrating the likelihood of more serious harm in the future. Thus, defining persecution by relying on its ordinary meaning generally results in an understanding of persecution as severe harm, whether aggregated or episodic.

A second, much broader conceptualization of persecution within refugee law has developed over the last thirty years: the failure of state-protection approach. Defenders of this model argue that the point and purpose of the Refugee Convention is to protect those whose states have failed them. Anker argues that the "state's legitimacy [is] based on its ability and duty to protect the basic needs and rights of its citizens."[15] This view has been cemented in James Hathaway's human rights approach, which combines the tradition of human rights law with international refugee law. On this view, asylum is a form of surrogate protection for the individual. Persecution, then, is defined as the "sustained or systemic denial of basic human rights demonstrative of a failure of state protection."[16] Several jurisdictions have adopted the human rights approach. The European Parliament noted in a Qualification Directive that persecution is harm "sufficiently serious by [its] nature or repetition as to constitute a *severe violation of human rights.*"[17] The British House of Lords likewise endorsed this approach in *Horvath v. Secretary of State for the Home Department* in 2000.[18]

This more expansive approach to persecution, which relies on identifying a lack of state protection, creates space for thinking about the persecution of queer and trans subjects. Within this framework, we can begin to consider how LGBTIQ people who are victims of extreme harm might lack the protection of their state, even in contexts in which the persecution is extremely localized. In situations such as Anu's, the state is not necessarily the persecuting actor, but its inability to curb the prejudice-based violence she experienced results in the significant violation of her rights. In other words, Anu was not protected from the intrafamilial violence that she experienced. The state either would not or could not help her.[19]

Although the failure of state-protection approach opens this space, it still relies on an implicit sense or instinct of what amounts to persecution, which requires recognizing certain types or patterns of harm as sufficient to meet this standard. In other words, the contours of the concept of persecution are determined by social and normative features of our world. What Anu experienced was not recognized as persecution, either when she presented it as a case of female genital cutting or when that violence was contextualized by her sexuality.[20] As noted above, there are two questions to distinguish here. On the one hand, there is the question of belief: did this violence really take place? On the other hand, there is the question of recognition: even if we believe Anu, is what happened to her *really* persecution?

While Anu was eventually offered asylum, after multiple appeals and interventions from specialized legal aid, her initial rejections were based on the fact that her sexuality was not believed (on account of her having been married). The physical violence she experienced, with its marks still visible on her body, was not recognized within the frame of homophobic violence, because she did not feel safe to disclose her identity. Without the framing of this violence as rooted in prejudice, it was not recognized for what it was. And when Anu's queerness was disclosed and subsequently doubted, then *again*, these acts of violence were denied the framing of prejudice and thus not recognized as persecution.

Unfortunately, Anu's story is similar to those of many LBQ women seeking asylum. Mengia Tschalaer has documented the challenges related to recognition that Black queer women face in receiving asylum—challenges exemplified by the story of Hope whom she met in Germany. Hope and her partner's home was broken into by the police during anti-LGBTIQ crackdowns in Uganda in 2017.[21] At that point, they had been together for ten years. Before they met, Hope was forcibly married by her father to an older man. She could only flee the abusive situation by convincing her family to let her go to university, where she met her partner. During the police raid, Hope's partner was injured and sent to the hospital, while Hope was jailed for ten days. With support from her mother, Hope worked with a local fixer to get a flight to Italy. Once there, she learned that she had been deceived. She was trafficked and forced to work in prostitution. A client eventually helped her escape to Germany, where she lived in a refugee camp in Bavaria. The camp was predominantly populated with asylum seekers from Sub-Saharan African countries, and maintained a similar social environment to the one Hope fled.

During her years in Uganda and during her time at a refugee camp in Germany, Hope kept her sexuality hidden. Visibility and other forms of unwanted attention would put a target on her back and expose her to prejudice. Like Anu, Hope's experience of violence and discrimination, of persecution, was not enough for German authorities. In August 2018, the German asylum office rejected her asylum application. As Tschalaer explains, according to German immigration officials, "[Hope] has not successfully established a substantiated fear of being persecuted. . . . Hope's homosexuality was not *explicit enough* for her to receive asylum."[22] In other words, the authorities did not believe Hope's story. But they also did not recognize the forced marriage and subsequent marital rape she experienced as substantiating her fear of being persecuted. Tschalaer contextualizes the story of Hope with shocking details from her research on LGBTIQ asylum seekers in Germany: 95 percent of Black lesbians had their asylum claims rejected after their first interview, as opposed to the wider rejection rate of 50 percent for LGBTIQ individuals and 30 percent for heterosexual women.[23]

Regrettably, the German interviewer's doubt in Hope's case represents a larger phenomenon; intersectional identities produce unique forms of vulnerability that lead to divergent forms of persecution. Black lesbian asylum claimants deal with a range of discrimination and violence related to homophobia, misogyny, and racism. Anu's and Hope's experiences highlight inadequacies in how the global refugee regime accounts for the differential experience of persecution.[24] In other words, how persecution occurs and is perceived reflects the intersections of one's identities. Meghana Nayak in her work on gender-based asylum in the United States finds that courts inherently evaluate the "worthiness" of a gender-based asylum applicant according to how well they fit into established frames that make certain claims more intelligible and thus more legitimate.[25]

Thus, queer women refugees like Hope and Anu are denied asylum because their experiences of persecution are not recognized, believed, or deemed sufficiently "worthy" of refugee protection. For Anu, the violence she faced was not recognized as a form of homophobic violence because her own experience as a queer woman did not match Western expectations of homosexuality—a topic well covered in the refugee status determination literature—where forced (or survival) marriage is less common.[26] Without a recognition of this violence as a prejudiced response to her sexuality, it becomes impossible for her claim of persecution to be intelligible. The violence that Hope and Anu experienced could not register as persecution to the authorities because it lacked the framing of sexuality that would allow for recognition of its homophobic nature.[27]

"Private" forms of violence that precede displacement are often depoliticized and uncontested.[28] As such, prejudice-based violence committed by family members in the domestic sphere becomes de facto legitimated by a lack of state action. In not problematizing familial violence, it merely comes to be seen as unfortunate, but also as unremarkable. Both Anu's and Hope's cases had a racial element, which further questions how the authorities recognize Black suffering. In Hope's case, as articulated by Tschalaer, there was an implicit judgment that while she experienced violence, it was not unique or severe enough to warrant persecution. With the initial failure of both cases, violence against a Black lesbian woman becomes normalized through a prejudice-based process that undermines any recognition of its particularity. How could Anu or Hope have been persecuted when what they experienced is simply what we have come to expect?

The unintelligibility of Anu's persecution to the British authorities and Hope's persecution to the German courts relates to how the courts themselves conceptualize this confluence of discrimination and violence. These courts recognize a supposed universal standard of persecution—one rooted in the conception established by the Geneva Convention of the refugee as fleeing to escape repercussions for political dissent—and apply this conceptualization to those with nonhegemonic sexual orientations and gender identities. They seek intelligibility through violent repercussions for any recognized action of "gayness," which is based on an "idealized gay experience" in the Global North. Without the recognized action that has come to define the expected presentation of persecution, the persecution goes unbelieved, or unseen.

QUEER INTERPRETATIONS OF VIOLENCE

While not all acts of discrimination and violence amount to persecution, these acts directly relate to how LGBTIQ people are targeted and failed by their communities and states.[29] Critical theorists working at the intersection of these two concepts reveal a way to think about persecution as a socially situated concept, akin to our previous consideration of relational harm. Scholars of anti-LGBTIQ violence recognize that the characteristics of violence resulting from one's identity will be impacted by the identity in question.[30] Indeed, it is through the exercise of this characteristic and prejudicial violence that meaning is made and exclusion is reinforced.[31] In seeing the meaning-making potential of this violence, scholars recognize how it can be normalized by a cisheteronormative society and thus, comes to be expected. It is in this normalization of violence that differential patterns of prejudice become unseen, such as those forms experienced by Black lesbians.

Scholars of queer and trans displacement have argued that the current asylum regime perceives anti-LGBTIQ persecution inadequately—namely, as a monolithic phenomenon tied to an "idealized gay refugee" experience that mirrors established Western narratives of the coming out experience of cis gay men.[32] This hegemonic narrative means that all queer and trans identities are interpreted through a particular script that is not representative of their experiences. Decision-makers in the West come to expect a certain universality—the imagined cis gay man's experience—in all queer stories. This results in the overlooking of other identities and ways of being queer and prevents more intersectional thinking.

All LGBTIQ asylum seekers come to be judged against this idealized cis gay male experience, which is not even universal for cis gay men in the Global North. In refugee status determination interviews and government narratives of inclusion, the assumed parallelism between this idealized queer and trans subject and the "classic political dissident" of the Geneva Convention is evident.[33] There are therefore two idealized subjects at play. When conceptualizing persecution, the accepted "standard" has been a political dissident who becomes targeted for their (or really, *his*) actions against a repressive regime. It is in comparison to this ideal that further acts of persecution are considered. As a political dissident only becomes targeted after putting their opinion into action (whether a physical act of protest or a speech act), the LGBTIQ person becomes a target because of how they exercise their nonhegemonic identities: frequenting of gay bars, coming out, engaging in relationships.[34] In these formations, the displaced person actualizes their protected identity, and the state reacts by repressing them in a violent matter. Within this established script, anti-LGBTIQ violence and discrimination must intermix in order to become an intelligible form of persecution. The person is targeted because of homo/transphobia, and they have therefore been discriminated against. When the form of targeting is violence, it can then constitute persecution.[35]

Of course, almost no displaced people fit into this narrative, even the more mobile cis gay men around whom it is supposedly structured. Not all LGBTIQ people have the same coming out experience; nor do they actualize their sexuality and/or gender identity in the same ways. As such, the specificity of their own lived experiences impacts the specificity of their persecution, rejecting this existing notion of an "ideal type" of LGBTIQ refugee. Anu's and Hope's forced marriages resulted from patriarchal social pressures that push women to become economically dependent on male members of their families, a dynamic documented by lesbian, bisexual, and queer women in many contexts.[36] The transition of economic reliance from father to husband leads to unique conditions for lesbian, bisexual, and queer women.[37] Anu's experiences of genital cutting and forced marriage become forms of persecution tied to the specific socioeconomic condition and social positioning of being queer *and* a woman in Nigerian society. Likewise, Hope's experience of marital rape and domestic abuse, though certainly not unique to lesbian women, becomes a form of persecution responsive to the socioeconomic condition and social positioning of a lesbian woman in Ugandan society. In these cases, persecution is a category of violence that reflects one's social environment and their position within that environment. The violence enacted upon Anu in Nigeria differs from that experienced by Hope in Uganda, which differs from that experienced by Victor and Ben discussed in the first chapter, precisely because they all navigate different social realities.

The specificity of violence and its effects is a focus of scholars of anti-LGBTIQ violence. Mercedes Gómez labels this confluence of discrimination and violence as "prejudice-based violence."[38] According to Gómez, the uniqueness of anti-LGBTIQ violence results from its social positioning, which, due to its invisible and amorphous nature, produces a form of anxiety.[39] Gómez explains that "individuals perceive or experiment [with] the boundaries between heterosexuality and nonheterosexuality as more flexible than those of race or gender; consequently, the need to mark the differences is more urgent." Gómez argues that it is through violence that difference can be made visible and thus marked. Gómez further explains:

> In the case of violence based on sexual prejudice, in which the differences are less visible, the construction of otherness also occurs *a posteriori*, that is, as a result of the violent gesture. The objective of executing the violent act is to eliminate danger, and in so doing, the perpetrator believes he/she simultaneously *fixates* his/her identity (as heterosexual) and that of his/her victim (as non-heterosexual).[40]

Gómez thus conceptualizes the situated nature of anti-LGBTIQ violence in her concept of prejudice-based violence as both *hierarchical* and *exclusionary*. These acts not only reject difference but also reinforce it. An act of violence based on sexual prejudice identifies the LGBTIQ person as an "other" and subjects them to a subordinate status as "lesser." Anti-LGBTIQ violence thus becomes constitutive in constructing an "us" and "them."

Difference as socially constructed and constituted through violent acts of exclusion becomes an important theme of anti-LGBTIQ persecution, for this form of prejudice-based violence is not always coordinated or state led.[41] A society that has a preoccupation with LGBTIQ identities, what Iris Marion Young refers to as a "border anxiety," will often inculcate a cultural setting where random, irrational acts of violence become a normal way to relieve this anxiety.[42] Judith Butler has recognized this violence as a result of gender's role as a disciplinary cultural agent—one that uses violence to force those who fail to meet societal expectations of their gender into line.[43] Thus, a broader societal public can perform this violence as a way to act on their anxiety related to sexual orientation and gender identity—or, rather, to condemn such identities and reinforce cisheteronormative patriarchy.

Intentionally or not, the prejudicial socialization against nonhegemonic expressions of sexuality and gender often has violent results. Young explains that this violence is not necessarily tied to a rational logic of repression:

> The violence of rape, random beating, the harassment of threats, taunts, display of pictures and symbols, and so on, is irrational in the sense that it is not explicitly instrumental to an end. It is performed for its own sake, for sport or out of random frustration, and has as its object only the humiliation and degradation of its victims.[44]

In other work, Samuel has articulated how prejudice-based violence in homo/transphobic settings produces a form of social transformation that cleaves these queer and trans populations from the broader body politic, denying them inclusion and recognition in the process.[45] The violence is legitimized through a moral framing that justifies the action as acceptable given the identity and social position of the victim. The violence becomes socially permissible. Here, the agent of violence and discrimination does not have to be the state, as it is normally conceptualized in the study of persecution, but local social actors. As a result, many LGBTIQ people retreat from public life. This conceptualization of persecution as resulting from this prejudice-based violence matches Rebecca's observations that persecution "undermines the minimal conditions of political life and changes the social and political world."[46]

Prejudice-based violence facilitates the subordination of the targeted group by changing social meanings to render the violence unremarkable.[47] The action of a singular actor becomes part of a recognizable broader pattern of society, in which certain acts of violence, such as *overkill*, or excessive violence beyond what is required to kill, becomes associated with the violent victimization of a specific group, LGBTIQ people. Samuel argues that when this violence becomes intelligible and normalized, it is depoliticized. The meanings produced by this form of anti-LGBTIQ necropolitics do not contest the violence but instead encourage social rejection and persecution. A witness might hear the horrific details of the act without questioning its occurrence, accepting it as normal for an LGBTIQ person, who they might even believe deserves it. The state, unable or unwilling to prevent the violence, might encourage such a narrative. The term "necropolitics" comes from Achille Mbembe's observation that the ultimate power of sovereignty results "in the power and the capacity to dictate who may live and who must die."[48] In her analysis of the Black Lives Matter movement in the United States and its relationship to violence against Black women, Shatema Threadcraft observes that through this necropolitical power, "states engage in efforts to convince those within their borders that the proper body for the subjects in question is, in fact, a deceased body."[49] Threadcraft's observation relates to Melissa Wright's work on lethal violence against women, or femicide, in Ciudad Juárez, Mexico, where the state tried to justify the rising levels of lethal violence against women as an expected result for women engaged in sex work. In so doing, the state justified and legitimized their murders and suggested that the threat only extended to women who "step out of line."[50] Wright thus acknowledges that gender and its associated prejudices are used by the state to evade responsibility for the death of its own subjects and to depoliticize the violence that it has failed (or does not wish) to prevent.[51] Thus, in many contexts, gender-based violence becomes normalized, and at times legitimated, because of the prejudicial social structures of patriarchy.

The necropolitical element of anti-LGBTIQ violence thus produces a broader societal normalization of this persecution. Eric Stanley has argued that severe brutality against queer and trans subjects in the United States, even during times of increasing "equality" and acceptance, becomes a way to deny the humanity of the victim. Stanley builds on the work of Frantz Fanon to argue that this negation of queer and trans lives is not an aberration but a result of "everyday cultural, legal, [and] economic practices and at the same time . . . [of] a consciousness that itself has been occupied by domination."[52] According to Stanley, the persistence of brutal intercommunal anti-LGBTIQ violence, particularly in a state marked as inclusive, demonstrates that "this space of nonexistence, or near life, forged in the territory of inescapable violence, allows us to understand the murders of queers against the logics of aberration."[53] Achieving this nonexistence, even in an "inclusive state," requires this overkill because such extreme violence denies the humanity of the subject, thus creating a meaning of nonexistence. Thus, in a modern inclusive state necropolitical power is reinforced when meaning is produced through violent acts of exclusion.[54] And as a result, these lives no longer become grievable as the victims' deaths are viewed not as a tragedy but rather as the logical conclusion of their existence.[55]

Anti-LGBTIQ violence subjugates queer and trans people, creating meaning in a broader society and excluding them from the body politic. This violence must be unique to these populations to produce these specific meanings. Melanie Judge has observed that anti-LGBTIQ violence relies on specific cultural, racialized techniques to reject the subjecthood of the victims and obfuscate the broader social environment that facilitated this violence. Exploring the case of violence against Black lesbians in South Africa, Judge notes "how homophobia-related violence, as a system of meaning-making, intersects with other forms of violent inequality that operate to legitimize and re-entrench its uncritical reproduction in post-apartheid South Africa."[56] Judge further observes how this sociocultural treatment of anti-LGBTIQ violence resulted in LGBTIQ individuals themselves failing to recognize this violence in the same way. This sociocultural treatment of anti-LGBTIQ violence, with its racial undertones, results in broader social understanding of this violence as resulting from individual or communal prejudice and not from broader legacies of patriarchy, colonialism, and apartheid in South Africa. Fernando Serrano-Amaya makes a similar point about Colombia, where he argues that paramilitary violence against LGBTIQ populations cannot be separated from the country's broader histories of structural violence, economic exploitation, and racial oppression.[57]

In recognizing discriminatory violence against LGBTIQ populations as a culturally situated site of meaning production, one can begin to see how it becomes both differentiated and unremarkable. When legitimized and normalized as something that happens to a deserving population, the violence becomes inconspicuous. When unremarkable, it then comes to be expected. This expectation, then, denies it as an aberration worthy of protection or redress. The specific forms of violence experienced by Anu—female genital cutting, forced marriage, physical abuse—and by Hope—domestic abuse, marital rape, trafficking—become so associated with racialized, queer women from the Global South that their occurrence does not register as severe or novel enough to constitute persecution. It is in the bigotry of this limited expectation that this community—and the violence inflicted upon it—becomes invisibilized.

These conceptualizations reinforce an existing understanding of persecution that necessitates a recognition that both the state and society can be perpetrators. While LGBTIQ people can qualify for asylum based on persecution by non-state actors, the state, even if absent, still has a role in this type of persecution, because of its duty to protect its citizens.[58] Such protections should extend to the relational harms produced from the broader social environment and perpetrated by fellow citizens. Anu experienced violence from society. Hope experienced violence from both the state and society. While in Hope's case, the violence of the police raid should be intelligible as a form of state-sponsored persecution, the domestic familial violence experienced by both her and Anu should also be considered state-abetted, as the state's public rejection of homosexuality and tacit endorsement of anti-LGBTIQ violence becomes the basis through which this violence is legitimized. Such a change in understanding adopted by many in the refugee regime can help to remedy the exclusion of Anu, Hope, and so many other Black lesbians from the realm of possible persecuted populations. In considering a baseline for the concept of persecution that might be inclusive enough to consider the varied experiences of LGBTIQ people, we might explore how cultural, social, and other political efforts seek to inhibit people's freedom to actualize their sexual orientation or gender identity how they wish.

LESBIAN REFUGEES AND PERSECUTION AS A SOCIALLY SITUATED PHENOMENON

What does it mean to say that persecution faced by LGBTIQ refugees is *socially situated*? LGBTIQ people are often fleeing pervasive forms of social oppression. These oppressions interact with and compound one another in ways that make the cause of the harm difficult to locate and therefore nearly impossible to escape. We recognize this form of harm as relational in the sense that it is produced through one's interactions with others and the broader society. All harms faced by refugees are to some extent relational.

People flee wars, climate disaster, or famine, all phenomena that are po-litically and socially produced. But LGBTIQ people face a social structure of exclusion undergirded by homo/transphobia (as a feature of the social world) that transforms and follows them wherever they go. You can, at least in theory, escape the direct threats of war by leaving the areas that have been impacted. But you cannot so clearly see where the danger lies when homo/transphobia might be present in the people all around you, both those on the move with you and those waiting to receive you.

A persistent observation of refugee scholars and lawyers is that lesbi-ans are less successful in their asylum applications than their cis gay male counterparts.[59] Cheryl Llewellyn identifies three ways that courts in the United States routinely undermine the cases of lesbian asylum applicants: by recognizing the violence experienced as unextreme, by dismissing the applicants' claims of violence as unsubstantiated, and by rejecting the vio-lence experienced as unrelated to the sexual orientation of the applicants.[60] As Tschalaer explains, LBQ women must deal with both the prejudices unique to being a woman and to those related to being queer.[61] As Stanley notes, for much anti-LGBTIQ violence, it is impossible to know if the vio-lence comes from one's sexual orientation or gender identity.[62] For many, it is the betrayal of the expectations associated with their perceived gen-der identity that causes this violence. But as Eithne Luibhéid has argued, rather than attempting the impossible task of identifying the exact source of this violence, it is more important to see how courts and the global ref-ugee regime treat lesbian women who experience a form of violence that results from these intersections of their identity.[63]

Lesbian women's struggle for recognition in the courts is impacted by the sexual imaginary established by the cultural narratives of the experi-ence of cis gay men in the Global North. The standard narrative of gay male development in the Global North—realizing one is gay at a young age, hiding it, and then finally coming out—which has been labeled by David Murray as the "staged model of development," does not match many les-bian experiences (nor experiences of gay male asylum seekers from non-Western environments).[64] Many queer women and nonbinary people do not have such a static identity or may realize it later in life.[65] Many live in highly violent contexts where same-sex relations between women are not explicitly criminalized, resulting in different risk mitigation strategies and coping mechanisms. As a result of this different development, queer women are often disbelieved because their narratives do not match the standard coming-out story—nor are they fleeing contexts of direct criminalization. A key indicator of this doubt is a common request in asylum interviews to explain the intricacy of lesbian sexual relations.[66] This disbelief of lesbian women results from what Mia Liinason calls the "Western visibility paradigm," according to which unless people engage in public space in a manner similar to cis gay men racialized as white, they are not to be believed.[67] Their experiences are dismissed, and they are denied inclusion in the global refugee regime. As noted by Roxana Akbari and Stefan Vogler, "When women attempt to use laws that are structured around straight, white, Western male perspectives and experiences, their pathways are limited and sometimes nonexistent."[68]

Lesbian women's experiences of persecution also differ from cis gay men as a result of their social position. LBQ women and non-binary people often experience more private forms of violence, exhibited by people in their social network, such as family members and partners.[69] As the National Center for Lesbian Rights (NCLR) notes, it is normally the family, not the state, that disciplines and controls the behavior of women.[70] Many LBQ women are forced into marriages with men, as seen in Anu's and Hope's cases.[71] Sometimes the forced nature of this violence is physical, but other times it is more structural. Women in many societies have a unique economic vulnerability that comes from their gender identity: when women are expected to be present and labor in the domestic space, their financial status is often tied to the man in that space who works. At first, this man is the father. Then it is the husband. These patriarchal structures enable dependency, economic coercion, and private forms of violence that come from within a social network, obfuscating much suffering and rendering persecution invisible. Sometimes the impacts of these conditions are visible—for example, having children as a result of forced marriage and marital rape. Other times, the impacts are harder to see—for example, when one has to make difficult, compromising choices as a result of one's economic precarity or when one suffers domestic violence that has been meted out with the intent to correct one's sexuality.

The NCLR identifies that the "primary challenge facing a lesbian asylum applicant is proving her persecution or well-founded fear of persecution in a world that denies her visibility as a lesbian and the visibility of her abuse."[72] As a result of the uncontested nature of familial violence in the private space, public remedies of support remain unavailable. Beyond the relegation of violence to the domestic sphere, there are other ways that the persecution of lesbian women is invisibilized. Because of cultural taboos regarding women's sexuality, many laws that criminalize same-sex relations or gender nonconforming behavior only refer to men.[73] As such, lesbian women may not be formally charged under anti-LGBTIQ criminal codes (often referred to as sodomy laws, in reference to a sexual act strongly associated with gay men), but they can be targeted in other ways.[74] They can be targeted by *not* being afforded protections—for example, when prejudice-based crimes committed by non-state actors are not prosecuted or when they are denied certain resources or protections as a result of their sexuality.

Remarkably, many asylum courts appear to ignore these elements of intrafamilial and state-abetted forms of persecution, further invisibilizing the abuse.[75] Numerous cases reject claims based on the believability of the applicant, without attending to or even acknowledging the claims of marital rape.[76] This ignorance could be as tacit as not addressing the marital rape in the court decision or as obvious as the court openly doubting that a "real lesbian" would ever have children. Other cases are rejected because the country does not formally criminalize same-sex relations between women, ignoring all the other ways that the state persecutes these women.[77] Other cases are rejected because they associate lesbianism with a certain gender presentation; they disbelieve an applicant because they consider her too feminine.[78] By ignoring these claims and refusing to recognize their persecution, the courts are identifying the violence that happens to LBQ women as unexceptional. This ignorance exists at an epistemic level; these women are discredited and doubted due to the ignorance of the court. These forms of nonrecognition could be understood as what Carol Bohmer and Amy Shuman label "epistemologies of ignorance," which legitimize the denial of redress to these women.[79] With little effort to change, the global refugee regime will continue to exclude LBQ women, and nonbinary people. As the asylum system is meant to protect queer women from persecution, their continued exclusion from the protections of that system is a notable failure.

By ignoring the suffering of these women and thus undermining the status of this suffering as persecution, courts further articulate a bias that says, "this is normal for women from these parts of the world." As Tschalaer further elaborates:

> The broken and violated racialized bodies of lesbian womxn from Sub-Saharan Africa often appear as mere casualties from violent patriarchal societies "back home" in asylum decisions. In this vein, Black lesbians' asylum stories that are shaped by human rights violations such as forced marriages, domestic violence, marital rape, sexual violence, forced pregnancies, and forced abortions—while relating to their sexual orientation—seem to echo the all too familiar and universalized canon of Third World patriarchy. As a result, their claims risk to go unrecognized and their individual stories are erased in bureaucratic deliberations around "true victimhood."[80]

These dynamics become even more complex as Black women are further sexualized by the courts. Tschalaer argues that these women are racialized in a way that punishes them for exercising sexual agency. In analyzing two cases of Black lesbian asylum, Tschalaer finds that these women appear to be punished for their actions in accordance with their sexual identity. Tschalaer argues that Black women's sexuality, particularly homosexuality, is obfuscated so that these women's actions become imputed as perverse and deserving of punishment.[81]

As such, it is in this context that the social positioning of LBQ women and nonbinary people, particularly those racialized as Black, becomes viewed less sympathetically by courts. As evidenced in the previous section, violence that is productive in reinforcing a norm associated with a deserving subject may be considered unremarkable and thus not be recognized as a prejudicial form of violence. And if it is not recognized as prejudice-based violence, it will not be considered a form of persecution.

Conceptualizing persecution as a *socially situated phenomenon* requires that we recognize how this targeted violence relates directly to one's identity. While queer and trans people become targeted for who they are, the form of their targeting itself reflects their specific and often overlapping identities.[82] In the case of lesbian women like Anu and Hope, the violence takes a more domestic form, reflecting their unique social positioning. This conceptualization extends the social imaginary of what persecution is and how it manifests in the real world. While there is an established understanding of what targeting looks like—one based on an "idealized gay refugee" who has followed the same stages of development as gay men in the West and actualizes their self-identity in a public manner[83]—for many LBQ women and nonbinary people, their targeting is only intelligible when the domestic space as a private sphere is explicitly considered. Recognizing the plurality of forms persecution can take extends beyond LGBTIQ populations and can encompass other examples in which a pattern of violence is visible but not yet clearly tied to the social concept of persecution.[84]

The standard model of the "political refugee" produces a unidimensional approach to conceptualizing persecution that does not reflect the fact that prejudice and harm are shaped by one's identities. Even the queered version of this ideal type within the global refugee regime cannot account for variation in persecution as experienced by LGBTIQ refugees. As such, the concept of persecution requires further fine-tuning. To build dynamism into the concept, it must better account for harm as a relational phenomenon that results just as much from one's behavior as it does from one's social position. By incorporating the relational element of harm into persecution, it becomes easier to understand persecution as a socially situated phenomenon.

With a more socially attuned approach to the concept, more nuanced forms of persecution can be recognized. Persecution, the harm resulting from prejudice being violently enacted, reflects the identities of the target. In neither Anu's nor Hope's case was the sole source of the persecution legal institutions, borders, or government; it was also social actors such as family. A violence resulting from intimate social networks in a broader environment of cisheteronormative patriarchy can be more insidious and therefore harder to flee as there are limited resources for protection. If one flees harm from within the home and, at the same time, cannot go to the state for support, they have no option but to escape. It is to this experience of escape through flight that we will now turn.

3 Flight

In February 2022, the Russian Federation launched a full-scale invasion of Ukraine. In response, the Ukrainian prime minister, Volodymyr Zelenskyy, announced that men between the ages of eighteen and sixty could not leave the country. Instead, they must stay and fight. Women, children, and the elderly began leaving in the thousands.

In March 2022, Judis, a trans woman from Svatove in the Luhansk region of Ukraine, attempted to flee across the border into Poland with many other women. After being strip-searched by Ukrainian border guards, Judis was denied safe passage because officials believed that she was a man, despite her recognition as female on government-issued documents. She told reporters that "one of the guards said, 'You're a guy, so get the hell out of here,' and told me I should be grateful they didn't call the police."[1] Another trans woman, Alice, recounted a similar experience: "[The guards] took us to a building near the border crossing. . . . There were three officers in the room. They told us to take off our jackets. They checked our hands, arms, checked my neck to see if I had an Adam's apple. They touched my breasts. After examining us, border guards told us we were men. We tried to explain our situation, but they didn't care."[2]

A few hundred miles away in the Ukrainian capital of Kyiv, many LGBTIQ people, particularly gender-diverse individuals, felt that it was not safe for them to step outside, let alone attempt to make it to the border. They were unable to seek assistance because of the violent homo/transphobia that they might face on the streets, both from fellow Ukrainians and now from the invading Russian army. One woman, Zi, described it as a "war within a war."[3] In Zi's case, it was not the border guards or formal legal structures that prevented her from seeking assistance but a more generalized social world of discrimination, persecution, and violence.

The political context of war and mass displacement can obfuscate these forms of immobility. In this landscape, LGBTIQ people are expected to remain quiet. When CBS network news covered the situation of trans women trapped in Ukraine, it sparked outrage, with people claiming that it is ridiculous to focus on LGBTIQ issues at the height of the Russian invasion.[4] Of course, the war in Ukraine has affected many millions of people in horrible ways. But opportunities to flee and access assistance remain unequally distributed. War affects everyone, but it does not affect everyone equally, especially when we focus our attention on mobility.

Targeted violence, discrimination, and lack of assistance can make it nearly impossible for LGBTIQ people to access protection; in this context, they are unable to reach a border or even to leave their houses at all. Most discussions of displacement focus on refugees as a specific category of displaced people who are entitled to international protection. But we should remember that most of the world's displaced population are *internally displaced*: At the end of 2024, there were 122.6 million displaced people throughout the world; 72 million of them were internally displaced persons (IDPs).[5] And yet, states in the Global North remain hyperfocused on the "refugee question," in part because those seeking international protection are perceived as threatening their ability to control the international distribution of migration opportunities.[6] The "invisible crisis" of internal displacement therefore remains, in many contexts, hidden from view.[7] But the invisibility of internal displacement is especially serious for queer and trans displaced people: eight of the ten countries with the highest IDP populations criminalize homosexuality.

Fear among gender-diverse LGBTIQ people about being unable to find support while internally displaced within their state is well-founded.

Refugees with diverse sexual orientations and gender identities are often denied humanitarian relief on precisely this basis, even if their exclusion is not intentional.[8] Gender-diverse populations displaced by the 2004 tsunami in India were denied emergency resources because their appearance did not match their identity cards.[9] During the 2022 floods in Pakistan, trans people could not access resources because of a lack of legitimate identification.[10] Humanitarian aid is often provided through state agents such as the police or military, which, in countries with criminalization or heightened anti-LGBTIQ prejudice, leaves queer and trans people outside the provision of humanitarian assistance.[11] This discrimination is often compounded during crisis by the breakdown of informal social networks of solidarity that queer and trans people rely on after leaving home. As a result, queer and trans populations are disproportionately affected by war, climate change, and economic upheaval because of how their social exclusion exacerbates their vulnerability.[12]

Of course, preventing LGBTIQ people from leaving can be a direct result of political decision-making. A 2022 Human Rights Watch report outlined the situation faced by LGBTIQ people in Afghanistan upon the return of the Taliban regime.

> Gender nonconforming individuals said they were afraid to go to the country's passport office or even pass through routine checkpoints on public roads for fear of being spotted by Taliban officials. The Taliban prohibits women from traveling without male relatives, so lesbians and bisexual women cannot escape on their own. Many LGBT Afghans have conformed to social expectations that they marry a different-sex partner and have children, and they do not want to abandon or uproot their families.[13]

In Kenya, amidst contemporary rising anti-LGBTIQ rhetoric and politics, reports have indicated that the government has stopped providing exit visas for those offered resettlement in a third country. At the time of writing, many LGBTIQ asylum seekers are either being kept in limbo within the country or are taking extraordinary risks to travel irregularly to other places, including toward conflict zones such as South Sudan, in order to access international protection, with minimal guarantees.[14]

Queer and trans people on the move are thus routinely denied assistance while trying to seek safety or support. In the case of Judis and Alice, they are actively prevented from crossing the border at all.

The current refugee protection regime depends on mobility. To access assistance, the displaced must flee to a border, an embassy, or a "safe haven" of some kind. Only then can they claim asylum or international protection. Nevertheless, some people simply cannot flee. The elderly and those with physical impairments and other disabilities may be unable to leave their homes without assistance. Others may face serious geographical challenges, like having to traverse mountains or dense forests, in order to access a safe crossing point. However, much contemporary immobility also has socio-political causes: It is not only geography that prevents people from escaping swiftly to safety, but also policies, norms, and practices that render people immobile. This chapter focuses on the immobility experienced by gender-expansive LGBTIQ people in their attempts to flee, either when trying to reach an international border or when searching for safety within their own state. But more fundamentally, drawing our attention to this lack of free movement helps to reveal the presumption of mobility in the global refugee regime.

Many displaced people face what we call *induced immobility*: a lack of options for movement made worse by social oppression and disadvantage. Induced immobility is a problem for displaced people as it frustrates their access to protection. But this focus also reveals a tension between the supposedly universal right to seek asylum and the centrality of mobility in the refugee protection architecture. In response to induced immobility, LGBTIQ refugees and organizers self-mobilize to assist one another through queer-led organizations. This need for self-rescue is a direct result of the current bounded nature of refugee protection and its inability or unwillingness to assist those who remain trapped within state borders.[15]

First, we outline the development of what we call *the refugee prevention regime* and the internalization and externalization of border controls, which shape the movement of those seeking international protection toward risky irregular pathways. Second, we extend this analysis by considering the concept of *induced immobility*, which is generated not by explicit movement controls but by oppressive social environments. For gender-diverse LGBTIQ people on the move, induced immobility often arises from pre-existing oppression and discrimination, such as in the case of trans women trapped inside Ukraine. Third, we critique the assumed equity in flight opportunities in the current system of protection for displaced people and ask what might be done about this in-state immobility. The

Rainbow Railroad, an organization that helps LGBTIQ people to escape persecution, offers a potential way forward.

THE REFUGEE PREVENTION REGIME

Appeals to immobility are often used to delegitimize the claims of displaced people who successfully manage to apply for asylum, particularly when they reach the borders of states in the Global North. Anti-immigration commentators bemoan the fact that those seeking asylum in the United Kingdom are disproportionately young men, who are criticized for leaving (their) women and children behind.[16] But the fact of women and children's immobility is not taken by such commentators as a reason to increase refugee resettlement numbers or to provide safe and legal pathways for women and children seeking asylum. Rather, immobility is raised precisely to justify an increasingly closed border that prevents even the most mobile from reaching the other side. This is not a necessary consequence of appeals to immobility. And, as we argue in this chapter, those considering the nature of asylum *ought* to recognize that some people are immobilized. But we should make sure that such arguments are not used to undermine the legitimate claims of refugees who have made it to some standard of safety, despite the odds being so purposefully stacked against them.

Despite the moralized appeals to the immobility of certain refugees (akin to Cynthia Enloe's construction of "womenandchildren"), states in the Global North continually create conditions whereby displaced people are unable to seek international protection.[17] They have done so by creating a border control apparatus that not only prevents people from legally crossing international boundaries but also makes it nearly impossible for them to reach these borders at all. "Fortress Europe," well known for its internal freedom of movement in the Schengen Area, takes drastic action to slow and prevent possible migration from the Middle East and North Africa.[18] This collective intervention by powerful states results in an "engineered regionalism": displaced people almost always remain within host countries in the Global South, with some seeking access to the Global North through dangerous irregular routes.[19] Such structures of border externalization consist of visa restrictions, carrier sanctions, advertising campaigns that attempt to convince would-be migrants to stay put, and international agreements that allow governments to push back those attempting to reach Europe.

Two obvious examples of this final tactic are the agreements between the European Union with Türkiye, and Libya. "The EU-Turkey deal," which came into effect in 2016, aimed to prevent onward migration from Türkiye to Europe.[20] Türkiye agreed to take action to prevent onward travel to the Greek islands, one of the safest ways to reach the European Union across the Mediterranean. Anyone who arrived in Greek territory from Türkiye could be forcibly returned to the country.[21] In exchange, the Turkish government received six billion euros. The International Rescue Committee argued that this policy has had the effect of "trapping thousands of asylum seekers and refugees in limbo with devastating impacts on their physical and mental health."[22] The agreement between the European Union and Libya is more dangerous still. This "cooperation agreement" between the Italian government and Libya, supported by the European Union, has resulted in increased support for the Libyan coastguard, which intercepts and pushes migrants crossing the Mediterranean back. People on the move are detained in Libya in horrific conditions, which are often compared with torture.[23] These policies directly result in the deaths of thousands of people in detention and as they attempt to reach safety through irregular migration routes. Between 2014 and July 2025, over 32,345 people have died in the Mediterranean while seeking to reach European soil.[24]

The use of the natural environment to immobilize people on the move is a key tactic. The Mediterranean functions as a scapegoat for powerful states in the Global North who claim that those drowning making these journeys have simply been taken by the immense force of the sea—as well as their own apparent poor judgment. We should remember that crossing the Mediterranean via regular routes is entirely safe; it is not deadly if you have a visa and a ticket to travel by air or boat.[25] This appeal to nature is used at other borders as well. In *The Land of Open Graves*, Jason De Leon shows that the deaths of migrants in the Sonora desert between the United States and Mexico are not natural but part of a policy that aims to funnel migrants into the most dangerous areas. The policy, dubbed "Prevention Through Deterrence," appropriates the desert as a mechanism, making it a key actor in the network of migration management.[26]

Policies like these prevent people from seeking international protection. But related policies also attempt to strike fear into those making migration plans from the very outset. In 2022, the British Government announced a new policy to "crack down" on human trafficking and smuggling: deporting asylum seekers to Rwanda. Those who arrived in the United Kingdom irregularly—that is, not through limited resettlement or legal pathways—would be at risk of being sent to Rwanda. The deported people would then choose whether to submit an asylum application to the Rwandan government, with no prospect of ever returning to the United Kingdom, even if their asylum claim was found to be successful. The Home Office itself has raised concerns about the treatment of LGBTIQ refugees in Rwanda but simply committed to keeping their position "under review" until the new Labour government came into power in 2024. The then–British Home Secretary, Priti Patel, argued that the new Rwanda policy would deter asylum seekers and save lives in the process.[27] But, at their core, such deterrence policies aim to undercut people's migration plans before they have even begun.[28]

All this paints the picture of an immense migration management regime that is more interested in preventing displaced people from seeking safety than protecting them. In an apparent age of hyper-mobility and globalization, this immobilization prevents people from reaching protection, shelter, and their families. These forms of immobilization are blatant, even though they are still often ignored by those who live within the borders of powerful and prosperous states. And still, there are other forms of immobilization experienced throughout the world that are more subtle but just as powerful in shaping freedom of movement.

INDUCED IMMOBILITY

Mobility is a core concept in many discussions of queer life.[29] LGBTIQ people must often move to find communities of care, whether across international borders or from one community to another within the boundaries of a state. Kath Weston famously called the movement from small towns to big cities in 1970s and 80s America "The Great Gay Migration," and these migrations have become central to Western narratives of homosexuality.[30]

Part of this mobility is based on the hope of building new communities. As Aren Aizura suggests, "at the root of many trans and gender non-conforming people's desire to be mobile is this persistent fantasy: that somewhere else other trans and gender non-conforming subjects are more free."[31] Conversations about queer mobility at the international scale almost exclusively focus on movement from the Global South to the North, which perpetuates the two-sided myth of "barbarism" in the South and "civility" in the North.[32] This framing also fails to capture the different experiences of people on the move.[33] Freedom and safety are, of course, not always the primary reasons that LGBTIQ people migrate.[34] LGBTIQ people are not moving exclusively to flee persecution in search of freedom. Instead, queer and trans people move for as many reasons as cishetero people do.

Studies of queer mobility focus on how queer and trans people negotiate public space but also on the various constraints on their movement. As we saw in the cases of Judis, Alice, and Zi, immobility is a key feature of LGBTIQ people attempting to seek protection, even when fleeing generalized warfare. This is because people are at risk of harm not only from invading armies, foreign border guards, or natural disaster but also from their fellow citizens.[35] Many queer and trans people are harmed not only by the original forces of displacement but also by others fleeing with them. This is compounded across lines of race and gender. Feminists have long recognized women's inability to move safely through intensely "gender-segregated space."[36] Women have adopted strategic practices to make it easier for them to be mobile, such as traveling in groups, seeking well-lit and busy conditions, or asking someone to accompany them. Questions of race change the picture again, with distributions of power shaping how people can move without threat or interference. The excessive surveillance of Black citizens in the United States, particularly when they are stopped by police while driving, suppresses their ability to move freely through neighborhoods.[37] Depending on who you are, and how you are gendered and racialized, immobility can concretely shape the way you live.

For LGBTIQ people, this intersects with questions of visibility and being "out." Those who do not fit within societal norms are punished for appearing in public space. Some can avoid this punishment more than others. Queer and trans people on the move who can conceal their identity may be able to evade some constraints on their mobility. "Passing" occurs when someone is perceived as a member of a social group that does not match their identity. Sometimes LGBTIQ people choose to "pass" and present themselves to the world in a particular way in order to avoid discrimination.[38] For those with nonhegemonic sexual orientations, this might mean presenting oneself as straight. For those with gender-diverse identities, it may instead mean successfully presenting as a hegemonic gender identity. For example, a trans man would "pass" when they are perceived as a cis man. "Covering" is often conceptualized as a more benign demand on LGBTIQ people. When someone covers, they do not attempt to fully disguise their identity, only to mediate and modulate it—for example, by not engaging in same-sex affection in public. Kenji Yoshino distinguishes between converting, passing, and covering, arguing that the history of gay rights has been a slow progression from demands to convert to demands to pass or cover.[39] This may seem like progress, given that people are no longer explicitly encouraged to fundamentally change their identities but simply to conceal them in certain contexts. But Yoshino points out that demands to pass and cover can often feel substantively like demands to convert. Being able to live openly as a queer or trans person is deeply intertwined with questions of identity and is thus a requisite to protecting one's dignity. Concealing and mediating how we act is another way of changing who we are.

LGBTIQ people can (and often do) avoid violence and discrimination by concealing or mediating their identities. But their doing so is not a benign form of camouflage. Besides the questions of identity and a life with dignity, the ability to conceal one's identity has often been used against LGBTIQ refugees when they seek asylum.[40] Until recently, asylum adjudicators around the world may have denied queer and trans people protection precisely on the grounds that they effectively or successfully passed, thus calling into question whether they require asylum if they could simply continue a life of concealment.[41] Thus, even if some LGBTIQ refugees might be able to avoid certain forms of induced immobility by passing or covering, they may also place their eventual application for asylum at risk by doing so.

Some LGBTIQ people on the move are unable to avoid pushing against encoded gender norms. This may mean being harassed and attacked in transit, including enduring homo/transphobic physical and verbal abuse. Again, queer and trans people often adapt to these circumstances in ways that they should not have to, for instance, by taking longer routes home, traveling with others, or concealing their identity.[42] Some trans people choose to dress contrary to their gender identities to access services. Others, like Zi in Kyiv, cannot leave the house at all.

This disparity in movement experiences, as well as the refugee prevention policies we outlined earlier, begin to paint a picture of what we call *induced immobility*: a lack of movement options that are additionally frustrated and compounded by social oppression and disadvantage. In contexts of induced immobility, the social environment can render it difficult or impossible for people to complete or even develop their migration plans. In the fields of refugee and migration studies, there have been several urgent calls for greater focus on immobility.[43] Stephen Lubkemann claims that this is a central gap in refugee studies, with a direct link being implicitly drawn between displacement and physical movement. In his study of war and conflict in Mozambique, Lubkemann argues that it is "those who move *the least* ultimately suffering most dramatically from the war's effects on migration precisely because their baseline mobility-strategies were profoundly disrupted through forced immobilization."[44] In the normative literature, Serena Parekh critiques political theorists' near-exclusive focus on the "ethics of admission," arguing that doing so obscures many people who are in a similar position to refugees but who cannot seek (or do not qualify for) international protection.[45]

Jørgen Carling offered one early attempt to think analytically about immobility in migration studies, arguing that the ability to move and the aspiration to move should be treated separately.[46] This pushed against the assumption that people simply migrated when they wished.[47] Not all immobility is involuntary: some people simply choose not to migrate. But as we have seen from just some of the cases so far, many people have immobility *imposed* upon them. Of course, people shift across these different categories throughout their lives. When LGBTIQ people come out to their families, they may face a sudden mobility deficit, with their networks of support being taken away. They may then eventually shift back to developing attainable migration plans as new communities are built or the old ones are reestablished.[48] While focusing on the mismatch between aspiration and capability is key to understanding the ultimate causes of immobility, it does not allow us to capture the many ways in which *immobilization* is often created and enforced by others. In shifting our attention away from the capability of the individual towards the relational forms of harm that they face, we can capture the more complicated ways in which people's capacities are structured vis-à-vis their ability to move.[49] *Induced immobility* allows us to take account of the fact that movement opportunities are upended by social and political prejudicial practices and the people who enforce them. It is another feature of a cisheteronormative order that shapes and controls the lives of queer and trans people.

Focusing on *induced immobility* allows us to recognize that immobility is causally complex: It results not only from political barriers (border guards) or physical barriers (mountains), but also from an oppressive social environment (homo/transphobia, racism, misogyny, ableism, etc.). Immobility is not, then, a feature that is bound up with the identity of the individual. Women are not immobile for the "natural" fact of being women but because their passage through gender-segregated spaces might introduce risks that they are not willing to take. Women's immobility is thus imposed by the patriarchal features of our world and how these features are normalized or enforced. In focusing on the contingent nature of immobilization, we can learn a great deal from the shift in disability studies towards the social model of disability, which emphasizes that the contingent construction of the built environment is often the primary cause of mobility deficits. Obvious examples of this might include buildings that are made without any form of accessibility: When people create these spaces, it is they who *immobilize* those who cannot enter. Earlier accounts of disability tended to focus on an overmedicalized and individualized approach to impairment.[50] The social model instead shifts focus to the collective and its failure to secure equitable conditions. In other words, people may be physically impaired, but it is society that "disables" people.

The same can be said for induced immobility more generally. It is not that LGBTIQ people like Zi in Kyiv are immobile *because* they are trans women. They are *immobilized* because of how the rest of society chooses to treat trans women and gender-diverse people. The inability to move, then, is compounded by different factors. In the case of LGBTIQ populations seeking safety, immobility is induced by the broader social environment and compounded by conditions of crisis. In this context, queer and trans people are immobilized in society. When they need to flee for their lives, immobility becomes a matter of life and death.

Even though the refugee prevention regime is one of generalized immobility, migration management systems can still have different effects. Some
displaced people are better able to seek assistance, whereas others are unable to reach a border or safe zone and may still encounter violence if they
do. People might lack financial capital and be unable to fund their travel.[51]
Individuals may lack the social networks required to help them escape.
There may be more basic reasons why people are immobilized: there are
sometimes no forms of transport available, or the land is simply too dangerous to cross. People might also be actively prevented from escaping, as
were Judis and Alice. There are many ways in which immobility might be
induced by certain actors, institutions, or social norms.

THE CONSEQUENCES OF IMMOBILITY

It is not difficult to show that some people are unable to move safely. The
concept of induced immobility helps to highlight how the forces that prevent
people from moving are often socially produced; for queer and trans individuals, they are features of a cisheteronormative social environment. Those
likely to suffer persecution, oppression, and discrimination while in public
space will find it difficult to move. Threats to mobility are often a large part
of queer life. Those who violate social norms, by having, for example, a same-
sex partner or a nonconforming gender identity, are at higher risk of harm
while on the move. This immobility is particularly common for trans and
queer people of color, who experience an intersection of different forms of
harassment.[52] As we have already said in our discussion of passing and covering, not all queer and trans people experience immobility in the same way.

But what are the consequences of paying attention to immobility on
these terms? The global refugee regime continues to treat sending-states
primarily as black boxes with sharp, easily discernible borders at which
people can claim protection—that is, as Gloria Anzaldúa describes "a narrow strip along a steep edge."[53] A clear outcome of induced immobility that
is unevenly distributed along social lines is inequality in the right to seek
asylum. To recognize this inequality is not, however, to make a claim about
the "fairness" of the distribution of protection among refugees. This inequality should be recognized instead to emphasize that some individuals

do not have access to the minimal conditions required to seek international assistance. Everyone has an internationally recognized legal right to freedom of movement within their state, even if many states do not respect this entitlement.[54] Internal freedom of movement is required precisely because it protects so many other important interests. In noting the different forms of immobilization faced by LGBTIQ people on the move, it is not our claim that they are the least mobile. To some extent, as we will see in the discussion of the Rainbow Railroad in the final section of this chapter, LGBTIQ have developed networks of escape in response to this context. Instead, what a focus on induced immobility demonstrates is that not everyone can exercise their freedom of movement, and this directly impedes their ability to seek safety.

We are also not arguing that states should prioritize some refugees over others. Discussions of prioritization buy into an ideology of scarcity that we reject.[55] States *do* have the capacity to accept and protect all refugees, but their governments lack the political will to do so. To highlight mobility differences is therefore not about fairness between refugees. It is rather to point out that some are unable to exercise their right to seek asylum because of constraints on their movement, either at the border or deep within the state. Rather than focusing on the potential inequity of asylum opportunities, this helps us to identify inadequacy within the structure and practice of territorialized asylum.[56] States can also reimagine their respective systems of asylum to account for the asymmetries in mobility. We have already discussed the externalization of borders as a result of anti-immigration politics, but there is also an analytical question about whether our current view of asylum as a territorially bounded good is sufficient. When many people cannot overcome limitations placed on their mobility, can we imagine an alternative approach that secures their right to flee?

OVERCOMING IMMOBILITY

We reach a tension: displaced people must be mobile in order to exercise their right to seek asylum, but some people in search of refuge are immobilized by prejudiced social systems of oppression, persecution, and discrimination. In our theoretical terms, this relational harm results from an oppressive cisheteronormative social world, which shapes how LGBTIQ people can move and form migration plans. The ideal solution, of course, is the promotion of freedom of movement for all. This entails the dismantling of various social and political practices and norms that create conditions of induced immobility: homo/transphobia, misogyny, racism, and ableism being among them. While this must be our ultimate goal, there remains the question of how LGBTIQ refugees can seek safety in the here and now.

First, some might rely on a commitment to safe passage. Humanitarian corridors are often demanded in cases of conflict and are logistically supported by international organizations, such as the International Committee of the Red Cross.[57] This presents itself as one way of alleviating at least some of the causes of induced immobility. In the first months of the Russian invasion of Ukraine, humanitarian corridors were agreed upon to allow civilians to flee Russian attacks on major cities. These were routinely closed due to credible reports that the Russian army was planning to attack civilians on the move.[58] Corridors used in other contexts have brought into question the aggressor's political motivations. Russia and Syria offered a joint proposal for a corridor out of Aleppo, but several organizations criticized the move, arguing that the statement implied those who stayed in their city would suffer illegal attacks on the civilian population.[59] Corridors can therefore sometimes be used to bolster objectionable political motives. Moreover, it is not obvious that humanitarian corridors structured in this formal way would assist people who suffer from socially induced immobility. While it clears the way, theoretically, for people to escape, the more structural causes of immobility are left untouched. Zi in Kyiv was unable to leave her house, in part because of the war and in part because of the violence that she would likely suffer on account of her gender identity while attempting to escape. LGBTIQ people on the move often also suffer harm from their fellow migrants. A broad commitment to safe passage, while important, cannot resolve the problem of induced immobility. Judis and Alice *did* reach an international border, but the guards who were left to decide their fate prevented them from moving onward to potential safety.[60]

If safe passage is insufficient, others might consider the possibility of humanitarian intervention to assist those trapped within the boundaries of states. If some are less mobile than others, then perhaps the international community should work *within* the borders of other states to assist those most in need. This interventionist approach is unpalatable to many, and for good reason. Much of the rhetoric surrounding international intervention on behalf of minorities has relied on ideas of a "barbarous," "uncivilized" population that required taming by a benevolent power in the Global North.[61] This is the narrative of the humanitarian "liberal" West, which intervenes in the best interests of those left behind in the Global South.[62] As Kimberley Hutchings puts it: "Within this imaginary, there is a clear asymmetry between the moral status of the humanitarian/liberal actor on the one hand, and the objects of their policies on the other. The only fully agentic player in this imaginary is the humanitarian/liberal."[63]

Induced immobility and its consequences remain unresolved by either of these two options. But a third way is presented by LGBTIQ organizations themselves, who challenge restrictions on mobility and the boundaries of humanitarian organizations through mutual aid efforts. Throughout the world, LGBTIQ activists and organizations have established safe routes to support the mobility of queer and trans people fleeing from harm to safety. In the Americas, a coalition of organizations have joined together to establish the *Red Regional por la Movilidad Humana LGBTIQ+* (Regional Network for LGBTIQ+ Human Mobility). In the face of ongoing violence, exclusion, and institutional neglect for the queer and trans displaced, these organizations have stepped in to provide life-saving support. The organizations operate a network of safe houses and shelter programs specifically for displaced LGBTIQ people, offering not only emergency accommodation but also legal assistance, psychosocial care, and access to health services. These spaces—often underfunded and at risk due to shrinking international aid—are among the few that explicitly recognize and respond to the compounding vulnerabilities faced by LGBTIQ asylum seekers in the region.[64]

Another organization, Rainbow Railroad, works globally to help queer and trans people escape from contexts of persecution. Their name references the well-known Underground Railroad: a network of safe houses throughout the United States that enabled enslaved Black Americans in the antebellum South to flee and travel to free states in the North, Canada, Mexico, and the Caribbean. Rainbow Railroad works globally to help LGBTIQ refugees find safety, but like the Underground Railroad, many of its efforts remain clandestine and rely on secretive social networks to enable escape.

The international refugee regime divides responsibility for assisting displaced people according to whether they have crossed an international border. Internally displaced people—those who remain within the boundaries of the state—have some avenues for seeking assistance, though these are constrained by their continued locality within their country of nationality or residence. When someone has successfully reached an international border, they can claim asylum or another form of international protection. Many organizations therefore refuse to cross over the boundaries of these protection frameworks. The United National High Commissioner for Refugees (UNHCR) is primarily responsible for assisting refugees, whereas the Intentional Organization for Migration (IOM) helps to assist internally displaced people.[65] What these organizations do not often do, however, is assist people in the act of *crossing* international borders. Rainbow Railroad ignores these usual categories and assists people wherever they happen to be, on either side of the border. They therefore work with local community groups within the state, helping people seeking refuge to access a network of safe houses. But they also enable travel out of the state. Their teams not only assist with money and visa applications; they also plot out travel routes based on a particular individual's passport power. This might include making several transfers in order to reach a country where they can seek asylum. In 2023, Rainbow Railroad received over 15,000 requests for support from LGBTIQ people throughout the world.[66]

These organizations are just two of many international protection networks that aim to subvert the norms that undergird the territorially segregated systems of protection for displaced people. In doing so, their operations represent an alternative model for remedying induced immobility. These organizations, working with local LGBTIQ groups, aim to upend the usual conditions of mobility inequality by providing support, creating networks, and offering a path through an otherwise often unworkable system.[67]

The international system of refugee protection is premised on the presumption of mobility. People who hope to seek refuge must make it to a border, a safe zone, a camp, or a humanitarian corridor in order to seek international protection. But, as the case of Ukraine shows us, many LGBTIQ people are immobilized in contexts of displacement, even when the cause of their flight is not directly related to their sexual orientation or gender identity. Alice and Judis were fleeing the Russian invasion, just like everyone else attempting to cross the border. Nevertheless, as trans women, they were rendered immobile by border guards and their subordinated position in a social environment that undermines their ability to flee. These relational forms of harm follow LGBTIQ displaced people when they attempt to seek international protection; the harms that they face are highly mobile and follow them throughout their flight.

Many LGBTIQ people attempting to flee war, climate change, or persecution face serious relational harms that immobilize them while they are on the move. Focusing on queer and trans people and the harms they experience therefore reveals a tension in the current institutions of asylum: People must move to seek protection, but they are immobilized by the world around them. What are we to do about this tension? The Rainbow Railroad and similar organizations, in subverting the international norms of refugee protection, offer a potential way out for LGBTIQ people. But they also demonstrate that it is possible to assist people who suffer from induced immobility. Doing so requires questioning the way we think about the division of labor in the protection of forced migrants and how prejudice and oppression can prevent people from fleeing for their lives.

4 Assessment

Please, have a seat.[1]

Do you feel comfortable?

I'd like you to answer some questions for me. Can you understand what I'm saying?

How did you arrive in this country?

Did you seek asylum as soon as you arrived? Why not?

Tell me about why you are asking for asylum here.

How did you pay for your travel to this country?

Why did you leave your country?

And why exactly are they persecuting you?

What was the harm that you specifically suffered?

Can you describe it for me?

What happened?

When did it happen?

Where were you?

Why did they do that to you?

Do you have proof?

Have you had a medical examination?

Do you have any photographs?

Would things be different if you went back now?

How would they find you?

Would you be recognized?

Could you just live in a different part of your country?

Is there a gay community where you are from?

How would you describe your sexuality?

Did you feel excluded from your community? Why?

Tell me about your relationship with your family.

Do you feel that people treat you differently?

Why do you think they treat you differently?

Do you feel different from other people?

Why do you feel you are different from others?

Do you prefer people refer to you as a man (he), a woman (she), or in another way (they)?

Do you think of yourself as a man (he), a woman (she), or in another way (they)?

What travel documents do you possess and what is the identity shown on them?

What kind of person are you attracted to?

What makes you special in the way you identify or express yourself?

How do you have sex with your partner?

Do you use dating sites?

Do you use video sites?

Do you have videos of yourself having sex with men?

Do you have any photographs?

When did you know you were gay?

What was your first gay experience like?

What does LGBT mean?

You don't know what it means?

What do you find sexually attractive about men?

When you had sex with your partner, did you put your penis into their backside?

When they were penetrating you, did you have an erection?

Did they ejaculate inside you?

Why did you use a condom?

What is it about men's backsides that attracts you?

What is it about the way men walk that turns you on?

Was it loving sex or rough?

So, you had intercourse with him not just blow jobs?

What have you found is the most successful way of pulling men?

Where do you go for nights out?

Where do you go for nights out in London?

Do you read Oscar Wilde?

Do you use sex toys?

Would you like a break? You don't have to disclose information if it is upsetting for you.

What turns you on about other men?

What turns you on about other women?

When did you last have sex with your partner?

Can you tell me about that?

Where did you have oral sex?

How long did you have sex for?

How long do you think it was for?

Did you each have oral sex?

After you gave him oral sex, what happened then?

Then what did you do?

Did he perform oral sex on you?

Did he do it to you first?

Did he ejaculate? Did he reach a climax?

How long did it take you to ejaculate?

Why was drinking his cum a problem?

You don't normally do that?

You've only done it once?

When you were having oral sex, did you usually use a condom?

How long after you had swallowed his cum, how long after that did you go for a sexual health test?

As a lesbian, you must go to clubs—which ones have you been to?

Did you attend Pride?

You don't look like a lesbian.

Do you have children?

Why do you have children if you are a lesbian?

Can you provide photographs of you and your partner together?

Can you provide videos of you and your partner?

What does it mean to be a lesbian in your country?

Have you ever had sex with a woman?

What does your family think about you sleeping with other women?

What does the bible teach about being a lesbian?

Does being a lesbian conflict with being a Christian?

Is there anything else you would like to add?

Displaced people seeking refuge on the grounds of their sexuality or gender identity often face intense scrutiny during their asylum interviews. State officials are tasked with determining whether such individuals are entitled to international protection and often hope to reveal some underlying "truth" about whether their request for sanctuary is authentic.[2] Interviewers and asylum caseworkers have historically demanded "evidence" of sexuality or gender identity, such as coming-out stories, narratives of complex inner lives, family dynamics, or stories involving illicit and hidden sexual desire.[3] These questions seek some fact about an individual's experience of persecution, but they also aim to uphold the state's right to exclude those who do not meet the correct standard to qualify for international protection. In the current international order, states have a right to determine their own membership and entry requirements and therefore the right to exclude or expel those who do not qualify for international protection. Refugees must demonstrate a "well-founded fear of persecution" to qualify for asylum under the 1951 Geneva Convention.[4] We saw in chapter 2 that the application of the concept of persecution can often exclude LGBTIQ people because of failures to account for its socially situated nature. This is a particular problem for LBQ women and nonbinary people who flee more private forms of violence.

Of course, there is a difference between claiming that a state has a right to determine its own membership and the question of *how* this process should be adjudicated. This is what Bernardo Zacka calls "the political theory of implementation."[5] As the questions above show, LGBTIQ asylum seekers have historically faced extremely invasive interviews in the name of catching "bogus" claimants. This could be thought of as part of the state's tendency to simplify, categorize, and sort in the name of top-down order. Or it could, quite reasonably, be seen as an outcome of blatantly homo/transphobic attitudes among some asylum adjudication officers.

In recent years, some of the harshness in this process has softened, particularly when it comes to asking for graphic details of sexual activities, preferences, and desires.[6] National and international guidance now recognizes the importance of special training for adjudicating LGBTIQ claims to refuge.[7] They also note potential complicating factors during the interview, such as the presence of family members, interpreters from the applicant's state of origin, or the possibility of the late disclosure of their sexual orientation or gender identity during the refugee status determination process. This final point is especially important, as many would-be refugees are never told that they can apply for international protection on grounds of their sexuality or gender identity.

This guidance is certainly welcome, though it is not clear that it has led to changes in practice beyond piecemeal adaptations.[8] There is well-documented evidence that asylum seekers still face upsetting lines of questioning, such as being asked to recount experiences of sexual violence. Others, especially LBQ women, are still denied international protection on the basis that their own testimony is not deemed "credible."[9] So, while people seeking refuge may be given more breaks and asked fewer intrusive questions, they still face many of the same basic assumptions about who is entitled to protection and on what grounds and, crucially, who is worthy of being believed.[10]

In the study of queer and trans displacement, the refugee status determination process (particularly the substantive interview) is a much-discussed topic. Dozens of brilliant studies reveal the failures of an assessment process grounded in disbelief and premised on Western conceptualizations of sexuality, gender, and displacement.[11] LGBTIQ asylum seekers are often misbelieved or explicitly viewed as deceptive.[12] Furthermore, state officials might impose a particular view of sexuality or gender as an identity, whereas in some contexts it is better understood as a set of practices; or they might assume that identity is fixed rather than fluid.[13] In the refugee status determination process, adjudicators often force their own framings and narratives onto the experience of queer and trans displacement, reflecting their own biases.[14] For example, asylum applicants are often implicitly expected to demonstrate that they feel ashamed of their sexuality or gender identity and are now on a determined path to "acceptance."[15] Other scholarship has emphasized how asylum systems fail to account for the intersectional identities and experiences of applicants.[16]

Aderonke Apata's case shows how the assumption of deceit can reshape the reception of one's claim during assessment.[17] Aderonke fled Nigeria after being charged with adultery and witchcraft because she was caught having an affair with a woman.[18] She was initially denied asylum by the UK Home Office because she had children from a previous heterosexual relationship and therefore was not believed to be a lesbian.[19] As part of her appeal, and out of desperation for her sexuality to be recognized (or believed) by the courts, Aderonke presented photo and video evidence of intimate relations with her fiancée. While the High Court judge rejected the Home Office's argument that she was not a lesbian because she had children, the judge agreed with the accusation that she was engaging in same-sex relationships "in order to fabricate an asylum claim based on claimed lesbian sexuality." The judge also accepted the claim that she was dressing and presenting herself in a particular manner "purely as a way of gaining refugee status." Aderonke was therefore viewed as deceitful by the UK asylum system, and any potential evidence of her sexuality was viewed as fabricated. LGBTIQ refugees therefore face a kind of double burden. They need to demonstrate that they have experienced (or will experience) persecution. But they also must prove *who they are*. Aderonke eventually did receive asylum, after thirteen years. During her asylum process, she founded the aid organization African Rainbow Family, and five years after receiving refugee status, she was called to the bar of England and Wales as a qualified barrister.[20]

Rather than repeat the arguments of our peers, we choose here to present the reality. In the composite that begins this chapter, the questions presented have been documented in asylum interviews in Australia, Canada, the United Kingdom, Germany, and the United States between the years 2010 and 2022.[21] It is not obvious that every experience of LGBTIQ asylum needs additional normative theorization. And, in particular, it is sometimes superfluous to explain why something is wrong beyond a mere confrontation of the facts. What this list of questions reveals is that the moment of legal adjudication by state actors, one that is perhaps often thought of as impartial, formal, or bureaucratic, is also a site of relational harm undergirded by prejudiced beliefs that are products of a cisheteronormative world. The homophobic social environment that people might flee in search of refuge also follows them into the state of asylum, and even into the interview room itself.

5 Containment

Victoria Arellano was a Mexican woman who came to the United States as a child and remained undocumented. As an adult, she was arrested for driving under the influence, arrested, charged, and eventually taken to an immigration detention center. Victoria was sent to a men's detention facility, the San Pedro Service Processing Center. According to various reports, she was friendly with the other detainees and often very positive about her situation. Before being detained, Victoria had been diagnosed with HIV; she was being treated with daily medication, and her symptoms had virtually disappeared. Upon entering detention, she was refused her prescription. As her health began to deteriorate, she requested to visit the nurse on several occasions but was still refused her medication by the detention center staff. Her fellow detainees began smuggling her extra food and speaking to the guards on her behalf. Once, when the guards forced Victoria to go outside despite barely being able to stand, the other detainees protested and began to chant, demanding that Victoria be taken to the hospital. The guards were forced to take her inside, but she was only given painkillers and water. Finally, she was taken to hospital, where she died an entirely preventable death.[1] Queer and trans people experience many forms of violence while contained—both by guards and their fellow detainees. Victoria's story is testament to the failure of the immigration detention system but also to the hardship trans women face in detention.

In the United States, migrants are routinely detained in unacceptable conditions. Detention centers run by US Immigration and Customs Enforcement (ICE) have come under extreme scrutiny following staff practices of physical, verbal, and sexual abuse; forced strip searches; unprovoked use of pepper spray; and a lack of support for medical needs.[2] Because of this, the American Civil Liberties Union has labeled ICE detention centers as "justice-free zones."[3]

LGBTIQ detainees frequently report experiencing extreme violence and abuse within ICE detention centers. According to the Center for American Progress, LGBTIQ people are 97 times more likely to experience sexual abuse in detention than cishetero detainees.[4] Many are housed in single-gender centers where they risk facing homo/transphobic hostility from other detainees.[5] For trans people who do not wish to be detained in such facilities, the only alternative is often solitary confinement, which can lead to acute mental anguish.[6] Research has shown that the experience of trans women in immigration detention has psychological effects comparable to torture.[7]

Thus far, we have explored how the persecution experienced by queer and trans refugees is socially situated and results from a relational harm that is the product of homo/transphobic social environments that enforce the cisheteronormative order. But this harm is not limited to the countries of origin, as its relational and capillary nature does not respect national boundaries. In this chapter, we explore how containment practices can change the locus of harm to the state of refuge itself. First, we turn to another story of such harms.

Kakuma is one of the largest refugee camps in Kenya, housing around three hundred thousand people.[8] Originally opened in 1992 in response to a rapid increase in Sudanese refugees, it is now home to displaced people from many countries, including Ethiopia, Eritrea, South Sudan, Somalia, Rwanda, and Uganda. The Kenyan government has threatened to close the camp many times, demanding more support from international actors such as UNHCR.[9] In June 2022, UNHCR was faced with an ultimatum: develop a new plan for camp management or Kakuma would be permanently closed.[10] Kakuma's closure would be an obvious problem for UNHCR, as would any issue with the Kenyan state. Kenya is an important partner for UNHCR; in addition to its role hosting hundreds of thousands of refugees in the region, Kenya was once the only country in East Africa willing to provide protection to LGBTIQ refugees, even though homosexuality remains a crime in the country.[11] However, the Department for Refugees in Kenya, which is responsible for registering applications, has recently ceased all processing of asylum claims on the grounds of sexual orientation or gender identity.[12] The right to asylum as an LGBTIQ person in Kenya has therefore been thrown into question. As a result of their inability to access asylum, LGBTIQ people have started leaving Kenya for South Sudan (an active war zone), Zambia, and Ethiopia in order to apply for protection in other camps where UNHCR has a presence.[13] Still, the Kakuma camp remains open, for now.

Multiple reports have documented the vulnerable situation of LGBTIQ refugees within Kakuma. Queer and trans displaced people had been informally grouped in "Block 13," an area that was meant to segregate them from other camp residents for their own protection. However, the grouping of LGBTIQ refugees together made them "hypervisible" to others, singling them out for abuse more easily.[14] The Organization for Refuge, Asylum, and Migration (ORAM) shared survey data from 2021 showing that 100 percent of trans respondents in Kakuma had been physically assaulted within the camp. This only dropped to 83 percent when expanded to all LGBTIQ respondents.[15] LGBTIQ refugees in the camp reported their concerns to camp officials, but the threats were not taken seriously. On March 15, 2021, a camp inhabitant threw a petrol bomb at two gay men as they slept outside on a mattress. A month later, Chriton Atuhwera, one of the men who had been attacked, died from his injuries. A spokesperson for Block 13, Gilbert Kagarura said, "It wasn't as though there were no warning signs. For years, we have been complaining about the threats we face and asking to be moved elsewhere yet nothing has happened." In response, Rainbow Railroad and ORAM have called for swifter resettlement pathways and new support for the LGBTIQ people displaced within the camp, including the right to relocate to an urban setting where protection is greater.[16] UNHCR has since issued a statement indicating that protection has been increased for queer and trans people living within the camp and that they remain committed to supporting and protecting LGBTIQ refugees.[17]

Here again, persecution is not limited to countries of origin, as the relational harms faced by LGBTIQ people follow them across borders. In this chapter, we explore how containment practices themselves exacerbate this harm and can change the locus of persecution to the state of refuge itself.

Why tell the stories of Victoria and Chriton together? Because both their deaths resulted from the consequences of containment in different contexts. Refugee camps and detention centers are not often spoken about in the same breath, but they represent different types within a series: two spaces within which refugees, people on the move, and the undocumented face extreme constraints on their movements and freedom, with serious consequences. In the Kakuma camp, the authorities failed to protect a gay man from physical abuse from another camp resident, eventually leading to his death.[18] In the ICE detention center, detainees pleaded with security guards who refused to acknowledge that a trans woman was slowly dying on their watch.

Displaced people often face extreme constraints on their movement. We have already seen that the process of attempting to reach an international border is fraught with challenges. Such challenges do not stop once a border has been crossed. Our argument here does not favor incremental improvements to detention centers and camps. Of course, it would have been better if Victoria had been given her medicine: this is the absolute minimum that we should expect. But focusing on queer and trans people deprived of their liberty in each context gives us a broader argument against containment practices altogether. We build this argument by drawing on the advocacy and organizing of LGBTIQ people themselves, such as the activists who fight against the existence of ICE detention centers in the United States. In their work, they show how the relational elements of harm become exacerbated by the structures of containment. In doing so, we make the argument that the containment setting can become a new site of persecution in the state of refuge, often exacerbated by state practice.

CAMPS AND DETENTION CENTERS: A JOINT APPROACH

This chapter explicitly treats refugee camps and detention centers under the same framework. Doing so requires justification. The standard understanding is that refugee camps are arranged to protect refugees, offering humanitarian assistance, shelter, food, and more. Detention centers, however, are where "bogus asylum seekers" and "criminals" are kept before a due process hearing or their eventual deportation. Each space therefore appears to operate under a unique logic: Camps are designed to assist the displaced in line with humanitarian ideals whereas detention centers contain the unruly and the illegitimate in line with punitive motivations. Criticizing them in the same way, then, might ignore this important difference. But detention and encampment are similar in several crucial respects.

First, camps and detention centers are heterogeneous in similar ways. Detention occurs both before and after state borders, at airports, buried deep in the countryside, or in an individual's own home. Encampment can occur within cities; on the edges or in between states; in large, organized facilities; and in self-established "informal" settlements. As such, both the camp and the detention center are difficult to define. The people who are contained within camps and detention centers are also deeply varied. Many people with protection claims are wrongly kept in detention centers.[19] For instance, in Yarl's Wood, a now-closed detention center for women in the United Kingdom, many detainees were found to have valid residence or asylum claims.[20] Thus, the idea that camps host the legitimate and detention centers host the illegitimate ignores reality. In many cases, the spaces of detention and encampment directly overlap. Yarl's Wood was closed as a detention center for women facing potential removal. But the British government has since proposed using the empty building to house asylum seekers arriving across the Channel in what has been described as "prisonlike" conditions.[21] Thus, the line between detention and encampment blurs.

Second, both camps and detention centers depend on a logic of containment. This does not mean that all camps and forms of detention always deprive people of freedom of movement. Camps can be more porous than traditional detention facilities, particularly when they develop from more informal settlements. Detention centers contain in sometimes more explicit ways. In being designed to mirror the prison system, they often lock people in buildings and sometimes in solitary confinement for months at a time. But even without absolute restrictions on mobility, both settings still represent a particular expression of state sovereignty and power.[22] In such instances, states retain the legitimate authority to contain and enforce containment when they choose to do so.[23] So, while camps sometimes do not contain, they still depend on a similar motivation: containment at the behest of the state.

Third, both spaces create new forms of vulnerability. This is partly because containment itself creates new harms, ones that cut across categories of race, gender, sexual orientation, disability, and class. For instance, in camps, refugees and asylum seekers face new challenges they had not encountered either on the move or in their state of asylum. Gemma Bird argues that standard gendered and racialized categorizations of vulnerability created by states to distinguish between "deserving" and "undeserving" recipients of asylum are disrupted in the context of the camp where groups that are ignored face extremely long waiting times, adverse conditions, and lack of medical assistance.[24] The camp therefore creates *new* contexts in which standard essentialized categories of vulnerability become disrupted. As we saw in the case of Victoria, detention centers also create new harms against detainees, ones that were not present before containment. Victoria was denied medical treatment at the hands of the detention center guards. She died in detention even though just months earlier she had been living without any symptoms. Part of this new vulnerability is generated because camps and detention centers are often geographically dislocated, often placed far away from other towns and cities, as well as being run by private corporations.[25] This all creates a system under which it is difficult for nonresidents to access information about what goes on beyond the walls or boundaries. Camps and detention centers therefore create new conditions that can have serious effects on the lives of those contained within them.

These three reasons justify a joint approach to the question of containment: one that recognizes the relevant similarities between the two settings. This does not mean that refugee camps and detention centers are the same or that all analyses of one can apply neatly to the other. There remain important differences in the constitution of camps, the people who work there, and the ways in which they assist (or do not assist) people on the move. They nonetheless share key similarities such that some critiques apply across both cases: the experiences of LGBTIQ people in both camps and detention facilities show that similar problems arise when queer and trans people are contained. As a result of state policy, displaced people are put in conditions of extreme danger with little attention paid to the conditions that exacerbate their vulnerabilities.

THE PROBLEMS OF CONTAINMENT

A queer critique of containment might simply begin with an account of the harms that LGBTIQ people face while contained. We know from the two cases above that camps and detention centers can have disastrous consequences for queer and trans people. But it is worth considering how these manifest and consequently, who might be responsible for remedying their harmful practices. The global expansion of immigration detention began in the 1970s but exploded post-9/11 when states used the new global agenda of counterterrorism to legitimize more extreme forms of border control. Detention is often justified by politicians and government officials on the grounds that holding people is necessary before their cases are heard or they are deported, but often these centers also contain people awaiting asylum procedures. States are legally entitled to detain migrants if they are deemed a threat to public safety or if they have committed a crime, but they routinely stretch this entitlement far beyond what is reasonable.[26] Detainees are therefore contained under the auspices of security, leading to their being conceptualized as criminals. What detention *is* therefore shapes how we think about the detained.[27]

Detention as a practice has come under sustained criticism from human rights and immigration justice organizations for many years. Even so, states resist the continued calls for alternatives and more humane treatment for migrants. Just a few years ago, criticism of the United States' detention regime reached a climax, when parents were being forcibly separated from their children while attempting to seek safety at the Southern border. As of January 2025, many separated families have still not been reunited.[28] Beyond the United States, global detention regimes within the refugee and asylum system create torturous conditions for people claiming asylum. Externalized border controls often involve detention in third countries, such as the European Union's involvement in Libyan detention centers, which have been found to use torture and blackmail to extract money from inmates and their families.[29] Detention centers therefore have a long history of harming many of those forcibly kept inside.

Victoria's story sits within a broader systemic failure across detention centers. For many LGBTIQ people, the general harms of detention are compounded and exacerbated.[30] Most detention facilities are segregated by sex, which is often not accommodating to LGBTIQ detainees. While there used to be some special recommendations and procedures for queer and trans people in detention, these were routinely ignored by immigration officials and detention staff. These procedures have ceased altogether during the current Trump Administration, as one of the president's first executive orders was to dismantle any federal government protections for transgender identities.[31] Queer and trans people in detention are therefore often placed in an impossible situation of having to either "out" themselves to receive accommodation (if even possible) or having to hide to avoid discrimination. In other words, disclosing their LGBTIQ identity might help someone access additional support, if available, but it could also make them vulnerable to abuse.[32] Stefan Vogler and Rocío Rosales argue that trans women are vulnerable because their classification as transgender can often morph into forms of punishment and exclusion.[33] Trans women are often physically isolated from other detainees and are threatened with "outing" by detention officials.

Even when LGBTIQ people do disclose themselves to staff, many face abuse, sexual and physical assault, social isolation, and withdrawal of medical treatment. One such case involved a queer asylum seeker from El Salvador, Laura Monterrosa, who filed a complaint of sexual assault against an ICE officer—in other words, an official of the American government. While the investigation was ongoing, Laura was kept detained while her assaulter continued working at the same facility—a situation so stressful that she tried to take her own life in order to escape it.[34] Laura was then forced into solitary confinement, where other ICE officials (American government officials) attempted to coerce her into withdrawing the complaint. She was eventually released, but only after many months. This form of solitary confinement is often called "administrative segregation" and is frequently justified for LGBTIQ detainees on the grounds of protecting them from other detained populations. But as we have seen in the cases of Victoria and Laura, it can be the detention center officials, not other detained people, who perpetrate abuse against LGBTIQ people in detention.[35]

Being confined alone, often in very poor conditions, has serious consequences for mental and physical health. In the United States, reports have indicated that, similar to Laura's case, solitary confinement has been used as a form of punishment for speaking out against abuse, as well as for requesting medical or mental health treatment in ICE detention. For example, many trans detainees reported considering or attempting suicide while in extended solitary confinement, revealing the severe traumatic effects of such treatment.[36] This confinement creates new forms of harm. In response to this, the European Court of Human Rights has ruled that isolating queer and trans people in detention "deprives them of meaningful access to detention center services or is tantamount to penal solitary confinement."[37] Nevertheless, the practice continues in many detention centers across the world.[38]

While there are numerous reports about LGBTIQ experiences in detention centers, there is much less available information about camps. Beyond Kakuma, where the queer and trans population have been organizing for themselves and involving international actors, there are limited studies of LGBTIQ displaced people in camp settings. News reports indicate that experiences similar to Kakuma occur elsewhere in the world. A queer Serbian couple was reportedly attacked in a refugee camp in Germany while attempting to seek protection; this happened after their application to leave the camp was denied.[39] In Dutch camps, Russian LGBTIQ asylum seekers have waited up to twenty-one months in deplorable conditions for their cases to be processed, with activists documenting five suicides of LGBTIQ asylum seekers in one year in these Dutch camps.[40] LGBTIQ refugees in camps therefore face the same challenge as queer and trans people in detention: they must choose between hiding or outing themselves. In a context where escape is impossible, exposing your identity is often extremely risky. In a recent documentary about LGBTIQ refugees in Greece, human rights activist Gregory Vallianatos observed, "Being outed in a camp is even more difficult than swimming across the Aegean."[41]

States compound the effects of containment with other measures that further punish those seeking asylum. For instance, many states adopt border externalization practices whereby refugees are relocated to detention centers or camps in third countries that have hostile social environments for LGBTIQ populations. In Australia, people who attempt to seek asylum are removed to detention-like facilities in Nauru and on Manus Island in Papua New Guinea in line with their third-country processing agreements.[42] In Papua New Guinea, homosexuality is criminalized, and many gay asylum seekers have written to the Australian government and human rights groups to outline their fear for their lives. One Iranian refugee, Ahmed, said the following:

> I have to hide my sexuality because in this country, like Iran, there are a lot of people—fanatics—whom if they find out anyone is gay they would harass them and maybe even try to kill them. I have to hide my personality once again. I have to live as someone else.[43]

B Camminga argues that in Kakuma, LGBTIQ refugees are asked to act with "discretion," leading to parallel experiences of invisibility and hypervisibility.[44] Once queer and trans refugees were segregated into their own zone in the camp, they became easier targets for other camp residents. As Camminga argues, living together provided safety in numbers, but it effectively outed the zone's residents, including those not previously known as LGBTIQ. Some non-LGBTIQ refugees thought that queer and trans people were receiving preferential treatment and threatened them. The case of the trans Ugandan refugee, Julia, demonstrates the challenges of hypervisibility in containment contexts such as Kakuma. Camminga writes, "Julia's gender expression, something which she found almost impossible to hide even when she did grow a beard, coupled with her nationality as a Ugandan in Kenya made her a lightning rod for anti-LGBTQ+ sentiment."[45] Of course, LGBTIQ people are often treated in violent and oppressive ways throughout their lives. The camp therefore acts as a microcosm for their lives beyond its boundaries. But the conditions of containment also expand and exacerbate these harms.[46]

ON INTRAGROUP HARM

Multiple themes have recurred throughout this book, but one that we have not addressed head-on is the question of intragroup harm: the perpetration of oppression, domination, and violence against refugees by *other* refugees. The Kakuma case appears to be a clear example of this phenomenon. LGBTIQ refugees were attacked by other encamped people.[47] Other examples we have used throughout the book are similar: When refugees attempt to flee, they face violence perpetrated by border guards and state officials, but also by other people on the move who are attempting to escape. If not treated carefully, the use of these examples could wrongly paint an image of those leaving the Global South as "uncivilized," people from whom LGBTIQ refugees need to be saved.[48] This way of conceptualizing LGBTIQ refugee protection can therefore represent an element of Jasbir Puar's theory of "homonationalism": a form of inclusion of LGBTIQ people by Western countries predicated on "saving them" from hostile "uncivilized others" that bolsters nationalist logics of exclusion and securitization in order to maintain the global order of power.[49] So, what are we to think about these instances of intragroup harm?

There are similar discussions around the question of refugee women. In "Saving Brown Women from Brown Men?" Heaven Crawley challenges the narrative that women in the South need to be rescued by supposedly noble actors in the Global North. Refugee women, Crawley writes, are understood through a neocolonial frame, which serves to "flatten out the complexity and diversity of women's experiences, in turn, decontextualizing and depoliticizing the specific circumstances under which violence and other threats occur."[50] "Refugee women" are therefore portrayed as one homogenous group of "victims," fleeing a single and clear perpetrator: men from the Global South. Such a view depends on assumptions about the supposed essential vulnerability of women but also reentrenches colonial articulations of who is violent and who is enlightened. Read (or written) in the wrong way, discussions of intragroup harms faced by LGBTIQ refugees could be thought to have a similar effect. Such discussions could flatten the experience of queer and trans refugees and paint them as a single homogenous set of victims considered in a political vacuum. This is dangerous because, as with the case of women, it perpetuates the idea that LGBTIQ refugees are "inherently" vulnerable, rather than *made vulnerable* by a dominant cisheteronormative ideology.[51]

This does not mean that cases of intragroup harm never occur or should be ignored. Instead, we should think about their context and effects in a complicated and careful way. The Kakuma case is a clear example of the importance of context. Conversations about homo/transphobic violence in the African continent, for instance, "paint Africans as inherently more violent towards, and less tolerant of, sexual and gender minorities than their Western counterparts."[52] But as Chan Tov McNamarah points out, these conversations often fail to highlight the colonial legacies of British imperial laws, which criminalized homosexuality and other forms of gender-diverse behavior. There remain regional variations in homo/transphobia across the postcolonial states in Africa. And this variation in part depends on whether antisodomy laws were actively enforced during the colonial period. Where they were, these imported attitudes tend to be more entrenched today.[53] But this framing of homophobia as something entirely imported from the outside might risk treating communities in the Global South as though they have no agency over their own destiny. Rahul Rao has critiqued different ways of locating homophobia in space and time, discussing in particular the debate around Uganda's 2014 Anti-Homosexuality Act. According to Rao, there are two dominant frames: one that views homophobia to be part of an African tradition and the other that frames it as a Western colonial import. Instead, Rao argues that in such contexts, homophobia "emerges as a transnational collaborative construction involving Ugandan and Western elites."[54]

It is obvious that some people on the move will hold social prejudices that put LGBTIQ people at risk. Acknowledging this is simply an outcome of recognizing that refugees are not a uniform mass. Instead, they are as politically and socially varied as any other population, unified often only by their need for protection. There is good reason to speak about intragroup harm in a discussion on containment. One key reason is that conditions of containment make all refugees vulnerable in new ways but also create the architecture for more instances of intragroup harm to occur. Refugee camps and detention centers bundle people from different backgrounds into close quarters, often forcing them to live in constant contact with each other and in situations of resource deprivation. In these contexts where people are physically trapped together, confronted with artificial scarcity, and denied their fundamental freedoms, the prevalence of intragroup violence is likely to increase. Camps and detention centers are often kept geographically distant from other community resources that could provide key services and oversight in the asylum state, so it should not surprise us that intragroup harm occurs. However, the prevalence of this kind of violence is sustained by practices of containment.

In containment practices, these intragroup harms directly relate to state policy. The conditions of intragroup harm obviously result from prejudice, but they are produced by both the extreme restrictions on mobility perpetrated through containment practices as well as the state's inability or unwillingness to curb such harmful behavior. This is made evident by the examples from Kakuma camp, where the Kenyan government put harsh restrictions on mobility for refugees and then UNHCR staff encouraged the self-segregation of Block 13 in a context in which security officers were unwilling or unable to guarantee their safety, effectively increasing their visibility and limiting their protection. Earlier in this book, we recognized that homo/transphobic acts of violence against LGBTIQ populations by non-state actors can amount to persecution when the state is unable or unwilling to safeguard the well-being of its queer and trans people. Here, in the case of intragroup harm occurring in containment spaces, we have a different case: The state cannot or will not safeguard the LGBTIQ population, and in fact, it *creates* the conditions for such homo/transphobic harm to flourish. Through this framing, new forms of anti-LGBTIQ harm thus result from the policies of the states of refuge, introducing new spaces for persecution to take place.

However, the relational harm faced by LGBTIQ refugees in containment is not limited to intragroup harm. Queer and trans refugees also face extreme violence and oppression at the hands of state officials.[55] This is obviously demonstrated in the case of Victoria, whose fellow detainees protested on her behalf against the ICE guards who were meant to care for her wellbeing. But this is also the case in Kakuma where police have demonstrated extreme disregard for the security of LGBTIQ people in the wake of violent attacks, exposing them to further risk by denying them protection.[56] These acts of violence perpetrated or abetted by state officials toward LGBTIQ people also amount to persecution as they result from pervasive prejudice against LGBTIQ populations. State agents who enforce containment policies can (and do) contribute to the social environment within which these forms of relational harm come to flourish.

While containment can create the conditions for intragroup harm to occur, in many cases, contained people work together to protect and assist one another.[57] There is a tendency to focus on intragroup harm and ignore these cases, perhaps, because the former buys into preconceptions about who is the perpetrator of anti-LGBTIQ violence. Intragroup harm, then, should not be ignored. But it also needs to sit beside a proper articulation of the contexts within which it takes place. In containment, this context is a government-led system that produces unique sociopolitical structures in which new forms of anti-LGBTIQ harm can be produced or existing harms can be exacerbated. It is a result of state practice and powerful international actors that people on the move are forcibly contained together, in situations from which no one can escape.

A QUEER CRITIQUE OF CONTAINMENT

As containment *itself* creates new forms of harm and vulnerability that can amount to persecution, a case can be made for its abolishment. However, some might be tempted, in response to the realities of LGBTIQ containment, to argue in favor of separation or prioritization rather than abolition. Separation, first, might involve segregating LGBTIQ refugees from the general population, perhaps into their own camps or detention centers. We know from previous chapters that queer and trans people often practice a form of self-segregation in order to create their own communities of care and support.[58] But in the case of continued containment, this option should be dismissed. First, as we saw in the case of Kakuma, segregation can often make people "hyper-visible."[59] Second, we know that queer and trans people on the move do not suffer *only* at the hands of their fellow migrants. In the case of Victoria, other detainees defended her from ICE officials. Segregation does not protect LGBTIQ people from government officials or NGO staff in positions of power. Sharry Aiken and Stephanie J. Silverman note that the Obama administration attempted to segregate queer and trans people, particularly trans women, in detention in "pods," apparently for their own wellbeing.[60] The consequence was that LGBTIQ detainees were even further separated from their communities and were left in conditions of extreme isolation. This separation model mirrors similar calls to create "transgender prisons" to respond to the specific needs of trans people in contexts of incarceration. But this method of separation as a kind of reform fails to take seriously the depth of the critique. As Eric Stanley puts it, "What abolition helps us understand . . . is that the only prison that would be responsive to gender is one that ceases to exist."[61] In other words, the very structure of containment itself makes queer and trans people on the move more vulnerable. Ayten Gündoğdu argues that containment practices compound vulnerability and precarity because migrants must rely on the "benevolence" of their captors.[62] Segregation, then, cannot resolve this vulnerability, particularly under the reigning paradigm of cisheteronormativity.

Others might argue in favor of prioritization: LGBTIQ migrants ought to be offered resettlement or release *over and above* other detainees. Doing so would resolve their vulnerabilities by taking them alone out of situations of containment. Indeed, this has been the response of organizations, such as Rainbow Railroad, who seek to reduce harm wherever possible. Similar arguments have been made about other groups who are deemed vulnerable, such as women and children or victims of torture. While prioritization could in principle help to ameliorate some of the vulnerabilities of LGBTIQ people on the move in the here and now, it does not fully recognize the breadth of the critique of containment that arises from what we have discussed so far. We might also note that prioritization policies can sometimes lead to the perception of "special treatment," resulting in backlash and an exacerbation of harm. Moreover, while LGBTIQ people are particularly vulnerable to practices of containment, their position also tells us about the nature of detention and encampment more generally. Noticing the structural consequences of containment practices offers a more general argument in favor of abolition; it is almost impossible to imagine an immigration detention regime that does not harm and dominate those who are contained within it, even when LGBTIQ people are removed from that system.

Aiken and Silverman distinguish between two forms of abolition as it relates to containment practices. Penal abolitionism critiques containment as a form of punishment, whereas carceral abolitionism more generally rejects all containment practices, including those related to immigration.[63] The case in favor of carceral abolition is substantiated by the growing evidence that detention provides no benefits to the detained or the surrounding community.[64] Detention is therefore not about the promotion of justice but the role it plays as a form of political spectacle.[65] Both kinds of abolitionists (penal and carceral) argue that resources should be distributed in more equitable and just ways.[66] Abolitionism is therefore not only a negative project of deconstruction, but a positive project of imagining something better.

Queer resistance and abolition have a long, shared history.[67] And queer-led organizations pursuing justice for LGBTIQ people trapped in detention often situate themselves within a broader carceral abolitionist framework. In other words, they not only argue in favor of justice for queer and trans people but critique the very institution of detention itself. For instance, many activists are part of the broader movement to abolish ICE.[68] This goal is not just about reducing individualized or piecemeal harm, which the practices of segregation or prioritization might contribute to, but about reimagining the world of immigration and freedom of movement. Jennicet Guttiérez, a founding member of Familia: Trans Queer Liberation Movement, describes the promise of ICE detention abolition in this way: "We wouldn't only be free, but we'd finally live in our full humanity and have opportunities to fulfill our dreams."[69] Importantly, this does not mean that harm reduction is never a part of LGBTIQ-led organizing on this issue. Many organizations do highlight discrete policies or argue in favor of release in particular cases. These two approaches are not zero-sum. As Eric Stanley, Dean Spade, and Queer In(justice) argue, when working toward carceral abolition, "we can do so in ways that both address/support the immediate needs of prisoners and use that work to expose, educate around, and organize against the evil of the system itself."[70] Put differently, it is possible to engage in the realities of the "here and now" while fighting for something different.

It is difficult to dislocate carceral forms of containment from modern politics. We are led to believe that such institutions are totally indispensable. As Angela Davis puts it in *Are Prisons Obsolete?*, "Prison is considered an inevitable and permanent feature of our social lives."[71] The same can be said for immigration detention. Politicians describe detention as "regrettable but necessary," claiming that mere reform is needed rather than total deconstruction.[72] Camps are also seen as necessary in many contexts, although alternatives to camps are often more successful in assisting people on the move.

Some may think that a move in favor of abolition is simply going too far; segregation or, failing that, prioritization are perhaps more reasonable and likely solutions to the problems of containment. It is not our aim to critique those who must do the hard work of attending to and supporting the lives of LGBTIQ people in camps and detention centers. As we have said, the harm reduction approach is often the only option. But a queer critique of containment takes us further than solutions that merely seek to amend current practice.

Critiques of abolition have pointed to the social function of imprisonment: that prisons are meant to protect the public from crime.[73] But, to seek asylum is not a crime and the default mass detention of asylum seekers and immigrants that we see throughout the world today cannot be said to serve this social function. If anything, the apparent role of containment in these contexts has been more about political signaling to local electorates that all migrants and displaced people are criminals first and people second. Contemporary immigration detention seems therefore to be far more concerned with serving this ideological function than with protecting people from crime.

So, what does it mean to imagine a world without containment? UNHCR's official policy since 2009 has been to pursue alternatives to camps, wherever possible.[74] In doing so, they recognize the ways in which camps might increase vulnerability and isolation. Refugees should therefore enjoy freedom of movement, access to local labor markets, and community support. Despite this policy, many states continue to insist on camps in order to contain refugee populations. Likewise, the United Nations Working Group on Arbitrary Detention has argued that "immigration detention should gradually be abolished."[75] The Working Group argues that detention practice "exceeds the legitimate interests of states in protecting its territories."[76] Despite this, states continue to invest millions in the building of new detention facilities, often in third countries that do not have robust human rights protection.

We are not alone in imagining a world without containment, though state policy in recent years has made this world seem much further away. Nevertheless, queer and trans people, through their experience, demonstrate that the stakes are much higher than they first seemed. Not only does containment have bad outcomes for queer and trans asylum seekers, but it can also obscure new forms of persecution undertaken by the very state that is supposed to protect them. When new relational harms can be created or compounded through practices of containment, we need to consider the possibility of relational solutions. How can the queer and trans displaced access and create a new social world free from the harms that follow them throughout their journey? It is to this question that we will turn in the following two chapters.

6 Reunion

In October 2018, a group of people began their journey from San Pedro Sula, Honduras, to the Southern border of the United States. Collecting others along the way in Guatemala and El Salvador, this group, who were fleeing persecution, poverty, and violence, came to be known as a "migrant caravan." Among those walking were over eighty LGBTIQ migrants from across Central America.[1]

News coverage at the time reported that many of the LGBTIQ people had chosen to separate from the main caravan because of abuse from other migrants.[2] As the LGBTIQ asylum seekers were fleeing the generalized violence that disproportionately targets queer and trans people, their vulnerabilities followed them even as they left their countries of origin. The social environment they fled remained with them, carried by the people walking alongside them and those they met on their journey. As we argued in chapter 3, on *flight*, queer and trans refugees often face difficult journeys while seeking protection as they are unable to rely on the same networks as other displaced people. The harms that they flee are relational because they result from the social prejudices present in others on the road to elsewhere. In this sense, relational harm can be thought of as capillary in how it extends through one's social network and persists even after changing location. LGBTIQ refugees therefore often organize to create alternative protection systems for themselves. Self-segregation as a protective practice has long been a tool utilized by members of the queer and trans community.[3] Unable to rely on traditional societal structures, such as their family or community, queer and trans people instead learn to rely on each other. When harm is relational, the solution must be also. In queer and trans community vernacular, this relationship is sometimes called "chosen family." In reports covering those waiting for safe passage from Mexico to the United States, journalists noted how LGBTIQ migrants embodied the kinship relations of chosen family: They described how migrants looked after one another through universal acts of care otherwise associated with the nuclear family.[4]

When the members of "the rainbow caravan" reached the United States' Southern border, they applied for asylum. Among them was a group of thirty trans women who presented themselves to the border guards in Tijuana together. Reports at the time indicated that ten of these women had won their asylum cases and been given protection in the United States. While many of the remaining twenty women were still being held in detention, waiting for court dates. Others had already lost their asylum cases.[5] Though these women presented themselves as a group, they were separated, sent to different detention centers, and were unable to communicate. Such separation is representative of the fact that the American asylum system—and indeed the global refugee regime itself—often pursues individual refugee status determination (RSD). Exceptions are made to this rule for families and married couples, for whom group determination and group resettlement become possible.[6] Of course, the presumption of family unity has itself recently been brought into question with the first Trump administration's policy of family separation, in which, most infamously, young children were forcibly removed from their parents. However, in principle, though perhaps not in practice, the family is understood as a special, privileged unit in the system of refugee protection—a unit from which the LGBTIQ displaced are often excluded.

Even when queer couples resemble a family in the cisheteronormative sense, they still face undue burdens. In March 2019, an openly gay couple from Honduras, Óscar Juárez Hernández and Darwin García Portillo, requested asylum at the United States' Southern border. They were separated and sent to different asylum processing centers in Louisiana and Colorado, where they could only communicate by mail.[7] In the case of cisheteronormative couples, the United States allows married asylum-seekers to apply to sponsor their spouse through "derivative asylee status" as long as the couple presents a marriage or civil union certificate.[8] Of course, this is not always respected in practice, and nonheterosexual couples are more structurally excluded from such procedures. In this couple's case, Honduras does not recognize same-sex partnerships. There was therefore no way for them to prove that they were a family.[9] While both individuals did eventually receive asylum on the grounds of their sexual orientation, their experience demonstrates how the refugee regime fails to consider the unique vulnerabilities of queer and trans people *as families*.[10]

By extending the discussion beyond individual status determination, we can see that cisheteronormative structures ground current practices of refugee protection. Our focus in this chapter is on the concept of the family; the chapter calls for a reconsideration of the practice of reunion and group refugee status determination to include queer and trans conceptions of kinship. In chapter 1, on *home*, we noted that intimate spaces are often the first site of relational harm for LGBTIQ displaced people. Interactions with loved ones, neighbors, or community members more broadly can often violently enforce the dominant cisheteronormative ideology. The idea of home therefore shifts from an origin to a destination, something that queer and trans people must create anew. Part of this reshaping sometimes involves finding or creating a new family for oneself. In chapter 3, on *flight*, we discussed how these harms can follow the displaced in their search for refuge. These harms sometimes come from fellow migrants or a violent border apparatus that seeks to curtail movement. In this context, communities of care, such as the rainbow caravan, can act as an important space of protection free from relational harms.

In this chapter, we make the normative argument for including queer conceptions of the family in cases of group status determination and family reunion. Exploring this area of refugee and migration policy allows us to unpack the question of who counts as a family under the current legal framework and to reveal the punitive results of our current assumptions. First, we discuss the moral case of family unity in general. Then, we outline the current approach to definitions of the family in refugee protection.

Here we show that the practice of family reunion and group status determination, as it stands, depends on a cisheteronormative conception of the family, which excludes queer and trans people from effectively seeking protection as a unit. From there, we consider queer conceptions of the family. We begin by outlining predominant discussions concerning kinship and family. We then argue that, since there is no relevant moral difference between cisheteronormative and queer conceptions of the family, both groups should be entitled to family reunion and group status determination. We also make the further claim that—as the family is often the primary persecuting unit in the case of LGBTIQ refugees—queer and trans displaced people have a compelling claim for the recognition of these different types of caregiving relationships.

THE CASE FOR REFUGEE FAMILY UNITY

International human rights instruments overwhelmingly recognize the importance of family life. Article 17 of the International Covenant on Civil and Political Rights (ICCPR) states, "No one shall be subjected to arbitrary or unlawful interference with his . . . family." It continues, "Everyone has the right to the protection of the law against such interference or attacks." The Convention on the Rights of the Child (CRC) recognizes the right to family reunification under Articles 9 and 10. Article 9 of the CRC outlines that "a child shall not be separated from his or her parents against their will, except when . . . such separation is necessary for the best interests of the child." Article 10 continues that "applications by a child or his or her parents to enter or leave a State Party for the purpose of family reunification shall be dealt with by States Parties in a positive, humane and expeditious manner." Article 16 (Paragraph 3) of the Universal Declaration of Human Rights asserts that the family is the natural and fundamental group unit of society and is entitled to protection by the state. The Inter-American Convention on Human Rights echoes these commitments to the family, stating that they are a key component of an individual's right to a private life.

The 1951 Geneva Convention on the Status of Refugees does not include any specific articles concerning family reunion. However, the Final Act of the UN Conference of Plenipotentiaries states that "the unity of the family . . . is an essential right of the refugee."[11] States therefore ought to "take the necessary measures for the protection of the refugee's family, especially with a view to . . . ensuring that the unity of the refugee's family is maintained particularly in cases where the head of the family has fulfilled the necessary conditions for admission to a particular country." In 2001, UNHCR's Executive Committee (ExCom) published a background note on family reunification in the context of resettlement and integration. UNHCR identifies five guiding principles to promote and facilitate refugee family reunification.[12] They argue that:

1. The family is the natural and fundamental group unit of society and is entitled to protection by states.
2. The refugee family is essential to ensure the protection and well-being of its individual members.
3. The principle of dependency entails flexible and expansive family reunification criteria that are culturally sensitive and situation specific.
4. Humanitarian considerations support family reunification efforts.
5. The refugee family is essential to the successful integration of resettled refugees.

Some, of course, argue that family reunion is not an acceptable mechanism for determining who ought to be admitted to a given state. Stephen Macedo argues that we should limit family-based immigration to only spouses and minor children and instead select immigrants on the basis of skill and economic output.[13] However, most accept the family network as foundational to the basic needs of human beings. Martha Nussbaum includes "affiliation" in her list of basic human needs, in which she recognizes the family as one important component.[14] Iseult Honohan likewise notes that "the reason a state may be considered to have a *prima facie* obligation to admit family members lies in the importance of such relationships, in which members have agent-specific obligations of care to one another. The right to family life may be thought of as a universal right to discharge special obligations, which recognizes the value of particular relations."[15] Matthew Gibney also puts this point forcefully:

It is not hard to understand the moral force that underlies the claims of family migrants to be admitted. Few things are more important to individuals

than their families and their spouse or dependent children. Without the opportunity to have these people around us, we would be deprived of those
who give meaning to our lives.[16]

We should note here that we are not making an independent argument
for the importance of family reunion. We instead take it as a given that
refugees have a right to be reunited with their families, even if this fails
to be respected in practice. Rather, we are making what might be thought
of as an argument from moral consistency. We argue that, if there is no
morally relevant distinction between heteronormative conceptions of the
family and queer and trans conceptions of kinship, the latter should be entitled to family reunion in the same way as the former. We also claim that,
as the family is often the primary persecuting unit in the case of LGBTIQ
refugees, they may have a particularly strong claim for the recognition of
different types of caregiving relationships. In the following section, then,
we will look at traditional cisheteronormative conceptions of the family in
refugee protection.

WHO IS 'THE FAMILY'?

According to UNHCR, "a broad definition of a family unit—what may be
termed an extended family—is necessary to accommodate the peculiari-
ties in any given refugee situation."[17] Likewise, The Human Rights Committee has affirmed that: the term "family," for purposes of the ICCPR,
must be interpreted broadly to include all those comprising a family in the
society concerned. Despite calls for a broad understanding of the family,
the right to family reunion is often applied restrictively. In the United
Kingdom, only the partner or child of an individual with refugee status is
eligible for family reunion.[18] Siblings, elderly dependents, or children over
18 therefore do not qualify. Notably, child refugees who receive status in
the United Kingdom cannot apply to be reunited with their parents; the
Home Office will only grant reunification in these cases in extreme circumstances. To qualify as "partners" (and thus receive group status determination) couples must be married or in a civil partnership. If the couple
is not married, they must prove that they have been living together for at

least two years before applying for asylum; this time restriction is not necessary in the cases of marriage or civil partnership. Notably, the updated UK Home Office guidance does ask case workers to consider whether living together would have put the couple in danger—as would be the case, for instance, in a country where same-sex relationships are criminalized.[19] In the United States, however, only legal spouses qualify for derivative asylee status, which allows an individual who has been granted asylum to have state protection extended to their significant other.[20] Therefore, if legal marriage is criminalized between same-sex couples or transgender identities are not recognized in the country of origin, then queer and trans people will be barred from the extension of this protection. We saw this in the case of Óscar and Darwin, the gay couple from Honduras, in this chapter's introduction.

Courts in other jurisdictions have accepted that different relationships may qualify for reunion and group status determination in certain circumstances.[21] For instance, in the case of *Boyle v. UK*, an uncle and a nephew were accepted as a family. Likewise, in the case of *Marckx v. Belgium* grandparents and grandchildren were also found to qualify for reunion.[22] Most jurisdictions also accept adopted children in cases of family reunion and status determination. However, parents must give documentation to prove that a formal adoption has taken place and, therefore, de facto adopted children do not qualify. The advice from the UK Home Office in cases in which a child has been taken into the home and is functionally a part of the family unit states that caseworkers must refuse the application and then consider whether there are any exceptional compassionate reasons for allowing reunion or group status determination.[23]

In the case of LGBTIQ parents, qualifying for legal protections and entitlements has been a consistent challenge. Court decisions in Latin America have made this contestation clear. For instance, in the case of *Atala Riffo and Daughters v. Chile*, the Inter-American Court of Human Rights (IACtHR) considered whether a lesbian mother should have custody over her children. Lower courts had argued that doing so would put the children's development at risk. The IACtHR ruled in favor of the mother, arguing that Atala Riffo had been discriminated against on the grounds of sexual orientation in a way that violated her right to a family life. A more progressive position was recently put forward in the *Advisory Opinion on*

Gender Identity, Equality, and Non-Discrimination of Same-Sex Couples from the IACtHR.[24] This advisory opinion confirms that same-sex couples are entitled to precisely the same treatment as heterosexual couples— states are therefore not entitled to any preferential policies, such as tax exemptions, for heterosexual partnerships.[25] Although this consistency is not reflected in current legislation (as there are states in Latin America and the Caribbean that do not recognize same-sex marriage), it does show a precedent for more expansive understandings of the family and calls for parity in the treatment of same-sex and heterosexual units.

Despite this recent progress, many states currently do not adopt the broad understanding of family as they are encouraged to do by the United Nations and other international legal instruments. In most cases, applications for reunion or group status determination are only accepted when the individual is either a spouse or a dependent child. Other cases, such as those outlined above, are outliers to the exclusionary focus on the family as a strict, nuclear unit. Conceptually, however, it is difficult to maintain these distinctions. Philosophers and political theorists writing about the nature of the family have historically taken a far more expansive view. G. W. F. Hegel, for instance, views the family not as made up of particular types of individuals but as reflecting a certain kind of relationship, one of love and mutual obligation.[26] Friedrich Engels likewise endorses an obligation-based account of family life. He writes, "the names of father, child, brother, sister are no mere complimentary forms of address; they involve quite definite and very serious *mutual obligations* which together make up an essential part of the social constitution of the peoples in question."[27] Both accounts, then, depend upon the kind of relationship and obligations that exist between people within a family unit. Another account of the family given by philosophers is functionalist in nature. That is, it focuses on the purpose of the family unit and argues that any group that functions similarly ought to be considered as a family from a moral point of view. Sarah Song, for instance, defines the family by its caregiving function.[28] She argues that using this approach is prudent as well as morally required and that, therefore, family reunion should include "pluralistic family forms and personal relationships."[29] Of course, these relationships of care and mutual obligation are not just found within cisheteronormative family structures. Instead, as Honohan puts it:

Such relationships may be found in cohabiting and same-sex partnerships (and other relationships) that do not all fit under the legal or genetic conceptions of family (though some are working to put them under the same or comparable legal footing) but they constitute a re-conceptualization of, rather than supersede, the family. Thus, there is a problem if states recognize as families only those falling into the strict legal or genetic category, rather than including these other kinds of intimate relationship.[30]

However, a more restrictive view of the family is often applied in practice for several reasons. First, states may want to limit the number of people who can claim to enter on the grounds of family reunion. Politicians often complain that family visas act as an open door to migrants who do not benefit the state in the same way as other immigrants selected for their skills. Since states are restrictive in this regard, they are unlikely to accept a more expansive understanding of the family when they believe that doing so would contravene their interests. Second, even if we attempt to build a more functionalist or obligations-based approach to the idea of the family, we are still inevitably measuring the new structures against the old. As Song notes, "the traditional model of the marital nuclear family is the standard against which all other forms of intimacy and kinship are judged."[31] Given these broader conceptual accounts, the next section considers what Honohan describes as the reconceptualization of the family to consider the implications for a more queer and trans inclusive refugee regime.[32]

QUEER KINSHIP

Queer rearticulations of kinship deconstruct the cisheteronormative assumptions behind the concept of the family. In recognizing the interwoven concepts of heterosexuality and the family, Eve Kosofsky Sedgwick explains that "the making historically visible of heterosexuality is difficult because, under its institutional pseudonyms such as Inheritance, Marriage, Dynasty, Family, Domesticity, and Population, heterosexuality has been permitted to masquerade so fully as History itself."[33] It is therefore difficult to separate the concept of the family itself from its relation to heterosexuality.

The relationship between the queer and trans person and family is fraught. As discussed in chapter 1, on *home*, for many LGBTIQ people, the family is the first locus of harm. And indeed, as analyzed in chapter 2, many acts of intrafamilial harm can amount to persecution. Sedgwick notes that "gay people . . . seldom grow up in gay families" and are often "exposed to their culture's, if not their parents', high ambient homophobia long before either they or those who care for them know that they are among those who most urgently need to define themselves against it."[34] In testimonies of refugees, many cite family persecution, in addition to societal or governmental persecution, as the reason for their flight. Simultaneously, it is the concept of the "traditional family" that is often used to justify societal and political persecution of LGBTIQ individuals. Throughout the world, public figures use the euphemistic discourse of "protecting family values" and "defending the family" to legitimize anti-LGBTIQ efforts.[35] Accordingly, many scholars have recognized the family as an institution of heterosexuality propagated by the state.[36] This propagation is maintained by the many ways in which the state recognizes a family: through marriage, inheritance rights, taxation, and custodial agreements. Butler refers to these institutions as part of the state's "regulatory control on normative kinship."[37] The cisheteronormative biases are self-evident: In many places throughout the world queer people cannot marry, queer couples cannot adopt children, and trans people are not able to have their identity recognized.[38] Thus, queering the concept of the family requires disentangling the many forms of regulatory control present in the normative conception of kinship. Sedgwick refers to this deconstruction as a way to "disengage . . . the bonds of blood, of law, of habitation, of privacy, of companionship and succor—from the lockstep of their unanimity in the system called 'family.'"[39]

Central to these clashes over the state recognition of queer kinship are what Butler refers to as the "bonds of blood" and the role of the child. Citing "the poor child, a martyred figure of an ostensibly selfish or dogged social progressivism," opponents to queer people's inclusion in state institutions that recognize the value of the family often argue in defense of the child.[40] Kath Weston summarizes this dynamic as cutting across "the politically loaded couplet of 'pro-family' and 'anti-family' that places gay men and lesbians in an inherently antagonistic relation to kinship solely on the basis of their nonprocreative sexualities."[41] Butler argues that these discussions about the child are often euphemisms for racial and gendered anxieties—controlling who can produce a state-recognized citizen is a way to control the demography of the body politic.[42] Lee Edelman similarly recognizes this child-focused politic as a form of "reproductive futurism . . . [that] affirm[s] a structure, [in order] to authenticate social order, which it then intends to transmit to the future in the form of the Child."[43] Recognizing the family as what Sedgwick calls "a mechanism to produce, care for, and acculturate children" through bloodlines becomes one of the strongest normative elements used in denying queer and trans people access to institutional support and recognition, as most queer couples cannot produce biological children without technological intervention.[44]

But of course, through adoption, the state recognizes non-bloodline forms of kinship every day. Butler argues that modern society does not have an entirely rigid conceptualization of kinship forced on us by political leaders. Instead, many draw on nonbiological relations.[45] Butler adds that:

> If we understand kinship as a set of practices that institutes relationships of various kinds which negotiate the reproduction of life and the demands of death, then kinship practices will be those that emerge to address fundamental forms of human dependency, which may include birth, child-rearing, relations of emotional dependency and support, generational ties, illness, dying, and death (to name a few).[46]

Thus, according to Butler, "kinship loses its specificity as an object once it becomes characterized loosely as modes of enduring relationship."[47] This echoes the functionalist approach to the family discussed in the previous section. Once the hypocrisies present in the cisheteronormative conception of kinship are revealed, a queer "reformulation of kinship" can be attempted and expanded upon.[48]

The many conceptions of queer family all follow a common theme: facing family or community rejection, queer and trans people seek one another out for support. This support can be emotional, such as providing acceptance and validation, or material, such as offering accommodation or financial support. In this way, queer and trans people rearticulate heteronormative conceptions of family using parts of the traditional model which serve them and doing away with that which does not. This queer approach to kinship relations represents chosen family. William Eskridge Jr. writes:

> Lesbians and gay men . . . do not usually follow the traditional husband-wife-kids model of family formation. Instead, we have turned to "families we

choose"—circles of consent-based intimacy among friends, partners, former lovers, children, and others.[49]

Kath Weston documented the various acts of care performed by LGBTIQ people in chosen families in San Francisco.[50] Weston explores how LGBTIQ people consciously form families made up of non–blood relations by demonstrating love, narrating shared histories, providing emotional and material assistance, and engaging in representations of solidarity across generations. They live together and provide each other with basic human needs and mutual support. Like more traditional understandings of family, these family members have a clear conception of their boundaries: who is in and who is out of the family. This conceptualization matches other broader approaches to the family present in Black American, Native American, and working-class American communities in the United States—communities in which family members often started as friends.[51] Weston argues that these queer and trans families produce a critique of traditional kinship by deploying and subverting symbolic materials of family (like the family tree) in the context of their "nonprocreative" relationships—relationships "that [contest] assumptions about the bearing of biology, genetics, and heterosexual intercourse on the meaning of family in their own culture."[52]

Despite being understood as "outside" the traditional conception of family, reproducing symbolic materials of family is central to queer kinship. American ballroom culture for instance, a form of queer kinship practiced mainly by LGBTIQ people of color in urban areas throughout the United States, reproduces the discourse of family in its structure. In ballroom culture, participants separate themselves into houses with mothers and fathers who take responsibility for their children. In doing so, they take on normative and gendered domestic roles. House mothers perform feminized domestic labor, such as monitoring the nutritional intake of their children and providing emotional support during times of crisis. House fathers take on the role of mentor, articulating their desire to impart the values of the house to their children. The children of these houses internalize and perceive these differences themselves. Many of them had been expelled from their homes by their biological parents on account of their sexual orientation or gender identity and, as such, these house mothers and fathers serve as guardians in their lives.[53] According to Emily Arnold and Marlon Bailey,

"Houses offer their children multiple forms of social support, a network of friends, and a social setting that allows free gender and sexual expression."[54] Often the father or mother of a house has an apartment at which their children are offered accommodation; as such, houses become both figurative and literal homes. These houses compete at balls, which are akin to themed beauty pageants that celebrate the sexual and gender diversity of the community. This culture came to mainstream prominence with the 1990 documentary *Paris is Burning* and Madonna's song "Vogue"[55] and has once again become prominent with the popularity of television shows such as *RuPaul's Drag Race* and *Pose*. Butler recognized the subversive potential of ballroom culture in the "reformulation of kinship" because of how its "appropriation and redeployment of the categories of dominant culture enable the formation of kinship relations . . . [and] form alternative households and community."[56]

While many queer conceptions of kinship are culturally rooted and context specific, there are commonalities between them. Reformulations of kinship, where older or more established queer and trans people support younger queer and trans people, have been documented within Argentina, Brazil, Peru, and Venezuela—as well as among Latin American migrant trans communities in Europe.[57] Interviewees in these situations consistently share how queer kinship structures provided material and social support during periods of precarity and transition. Julieta Vartabedian Cabral observes how queer and trans Latin American migrant communities in Europe employ "house verbiage," as seen in *Paris is Burning*, to describe their rearticulated queer kinship structures.[58] In testimonies of the first-ever high school for trans people in Argentina, students shared testimonials like, "The high school was a family that rescued me" and, "To me, the high school signifies care, help, study; it signifies family."[59]

Critically, however, there are complexities within these broader narratives that highlight the importance of culture and context. Katrin Vogel notes in her ethnography of Venezuelan trans migrants in Europe how many "put much emphasis on their love for their *mamás* [natural mothers]."[60] As such, while the family can be the first locus of persecution for many queer and trans asylum seekers, it is not right to say that all of them suffer alienation from their natural family unit. In certain settings in Latin America, the closeness between queer and trans people and their mothers can survive the intrafamilial or community persecution that might produce displacement. While there are a host of possible explanations for these dynamics, Giuseppe Campuzano argues that rigid, cisheteronormative conceptualizations of gender are colonial imports to Latin America and that many indigenous cultures included variant gender identities, especially in mother-child relations.[61]

These queer kinship practices have also been observed in LGBTIQ refugee support networks throughout the world. For instance, Elif Sari details similar practices of family making among LGBTIQ displaced populations in Turkish refugee camps: "Most of them stay with other LGBTI refugees, establish alternative families through queer rearticulations of heteronormative kinship ties, and form their own financial and emotional support mechanisms."[62] Such commentary parallels language from a collective of queer and trans refugees in Greece. In an interview in *The Guardian*, Maha, a trans woman who fled persecution in Iraq, shared that the group helped her to recreate the loss of family life. In explaining how the group became her chosen family, she said: "They gave me moral support. They helped me talk about things I had never really talked about before." She continued, "Family doesn't just protect, it gives you substance, it gives you context."[63] There are similar reports of such articulations of kinship and care among queer and trans refugees in Kenya and South Africa.[64] These dynamics and their importance to the normative case for the inclusion of queer kinship in refugee protection are well summarized by Sari: "queer kinship ties, and everyday relations of love, care, and support seem to prove the truth of a Turkish immigration officer's bitter remark: "At the end of the day, a refugee's problems are solved by other refugees."[65]

As mentioned in this chapter's introduction, journalists traveling with the LGBTIQ migrant caravans noted how its members took care of each other in a manner akin to family.[66] The creation of this "rainbow caravan" is another example of how queer and trans people self-segregate to protect themselves and each other. Indeed, other reports of LGBTIQ asylum seekers in the border cities of Mexico, where many wait in hope of gaining refuge in the United States, often note the nature of care found in local shelters.[67]

LGBTIQ refugees continue to experience violence and persecution in Mexico (both from other migrants in accommodation as well as the broader Mexican society) and, as such, often seek LGBTIQ safe houses, where they can look after each other in a domestic environment free from discrimination.[68] One report summarized the experience of a refugee who had been waiting for ten months in Mexico for his case to be considered by the American government as follows: "He may not have found safety, but he did find a family that loves him."[69]

With such clear interdependent relations of care, it is no wonder that many of these individuals often seek asylum together. Were they to receive asylum as a group, they would most likely continue to rely on each other as a family unit in a new land. However, as we have already seen, being considered as a group is exceedingly unlikely, as American refugee status determination processes treat these queer and trans asylum seekers as individuals rather than as a family unit. Most will not be fortunate enough to receive asylum, and those accepted into the asylum system will be separated and sent to different detention centers, where they will lose access to technology. Supportive units of LGBTIQ people, or chosen families, are therefore regularly dispersed throughout the country and likely only able to communicate by letter—that is, if they know each other's locations at all.

While the global refugee regime accepts applications for asylum from the queer and trans displaced on the grounds of sexual orientation and gender identity, the broader protection system is not fit in its current form to accept them as people, whose success in a new land depends on their ability to form relationships and rely on community, as well as family. These universal needs are already recognized by states, which permit family reunification and attempt to settle refugees from the same region together. However, as homo/transphobic persecution often occurs at both the family and community level, simply relocating LGBTIQ refugees into national enclaves in host states risks extending their persecution into new lands. If the premise of keeping a family together is to provide support and improve the likelihood of survival in a new state, the chosen families of LGBTIQ refugees should be honored.[70]

A RIGHT TO QUEER FAMILY REUNION

As we have seen, the current regime of refugee family reunion and status determination depends on a cisheteronormative conception of the family.

We noted at the outset that chosen family units are often separated and held incommunicado when seeking asylum; they are not eligible to be reunited or considered for group status determination. Traditional modes of family reunion or status determination do not mitigate the relational harms experienced by LGBTIQ refugees in host states because the cisheteronormative family unit can be a key persecuting agent for the queer and trans displaced. As such, a relational solution that can redress intrafamilial harm and the challenges of displacement is required. LGBTIQ populations have already found a solution in the development of chosen family, which helps them overcome the effects of exclusion and social prejudice. Here states of asylum can contribute to these solutions by allowing LGBTIQ refugees to access group status determination or eventual reunion with their chosen families.

We have argued that, given the moral equivalence of queer conceptions of the family to traditional cisheteronormative understandings, the two ought to be treated equally. This means that queer chosen families should be able to apply for asylum as a unit, apply for derivative asylee status (in the context of the United States) and apply for reunion if one member has successfully been granted asylum.

Some may argue that this is an overextension of protection currently offered to refugee families. States are already unwilling to offer refugee family reunion to even those relationships that clearly fit within the scope of the cisheteronormative conception of the family. Therefore, some may worry that asking states to offer such protection to more groups might lead to a retraction—rather than an expansion—of the overall level of protection. While we do not predict that the change advocated in this chapter is forthcoming, we also do not believe that this justifies distinguishing between cisheteronormative family units and LGBTIQ family units from a moral point of view. While it may be that states would likely push back against the expansion in protection, if we have shown that there is a moral equivalence between the two broad types of family unit, then we have no justification for distinguishing between them—whether this equivalence will be recognized or implemented is another point altogether.

Additionally, some may reply that, in the case of queer and trans chosen families, it is more difficult to determine the boundaries between family and friends—that is, there may be a worry that this expansion would lead to more fraudulent claims of reunion, as biological testing is not available to determine who is a "genuine" family member. However, there are many ways—beyond biological testing—that are already used in current systems to determine genuine family relationships. For instance, the United Kingdom accepts (at least in principle) the claims of couples who have lived together for more than two years or those who have de facto adopted children (though admittedly only in extreme circumstances). Similar policies could be put in place to determine members of a given chosen family. These could mirror policies that already exist within the current refugee reunion regime.

Refugees are entitled to family unity. However, this right has rarely been extended to the queer and trans displaced. Instead, cisheteronormative assumptions and more active forms of exclusion often prevent LGBTIQ refugees from being with their loved ones. We have argued throughout this chapter that a more expansive understanding of "the family" is required in refugee law and policy to accommodate the chosen families that queer and trans people create for themselves. This is even more important as LGBTIQ people are often excluded from their biological family units and therefore lack more common networks of support and care.

This emphasis on new forms of community and belonging is one step towards confronting the relational harms that we have highlighted throughout the book so far. LGBTIQ people often flee harms enforced through homo/transphobia that are reflective of a broader cisheteronormative environment. They are targeted by acquaintances, family members, loved ones, and neighbors, as well as by active state policy. But these small family units can only do so much to resolve relational harms. They can provide a form of temporary protection from the hostile outside world. The next chapter considers what broader relational solutions might be required in the queer search for refuge, turning to the role that solidarity can play in creating new social environments within which the queer and trans displaced might flourish. Only then can we have a proper understanding of what *sanctuary* might mean at the end of the queer search for refuge.

7 Sanctuary

Abderrahim El Habachi fled Morocco for the United Kingdom in 2017 to live openly as a gay man. In his home country, being gay was a crime and also put him at risk of violence from the police and fellow citizens.[1] Abderrahim filed for asylum and was relocated to Cardiff, Wales, where he hoped to begin a new life. However, in Wales, Abderrahim continued to encounter discrimination because of his sexual orientation. While his asylum application was processed, the state placed him in temporary housing run by the National Asylum Support Service, where he became targeted by fellow asylum applicants. He told reporters, "It was as though there was no effort to make LGBT+ people welcome. The drop-in centers for asylum seekers and refugees weren't LGBT-friendly; they were mainly aimed towards cis men. I was made to feel unwelcome." Other LGBTIQ asylum seekers echo the experience of Abderrahim, as the discrimination and lack of safety in state-provided accommodation, both during and after status determination processes, is a frequently identified problem throughout states of asylum.[2] Abderrahim has since called for specialized housing for LGBTIQ asylum seekers to avoid the continued homo/transphobic abuse in their country of refuge, from both the host community and from other migrants. He told reporters, "I had fled a country that was dangerous for me because of who I am, and *I was put in an environment that felt more dangerous than the situation that I left.*"³

Throughout the book we have recounted diverse stories of displacement. A central theme of these stories has been the way that the relational harms associated with homo/transphobia follow people wherever they go. We have already shown that harms can be compounded during attempts to reach the border, transfigured in assessment and detention, and exacerbated through lack of reunion. But we often assume (or perhaps hope) that once refugees reach their final state of asylum, they will be safe, at last. Abderrahim's case shows the persistent harm refugees often experience in the state of asylum, even after territorial admission. For some LGBTIQ refugees, including those who successfully receive full status, injustices can continue or transform in the state of asylum even *after* inclusion. In other words, even once LGBTIQ people have successfully made it across a border, they remain unsafe.

Many of us operate under the assumption that once someone is admitted to a state in the Global North—either territorially or by receiving formal refugee status—their security is guaranteed. That is, we have often treated *entry* as our primary focus, rather than what happens *after* admission. Given the prevalence of misogyny, racism, xenophobia, homophobia, and transphobia in the Global North, this assumption of ensured protection is mistaken. In not considering the postasylum experience, those of us attending to the ethics of refuge potentially ignore these harms and the related normative questions that only arise after admission. The risk of this silence is that many problematic dynamics go unquestioned and existing conceptualizations of asylum-granting states obscure continued injustice. Normative approaches here are essential, as any understanding of a just and effective refugee regime must consider the full experience of the displaced, including postadmission. The question of what it means to seek and receive sanctuary does not end once the border has been crossed. And so, justice for the queer and trans displaced must also consider what it means to be truly safe in the state of asylum.

This chapter offers a conceptualization of sanctuary after asylum that accurately reflects the diverse experiences of the queer and trans displaced. It therefore traces the relational harms that persist or are created in the state of asylum and offers a path forward in the form of relational solutions through networks of solidarity. First, we outline the current landscape of the political theory of refuge regarding the question of admission. Second, we consider the many ways in which new harms can emerge postadmission. Third, we ask what the experience of the queer and trans displaced can teach us about sanctuary after asylum. We argue that shifting our attention away from entry and towards a richer idea of sanctuary helps to demonstrate the current limits of the refugee regime, while also demonstrating our capacity to imagine something better. In doing so, we turn towards the networks of solidarity that are built between LGBTIQ people and other marginalized groups, arguing that such spaces help us to imagine new social worlds that can provide visions of true sanctuary for the queer and trans displaced, even if they feel distant.

THE ETHICS OF ADMISSION

Queer and trans displaced people seek safety for many reasons: because they are persecuted for their sexual orientation or gender identity or because they are fleeing crises such as war, climate disaster, or political unrest. In taking seriously the entangled nature of the harms that queer and trans displaced people face, we often note that this distinction is difficult to locate in the world.[4] Whatever the "first cause" of their displacement, if indeed there is one, LGBTIQ refugees become enmeshed in systems of oppression that prevent and curtail their mobility as they search for freedom and safety.

It is unsettling that this suffering continues even when supposedly durable solutions have been secured after admission. The focus on admission as the key goal of refugee policy is at its clearest in the political theory of refuge. Within this burgeoning literature, many focus on conditions for entry into the state of asylum, or what Serena Parekh has called "the ethics of admission."[5]

This emphasis echoes Michael Walzer's early conceptualization of refugeehood as a forceful moral claim against the usual boundaries of the state. The claim to asylum is therefore a distinctly powerful force. As Walzer explains, "'If you don't take me in,' they say, 'I shall be killed, persecuted, brutally oppressed by the rulers of my own country.'"[6] The obligation to accept refugees therefore acts as a constraint on the state's right to exclude outsiders.[7] The duty to admit refugees is not always taken to be absolute, but even the most stringent defenders of the state's right to control borders generally make exceptions in the case of refugees.[8] Two core debates have arisen from the focus on admission: (1) Who counts as a refugee? and (2) Why do states have obligations to assist refugees at all? The first debate considers to whom states have these more stringent obligations, with some focusing on broad criteria such as human rights protection or violations of basic safety and others defending the Geneva convention's emphasis on persecution.[9] The second debate concerns how we should ground the state's obligations to refugees: through duties of rescue, duties of legitimacy, or duties of reparation.[10] In considering who exactly ought to be admitted and for what reason, all these debates focus on admission. Of course, admission to an alternative state is important, given the nature of displacement and the paradigmatic framing of durable solutions. Indeed, some argue that this need for admission is precisely what makes refugees distinct from other "necessitous strangers."[11] But Serena Parekh argues that the focus on admission precludes us from considering other important normative topics, such as what happens to those who do not qualify for international protection in the first place—for example, those who are born legally stateless.[12] Parekh is right that the current debates in the political theory of refuge have obscured or ignored some of the most serious harms faced by displaced or stateless people. But they have also prevented us from turning to the question of what happens to refugees after entry into their new state.[13]

Where political theorists do discuss the obligations of states to refugees beyond admission, they usually adopt a blanket approach, treating all refugees as entitled to similar remedies. David Miller argues that refugees require the protection of their basic human rights, and similarly, Michael Dummett views refugees as entitled to a minimally decent human life.[14] Both accounts include the possibility of differentiated protection for specific sets of refugees: Living a minimally decent human life presumably includes freedom from homo/transphobic persecution and other forms of prejudice. What is missing, then, is not the ability to subsume these cases, but the lack of explicit consideration of those fleeing relational harms that extend across borders. David Owen discusses differentiating refugees on the basis of the harm that they have fled, arguing that those escaping persecution are entitled to citizenship in their state of asylum, whereas others fleeing generalized violence require the protection of their human rights with an entitlement to membership developing over time.[15] However, this account alone cannot address the complex and varied harms faced by displaced people, especially those fleeing pervasive systems of social oppression. Such relational harms often transcend borders and transform depending on context; the harms produced by displacement depend not only on their cause but also on the sociopolitical conditions that constitute vulnerability while searching for protection.

Most of these debates assume that we are solely discussing admission *from* states in the Global South *to* states in the Global North. They do so even though the vast majority of refugees are hosted in states outside of Europe and North America.[16] But this assumption is also based on the expectation that these states are particularly well placed to protect displaced people, especially queer and trans refugees. Annamari Vitikainen argues that liberal-democratic states should prioritize LGBTIQ refugees for resettlement on the grounds that these states are best able to protect against further injustice.[17] According to Vitikainen, such a claim to priority only occurs in situations of extreme scarcity in which the state must choose between claimants and when they are equal in every aspect of their claim to asylum.[18]

While states in the Global North do offer important protections for the queer and trans displaced, this can sometimes obscure injustices that persist even after admission. As we have seen throughout the book, the experiences of the LGBTIQ displaced reveal complex social harms that challenge the assumptions about postadmission protection. Thus, stories such as Abderrahim's at the beginning of this chapter call into question what sanctuary might mean in states of asylum that are supposedly best placed to protect them.

LGBTIQ REFUGEES IN THE STATE OF ASYLUM

The queer and trans displaced often face forms of violence that persist after admission into the state of asylum. We have already seen how LGBTIQ refugees face extreme hardship in the contexts of their home, flight, assessment, and containment. But even beyond these experiences, refugees can face a form of enduring injustice when they have supposedly already secured durable solutions.

The experiences of LGBTIQ refugees thus challenge assumptions related to the territoriality of persecution. We often assume that the harms faced by refugees are territorially bounded and that legal or territorial admission to a new state will resolve them. There are two ways of understanding admission in this context. First, one could address injustices faced during the refugee status determination process. In these cases, claimants would be within or proximate to the borders of the state but would not yet have been offered formal status. Such claimants would include people who have just entered and lodged an asylum claim. Second, one might attend to the injustices faced by individuals after they have received legally recognized status.[19] Both approaches to thinking about postadmission are required.

The first focus on the process of seeking asylum has been addressed by much of the scholarship on LGBTIQ displacement within migration and refugee studies, as seen in chapter 4, on *assessment*.[20] Once the acceptance of LGBTIQ refugees became established within the global migration regime, scholars focused on the RSD process, particularly during the interview stage when prejudice can compound based on the applicant's sexual orientation, gender identity, sex characteristics, race, religion, disability, and culture.[21] These assessment processes privilege Western conceptions of sexuality and gender and unethically mine traumatic experiences.[22] Furthermore, we, along with other scholars, have identified how practices of the global refugee regime exacerbate vulnerabilities—for example, in chapter 5, on *containment*, we discuss how detention and encampment expose LGBTIQ refugees to prejudice from other refugees and host communities thus producing new harms.[23]

This scholarship has also addressed the normative—and exclusionary—impacts of current systems of inclusion. Meghana Nayak's work reveals how the refugee regime in the United States reinforces a narrow narrative of LGBTIQ vulnerability that performs inclusion while distracting from prejudicial exclusions in its own asylum system.[24] Satvinder Juss argues that this acceptance of LGBTIQ refugees has become a way for the Global North to signpost their "civility" against the "barbarism" of the Global South.[25] Fatima El-Tayeb has explored how actors weaponize the values of LGBTIQ inclusion to racialize and other minorities in Europe, and thus deny these minorities inclusion in the European body politic.[26] These accounts again reinforce Jasbir Puar's theory of "homonationalism," whereby Global North countries use their supposed concern for LGBTIQ populations in the Global South to justify intervention—often through homo/transphobic institutions like the military—in the domestic politics of other countries.[27] This scholarship reveals serious injustices in the refugee status determination process and in supposedly inclusive reception policies. As a result, on the first understanding of postadmission as focused on the asylum-seeking process, we already know that serious injustices and harms persist once someone has been territorially admitted into the state of asylum.

The second stage of postadmission—what happens to refugees after they have received formal status, if still on a temporary basis—shows a further weakness in the assumption that the granting of legal or territorial admission prevents future relational harm. LGBTIQ refugees will often face continued homo/transphobia in their state of asylum. This can harm their potential integration or access to durable solutions, but it also might violate state duties to support displaced people. These failures are a violation of what Patti Lenard calls "duties of resettlement," which are owed to displaced people who have been admitted to the host state on the presumption that they will become permanent residents.[28] Lenard argues further that states have a particular duty to resolve oppressive conditions for refugees, especially when those oppressive forces are the very cause of their displacement. She writes, "In resettling refugees who have fled group-membership-based persecution, host states have a duty not only to protect their rights on an equal basis, they additionally have a duty to protect them from the particular forms of danger that they have fled."[29] While Lenard notes that LGBTIQ people flee home for many reasons, this special duty only attaches to queer and trans people who have fled *because* they are LGBTIQ; it amounts to an enduring injustice. But as we have seen, LGBTIQ people who flee for their lives for other reasons *also* face extreme relational harm in their search for refuge—harm that can amount to new forms of persecution.

LGBTIQ refugees require more than simply admission. When LGBTIQ people flee generalized societal persecution, they often cannot be resettled in communities with refugees from the same nation, as the social structures that permit prejudice-based harm and persecution can persist in diaspora communities.[30] However, the sites of continued persecution for the LGBTIQ displaced are multiple, and they do not only arise within migrant communities. An individual's state of origin can also make it harder to find refuge as an LGBTIQ person. The recent displacement of millions of people from Ukraine demonstrates this point. War affects everyone, but its impact is discriminate.[31] We know from chapter 3, on *flight*, that the gender identity of trans Ukrainians attempting to flee has an immense impact on the harms that they face while on the move. Trans people, in Ukraine and elsewhere, struggle to cross borders if their documentation does not reflect their gender identity, and when it does, they remain subjected to invasive practices such as strip searches. In Ukraine specifically, many trans women have been forced into military conscription, even if the government formally recognizes their gender identity.[32] But beyond the harms that manifest throughout the process of fleeing towards the international border, these forms of social prejudice and persecution can persist after the state's boundary has been crossed. For Ukrainian LGBTIQ refugees who sought asylum in neighboring countries, their precarity did not end as they entered two states, Poland and Hungary, whose governments at the time had been harassing their own LGBTIQ populations for political gain.[33] Such complications in the supposed state of refuge are obfuscated when the focus is primarily on admission, as we fail to notice that the border does not protect from all harms.

The question of postadmission security also arises in cases where specialized medical care is a basic condition of adequate protection. For instance, intersex people require access to specialized medical care that takes their unique needs into account, while treating them with dignity and respect. This is particularly important because violence against intersex people often functions through institutionalized medical care, such as through practices of forced sterilization.[34] Being admitted to a state that is not able or willing to protect intersex people from these harms does not meet the standards that we should demand for international sanctuary.[35]

Continued harm in the state of asylum is not unique to LGBTIQ refugees, who also have many other identities.[36] Cishetero women seeking asylum from domestic violence, for example, might be situated similarly to LGBTIQ refugees in terms of their access to family and informal networks of support.[37] Those living with disabilities might not be given adequate support in the form of specialized medical care and reasonable accommodation in the state of asylum.

Other forms of continued harm also persist within the host state. Scholarship outside of political theory on LGBTIQ refugees shows that though these displaced populations might enter a new state, they are rarely fully included. Their unique needs are not met and so, in addition to violence and discrimination, they experience isolation and exclusion.[38]

More disturbingly, *new* harms can be created in the process of seeking durable solutions. We have already seen that the state of asylum can generate new harms in the process of assessment and containment, sometimes amounting to forms of persecution in their own right. But these new harms can also develop even when displaced people are supposedly in the process of being incorporated into their new state. For instance, displaced people of color relocated to neighborhoods in countries with a history of racism or xenophobia are likely to face discrimination and hatred even when they are supposedly protected.[39] Many of these refugees might be experiencing certain forms of prejudice for the first time from a hostile local population. Again, this demonstrates that admission alone is insufficient for ensuring protection. In recent years, there have been a series of incidents of resettled refugees (often dissidents) in the Global North who become violently targeted by repressive regimes, including Belarus and Russia.[40]

Even when someone is not being actively targeted, new forms of harm can emerge that make life exceptionally difficult for those seeking refuge. Victor, whose story began chapter 1, on *home*, was rendered homeless when seeking sanctuary in the United Kingdom because of the policy barring asylum seekers from working while waiting for their claims to be processed.[41] His experience reflects that of many queer and trans asylum seekers who confront homelessness during and after the asylum process because of these labor restrictions and very limited housing benefits. A recent report from the NGO Micro Rainbow found that 39 percent of LGBTIQ refugees in the United Kingdom had become homeless after receiving a *positive* decision on their asylum claims. Many asylum recipients are only given seven days' notice to leave state-provided accommodation and secure new housing. As asylum seekers cannot legally work in the United Kingdom while their claim is being processed, many are not prepared to find or finance their own housing on such short notice. [42] Sima Shakhsari argues that the state of refuge's failure to provide proper support to LGBTIQ refugees is its own form of violence.[43] They recount the story of Mahtab, a Turkish trans woman refugee in Canada, who took her own life after learning that her state-provided housing support would be discontinued. The tragedy of Mahtab's story reveals the severe relational harm experienced even after admission to a new state has been received. All of this complicates the image of the Global North as a place of total safety free from violence and persecution for LGBTIQ refugees.[44]

The literature on LGBTIQ refugees from beyond political theory raises at least two substantive questions. First, can LGBTIQ refugees be assisted through the usual standards of protection? Second, does the existence of harms that transcend and mutate across borders throw into question the very efficacy of the current asylum regime itself?

SANCTUARY AFTER ASYLUM

Persistent harms faced by LGBTIQ refugees in the state of asylum challenge existing theorizations of sanctuary. The political theory of refuge has yet to address the obligations of states with respect to these marginalized groups after admission. A lack of focus on domestic injustice potentially mirrors Inéz Valdez's critique of the global justice literature.[45] When theorists *do* discuss the existence of injustice within the "prosperous West," they do not consider "forms of domestic injustice . . . whose redress might be empirically, normatively, and politically connected to causes we tend to identify with cosmopolitan justice." Most existing theories of refuge conceptualize harm as an external threat, outside of the Global North, posed to a specific kind of refugee—a dissident fleeing individualized persecution or someone escaping generalized harms such as the breakdown of state protection. But there remains little discussion of those fleeing social harms that recur across borders perhaps more readily than other drivers of displacement.

A lack of focus on postasylum protection contributes to a worrisome assumption: that once entry to the liberal-democratic state has been secured, there is little left to discuss. We know from the above cases, including

Abderrahim's, Victor's, and Mahtab's, that this is not true: The assumption that the liberal state always provides a minimal standard of protection forecloses any discussion of relational harms like homo/transphobia that can move or transform across borders. The universality of protection that is assumed postasylum puts particular refugees at risk of further injustice and persecution.

What does this mean for how the refugee regime and postasylum protection should be restructured? LGBTIQ refugees may be entitled to distinct remedies that take account of the relational harms that they face. As requested by Abderrahim, LGBTIQ refugees could be offered specialized housing or a choice in where they are resettled. This would give them access to places that have existing support structures, appropriate medical care, and established practices of community inclusion for queer and trans populations. The demands of advocates, like those of Abderrahim, often identify the salient issues that these populations still face in their countries of asylum and should be taken seriously by scholars and policymakers.

However, the implications of this focus reveal deeper and more challenging questions for political theorists of refuge: If homophobic persecution can *worsen* once in the state of asylum thus undermining the idea that admission into the Global North is a sufficient condition to guarantee protection, then the structure of refugee protection, which is built on the premise that *admission is protection* becomes unstable. Our assumption that admission should be the central focus of discussions of refugeehood is insufficient if entry can make matters worse. LGBTIQ refugees pose a more fundamental challenge to our thinking—not only about what the territorialized state can achieve but also about what justice and protection mean for the globally displaced.[46]

In response to this reorientation, we might diversify the kinds of displacement around which we center our approaches. Shifting our attention to LGBTIQ refugees (and others fleeing generalized forms of social exclusion and oppression) can reveal new conceptual challenges. We may also wish to further consider how LGBTIQ refugees and LGBTIQ migrants alike may have similar experiences of state protection or dereliction. And we might examine the extent to which legal (and theoretical) regimes tied to displacement obscure certain state features when it comes to meeting these obligations, again listening to how advocates frame and engage with these issues. We have shown that some sources of persecution and harm render physical borders inconsequential as they do not by themselves resolve the relational harm experienced by marginalized groups seeking refuge. As such, there may be a need to reconsider the efficacy of entry as the central mechanism of protection.

FINDING SANCTUARY IN SOLIDARITY

It is one thing to seek sanctuary; it is another to truly find it. Queer and trans people have always sought out new ways of imagining the world and their place within it. Part of what it means to be queer is to be *different* and therefore to challenge pervasive ways of thinking about how the world ought to be. As described in previous chapters, the queer person and the refugee are not so different from one another: They both sit on the margins of standard ways of being, and they both offer, in their existence, a challenge to that order—a revelation of its limits and an articulation of how things could be otherwise. In turning our attention to the world after asylum, we see that LGBTIQ people in the state of refuge have much in common with queer and trans people seeking protection. The question of safety for the local queer and trans population is often bound up with the same injustices faced by those seeking a new life after admission. This is clear in the context of a growing backlash against both LGBTIQ people and migrants as proximate categories of "outsiders." Right-wing populist politicians simultaneously target migrants and LGBTIQ people. The first wave of executive orders signed by President Trump during his second administration included declarations made to "protect women from gender ideology" as well as efforts to strip Americans born of immigrants of their birthright citizenship. Both groups are viewed as priority targets; they were the first to have their rights questioned and curtailed by the new administration.[47]

This intertwined fate has been recognized by many LGBTIQ people. As already mentioned, LGBTIQ organizations in Latin America have come together to create a network that identifies safe havens for LGBTIQ asylum seekers moving throughout the continent.[48] Furthermore, LGBTIQ organizations made up of citizens in states of asylum regularly demonstrate and practice solidarity with displaced queer and trans people. They do this in recognition of their own position but also in reference to shared forms of social exclusion. For instance, in the United Kingdom, the *No Pride in Detention* campaign brought together many LGBTIQ advocacy groups beyond those focusing on displacement.[49] This campaign sought to center the harms faced by LGBTIQ populations in immigration detention—as part of a bigger conversation about forms of exclusion faced by all queer and trans people. Furthermore, in some contexts LGBTIQ citizens or community groups in states of asylum, such as Canada, can sponsor LGBTIQ refugees directly or assist those who have arrived in adjusting to their new lives.[50]

What is noteworthy is that queer solidarity often extends beyond those whose identities fall within the LGBTIQ acronym, challenging our understanding of shared systems of oppression. Traditional debates on solidarity split the concept in two: solidarity *with* and solidarity *among*. Solidarity *with* implies no existing relation between the actors.[51] We can act in solidarity with someone when we offer our political power, money, or voice in service of their cause. But on this reading, there is no symmetrical relationship required and no obvious sense of a shared fate. Solidarity *among* "names a relation among members of the same group."[52] In instances of queer solidarity, it is often difficult to make such a distinction between "with" and "among." Queer solidarity often takes this expansive form by identifying the intersections of oppressions that might seem disconnected or unrelated to one another. One example of this is the strength of queer solidarity with movements for justice in Palestine. For example, the 2024 Capital Pride march in London was blocked by queer Palestinians and allies chanting, "Queers of the world, unite. Palestine is *our* fight." This support must balance advocating for Palestinian self-determination and an end to war in Gaza and the occupation of the West Bank with advocating for the improved conditions for LGBTIQ people in Palestinian society, including an end to criminalization in Gaza. The queer Jewish-American activist Matt Bernstein, explains, "My belief in human rights for others is not conditional on what they would do for me. All forms of oppression—homophobia, racism, misogyny, transphobia, occupation, and colonialism—are interconnected. You cannot end homophobia with a bomb."[53] Sa'ed Atshan articulates the tension and possibility present in this solidarity, arguing that queer solidarity for justice in Palestine can call both for a right to Palestinian self-determination and improved conditions for queer and trans Palestinians within the territory.[54] Atshan's effort to understand the relationship between LGBTIQ oppression and Palestinian liberation reveals how queer solidarity can create new political imaginaries and make evident new social ties that were not previously perceived as possible.[55] Again, queer activists challenge our assumptions about what solidarity means and how it might be shared with others in furtherance of fundamental human rights. Queer organizing provides a blueprint, then, for how solidarity could become a key practice in making sanctuary possible for queer and trans refugees. Refuge for the LGBTIQ displaced might be possible when a broader public takes responsibility for securing their safety, even when the state fails them.

We often assume that when LGBTIQ refugees are admitted to states in the Global North, their protection is guaranteed. However, states of asylum often fail to protect queer and trans displaced people from the relational harm that follows them across borders. The state of asylum can also create *new* harms, partly by failing to combat pervasive social prejudice, but also by not ensuring access to basic rights such as housing, work, or healthcare. In this context, state protection is absent; the state of asylum is either unwilling or unable to protect the displaced any further, particularly when admission is assumed to be the most important duty of states. These harms sometimes result from explicit state policy, such as denying asylum seekers the right to work and thereby rendering them homeless. But as these harms are relational, they also travel and transform in a more capillary manner throughout the social environment. Many displaced people face social prejudice from fellow refugees, community members, state officials, and citizens in their new neighborhoods. The relational harm they confront is reflective of the cisheteronormative orders that have shaped their experience throughout their search for refuge.

Relational harms require relational solutions. Our current moment of growing political backlash means that more expansive forms of solidarity have become indispensable. Active state aggression against fundamental human rights, even in supposedly LGBTIQ-friendly states, makes these commitments to one another a form of joint protection. The importance of solidarity does not mean that we need to be exactly aligned in our thinking or goals; solidarity does not demand perfection.[56] Instead, it requires a more capacious understanding of whom we should stand with and among in the face of political repression.

Our relational account of harm has described how homo/transphobia pervades different social environments and shapes the experiences of the queer and trans displaced. But solidarity can help us to reimagine what our social world should be, even in the face of what it is not.[57] If we conceptualize solidarity as a project of both political and social change, then it becomes clear that we need to organize to confront both the political actors that persecute as well as the social environments that facilitate the diffusion of this harm. As Sarah Schulman puts it, "solidarity *builds an infrastructure for the future*."[58] This means that solidarity requires a more forward-looking approach that focuses on developing networks of information and protection in the present, while also prefiguring how the world could be otherwise.[59] Only by understanding the nature of the harms faced and thinking through how we might change the world for the better can we turn to the question of justice in the queer search for refuge.

Conclusion

In Venezuela, Sebastián, a gender-nonconforming gay man, was thrilled to have good work in a government ministry. His professional qualifications secured him the job, despite being a registered member of an opposition party. Things became more complicated for Sebastián when a new boss arrived and started to request that employees participate in progovernment demonstrations. Sebastián refused and, as a result, was put on a watchlist.

Soon after, he became a persona non grata in his office and community. At work, colleagues began directing homophobic slurs at him and suggesting that the local progovernment militia, *los colectivos*, were monitoring his movements. In public, members of the *colectivos* began threatening him and strangers accosted him with homophobic language and threatened further violence. Soon after, a bullet was left outside his home, etched with his name.

Fearing for his life, Sebastián fled. With the help of a friend, he crossed the border into Colombia via informal routes. The journey removed the initial threat of the *colectivos* but brought little relief. As an undocumented migrant, Sebastián struggled to find work in Colombia. He sold sweets on the street, but his earnings were meager. Employers refused to hire him, citing his perceived femininity or lack of documentation. Landlords turned him away, and both homophobic and xenophobic slurs followed him in public spaces. Even access to the large and vibrant Venezuelan community proved difficult as he encountered further homo/transphobia from his fellow expatriates.

The compounding pressures of survival and rejection led Sebastián into sex work. It was not a choice he wanted to make but one he saw as necessary to live. This work exposed him to further risks. During one encounter, a client, claiming to be a police officer, assaulted him, leaving him with physical scars and trauma.

Seeking justice for the assault proved futile. The Colombian police in the town dismissed his complaint, saying "this is what happens to faggots." They erased evidence from his phone and refused to document the incident. The experience underscored how little protection or support was available to someone like him—an undocumented, queer migrant.

Not long after the assault, Sebastián learned he was HIV-positive. The stigma surrounding HIV added another layer of exclusion to his life. Many healthcare providers turned him away because of his lack of formal documentation, and others treated him with disdain when they learned about his HIV status.

Despite his efforts to rebuild, Sebastián's undocumented status, sexual orientation, gender presentation, and HIV diagnosis limited his access to healthcare, stable housing, and employment. After a year in Colombia, Sebastián connected with an HIV-support group, who put him in touch with an LGBTIQ-refugee aid network that is providing him with psychological counselling and working to formalize his status in Colombia. These humanitarian organizations provide temporary relief but are only the beginning steps to a longer-term solution.

Sebastián's story demonstrates the complex and compounded vulnerabilities faced by LGBTIQ people in situations of displacement. The harms of homo/transphobia, xenophobia, and the stigma of HIV intersected to shape his experience in both Venezuela and Colombia. His journey reveals the systemic barriers that queer and trans individuals encounter at every stage of displacement, leaving them marginalized and unsupported.

Samuel met Sebastián at a community space for LGBTIQ Venezuelan migrants in a Colombian border town.[1] At the time of their meeting, Sebastián still carried the effects of life-threatening violence by state and community agents in both Venezuela and Colombia and remained at extreme risk of more existential injury as well as secondary cycles of displacement. Sebastián's experiences also demonstrate the relational nature of harm that drives multiple cycles of queer and trans displacement. The prejudice that undergirded his persecution adapted to each new social environment, following him across borders. His story reveals both the stakes and limits of our current approaches to conceptualizing justice in the queer search for refuge.

We began writing this book against what appeared to be a context of slow but progressive change. The refugee regime had, over the last thirty years, demonstrated its capacity to expand. This expansion was slow, piecemeal, and incomplete, but nevertheless meaningful. At least thirty-seven countries now grant asylum to queer and trans populations, with some developing special policies and migration pathways to help LGBTIQ people seeking protection. We were ready to frame our book as an intervention on what an *even more* progressive refugee regime might look like; one that genuinely includes and protects the queer and trans displaced.

But we find ourselves in a new context. While hateful backlash against migrants and LGBTIQ people had been growing for some time, it is now explicit government policy in many countries that once championed inclusion. Since early 2025, the International Organization for Migration has cut over three thousand jobs due to loss of funding and can no longer support other countries in their resettlement efforts.[2] Simultaneously, diversity, equity, and inclusion (DEI) initiatives have been scapegoated as a source of society's ills by the Trump administration, resulting in their demolition and a broader silencing of these topics. Policies that seek to protect and uphold the interests of marginalized social groups have become politicized. Many of the bulwarks in the United States that might stand up for these ideals have been undermined. Universities, a space for intellectual engagement where the values that undergird the demands for justice for the queer and trans displaced are articulated, have come under fire.[3] Large corporations (the ones that used to so loudly sponsor pride floats around the country and celebrate the rights of LGBTIQ people with special pride collections to benefit from the "pink economy") have receded from these debates.[4] So, although when we started this book there was a sense of slow and steady progression and hope for what might come next, we are no longer able to tell that story.

In the wake of this new reality, we must defend the rights that have been gained, while still working towards a more just future. Even in a non-ideal world that is hostile to LGBTIQ refugees, questions of justice still matter. We cannot abandon ambitious thinking on how the world should be for those seeking sanctuary, even as we are simultaneously forced to secure our position.

We subtitle this book *justice in the queer search for refuge* to emphasize the importance of philosophical thinking in the face of real world crisis. Normative debates in the political theory of displacement have consistently revolved around whether states have an obligation to admit refugees and on what grounds.[5] This discourse has focused on finding the 'proper' definition of refugeehood and therefore on drawing contours around who is entitled to protection. As Phil Cole has argued, this definitional project will always mean leaving some people out; in placing parameters around the concept of refugeehood, we also exclude many from the protection that it is meant to guarantee.[6] Recent work has attempted to move beyond this paradigm by drawing our attention to more expansive and non-ideal ways of thinking about displacement. This has involved analyzing the real-world contexts of forced migration, the unfair distribution of asylum protection between the Global North and South, and how powerful states work collectively to prevent people from seeking refuge.[7]

In a sense, existing work in the political theory of displacement has already undergone a shift towards more non-ideal theorizing that is responsive to the conditions of the real world. One might reasonably conclude that, in turning our attention to the experiences of the queer and trans displaced, we might be in the business of what Judith Shklar called "damage control." However, the project of this book is not just to document the many injustices faced by LGBTIQ people in situations of displacement. Rather, we are working to ensure that those most vulnerable to the power of the state and broader social forces are not ignored in our considerations of justice. The inclusion of their experiences is central to this more ambitious project of building a theory of justice that can also attend to the queer and trans displaced.

This book is our attempt to account for the theoretical indispensability of queer and trans people seeking refuge in any broader theories of displacement justice. In doing so, we develop a concept of relational harm that reflects LGBTIQ people's experiences of displacement by elaborating how anti-LGBTIQ prejudice mixes with different environments to produce new sources and sites of persecution. This concept of relational harm therefore offers a new way of thinking about the search for refuge that better reflects the social injustices of displacement. We are motivated by a concern that the majority of theories of displacement justice thus far have not properly considered differential experience, and as a result, we recognize a theoretical impoverishment regarding intersectional claims for justice. *The Way Out* is therefore not only a project in theorizing from the experiences of the queer and trans displaced; it is about seeking a new way of understanding displacement justice.

Part of this story is understanding the harms that LGBTIQ people must flee from. But it is also about the harms that they face on the move and how the refugee regime compounds and reconstitutes their exclusion. We have sought to highlight the fact that the harms suffered by LGBTIQ people are social, relational, and highly mobile. In other words, the harms that the queer and trans displaced flee can follow them within and across borders as they are fueled by an ever-present ideology of cisheteronormativity enforced by both people and states. This means that the homo/transphobic social world persists with the displaced throughout their journeys; it often begins at home, forces their escape from persecution, immobilizes them during flight, affects how their claims for protection are understood during assessment, worsens the harms of containment, limits access to support in the new country of asylum, and ultimately denies them sanctuary. Because this harm is a relational phenomenon, it requires relational solutions. Such solutions might include allowing the displaced to seek refuge with their loved ones, ending the practice of containment, or enabling new communities of solidarity to flourish after legal and territorial asylum has been found. This approach to displacement justice focuses on the entire experience of seeking asylum, from its beginning to its supposed resolution.

Emphasizing the importance of *justice* in this context shifts our attention away from duties of charity, which is a framing that haunts discussions of refugee admission.[8] Duties of charity allow the agent to be "morally at liberty" to choose when such obligations are discharged.[9] But duties of justice require individuals or groups to be entitled to something by right; on this view, these duties are more than options that various actors are free to choose between. Instead, they are requirements of justice, and a violation of these duties is not only a misfortune but something more serious.

Many of the harms articulated throughout the book are not merely harms but also *wrongs*.[10] They constitute an abdication of the state's duties of justice, especially when they compound or create new forms of persecution. Thus, while the inclusion of queer and trans displaced people does not tell us a clear story about what an ideally just system might demand, it can tell us how exclusion continues to shape our understanding of displacement justice and therefore might prevent its realization. In this sense, justice in the queer search for refuge concerns not only what displaced people are entitled to but how we approach the concept of justice when building and creating theory. When we fail to include entire populations of displaced people, such as LGBTIQ refugees, our tools and concepts in the debates on displacement justice are insufficient.

How might our current thinking be reshaped in light of the more expansive account of harm articulated throughout this book? For one, the complexity of LGBTIQ displacement tells us something important about our current theories of justice for people on the move: principally that they are built around an imagined refugee who flees state-led persecution and seeks protection at the border. In reality, the world of displacement is far more complicated, and this complexity does not only arise in the case of LGBTIQ refugees but also of those fleeing other pervasive social harms.[11]

We might think that queer refuge is just another consideration to add to our theories of displacement justice. We need only "add LGBTIQ people and stir." In this view, the way to respond to the puzzles raised by queer and trans displacement is simply to incorporate them into our current thinking about forced migration. Their inclusion may push us just beyond the boundaries that we have set for ourselves, but never by too much. Instead, throughout the book, we pursued an approach that highlights how the inclusion of queer and trans people in our theorizing about displacement challenges our conceptual approaches in a more fundamental way. The contribution of this approach varied throughout each stage of the imagined displacement journey adopted in this text. Sometimes this approach demonstrated how our legal and theoretical commitments are not extended to certain groups, as in the case of lesbian, bisexual, and queer women seeking asylum. Elsewhere it revealed that our focus on admission in debates of displacement justice obscures what happens within the state of refuge or what happens to those who are rendered immobile and never reach the border. In other cases, a focus on queer and trans refugees reveals the harms of certain practices for *all* displaced people, as in the contexts of assessment and containment. They demonstrate that seeking refuge on equal terms with others requires more radical thinking about the practices of reunion and sanctuary.

But Sebastián's story also reveals how complicated all of this can become. His sexuality and gender expression mixed with many other forms of prejudice, oppression, and exclusion. His political views were the "source" of his displacement—he refused to participate in progovernment demonstrations—but this led to homophobic attacks, death threats, and his eventual escape from the country. After his escape he faced experiences that many people on the move face, but the harms were exacerbated by his sexuality and gender expression. The homophobia adjacent to his persecution magnified the threat he faced because of how gender-nonconforming gay people are treated in much of Venezuela: as hypervisible minorities and legitimizable victims of state and communal violence. In Colombia, employment discrimination on both xenophobic and homo/transphobic grounds pushed him into an informal economy in which violence and abuse manifested from an ever-present risk to a reality.

Sebastián's experiences differed from the imagined refugee fleeing state-led persecution, and they challenge us to think differently about displacement justice. It cannot simply be a case of "add LGBTIQ people and stir," because the genuine inclusion of queer and trans displacement into our considerations of justice requires a recognition of how gender and sexuality, like many other identities, affect nearly every interaction in a person's life. Thus, the harms that Sebastián experienced during displacement reflected the interaction between the social world and his various identities. As these harms do not respect borders, a cisheteronormative social world followed him and shaped his journey and search for protection.

The theoretical framing of this book reinforces the importance of theory built from the lives of real people because their experiences demonstrate that our normative starting points must be constantly rearticulated. LGBTIQ people in situations of displacement are doing this work already.[12] In their queer search for refuge, they identify injustice, frame their needs, make claims for dignified treatment under international protection, and state their demands more clearly than we ever could. But we can contribute to their cause by echoing their efforts to challenge prevailing paradigms that accept the global refugee regime as it is, as opposed to articulating what it could be.

Our aim is therefore not just to include LGBTIQ refugees within current institutions of asylum protection, but to use queer and trans experiences to question those very institutions. Queering our understanding of refuge is therefore not only necessary from the perspective of inclusion; it is also conceptually indispensable. In other words, our conceptual tools will remain impoverished as long as exclusion persists. And with an impoverished theory, it is questionable how well we can hope to dream of a better future. Queer and trans refugees, while facing unique intersections of harm and injustice, thus teach us something further. They lead us to recognize fault lines and loaded hypocrisies within an unjust system that is meant to protect them.

Some of the changes suggested throughout this book are not piecemeal or surface level. Queer perspectives disrupt not just the practice of refugee protection but the very concepts that we employ. Thus, within the global refugee regime, implementing displacement justice must challenge existing political and legal frameworks, which seek to incrementally expand existing concepts to apply to new populations as opposed to revisiting the underpinning concepts themselves. We should not force the queer and trans perspective to fit within our existing frameworks. Instead, we should allow their perspectives to create change. This reorientation has significant potential in asylum law, as lawyers may build on our concept of relational harm to advocate for a more robust conception of persecution that better reflects its situated nature and malleability to the social world. Such an understanding of persecution might help courts to recognize that its nature is ever-transforming depending on a given individual's social position and thus end the serious injustice of the extreme harms experienced by certain populations being considered outside the bounds of asylum.

With this book, we hope to encourage *more* disruptive thinking on the question of refuge—thinking that takes seriously the constant ways in which our concepts must be reconsidered to reflect the experiences of those most affected. In centering nonhegemonic perspectives to question core assumptions, we lay a methodological blueprint that goes beyond the queer and trans displaced. Recognizing the impact of our assumptions related to the global refugee regime opens a new discourse about how such approaches block our understanding of what's right and what's possible.[13] This book demonstrated that such an approach matters for understanding the conditions of LGBTIQ people seeking safety, but we hope it leaves the door open for a dynamic conceptual approach that can respond to the needs being articulated by a range of communities.

It has been thirty years since LGBTIQ people began to be formally incorporated into the global refugee regime, and yet the status of their inclusion has never been more urgent. After decades of uneven progress that advanced legal inclusion for some while leaving others behind, we complete this book in more uncertain times. Regrettably, around the world, queer and trans people have become the scapegoats of targeted campaigns by conservative actors, political elites, and religious leaders. As a result, the very premise of inclusion as a sign of progress has become contested. That foundational idea may now be under threat.

The countries that have long touted their histories of accepting refugees—as well as their involvement in expanding inclusion to the queer and trans displaced—now appear to produce queer and trans displaced populations themselves. As anti-LGBTIQ rhetoric has become an effective mobilization framework around the world, queer and trans people have become the battleground for culture wars. There soon may not be sanctuary after asylum for queer and trans people seeking refuge in many states across the world. We cannot predict anyone's experience, nor are we here to diagnose the climate of an individual country, but we can provide a framework of analytical thinking that lets us reflect on and normatively adjudicate our obligations to those most in need.

Today, many LGBTIQ activists around the world organize to resist the backlash, refusing to cede hard-won gains to creeping authoritarianism. In developing normative theory grounded in the lives of those most affected by the exclusionary effects of cisheteronormativity, this book is our contribution to a global movement led by refugees and activists themselves. Ours is a joint project of understanding and seeking justice for the queer and trans displaced, and we have learned much from them. We hope this book is a testament to their effort, as just one step toward displacement justice. There are many yet to be taken.

Acknowledgments

We would like to extend our heartfelt thanks to a range of people who made this book possible. First and foremost, to our editor Naomi Schneider, for believing in the work of two early career researchers trying to do something different, as well to the broader University of California Press team, including Aline Dolinh and Summer Farah, and the BookComp team, including Jon Dertien, Artemis Brod and Bob Ludkey. Second, to our respective dissertation supervisors who believed in this project and encouraged us to pursue it during the intensity of doctoral study; Rebecca thanks Matthew Gibney and Samuel thanks Alexander Betts and Masooda Bano. A special thanks as well to the Refugee Studies Centre and Department of International Development at the University of Oxford for being an intellectual home for this research. Many of the foundational discussions for this text took place in the special place that is the DPhil loft of Queen Elizabeth House.

We also wish to express our gratitude to Carlos Saavedra for granting us permission to use his magnificent photo as the cover of our book as well as to Rufaro Muchaka and Ila Zelmanovitz Axelrod for providing research assistance.

We would like to acknowledge the institutional support that we received during the writing of this manuscript: Rebecca, from the University of Bristol (Department of Philosophy) and University of Cambridge (Department of Politics and International Studies), and Samuel, from the University of Oxford (Department of Politics and International Relations) and the European University Institute (Max Weber Programme, Department of Political and Social Sciences).

Work from this book was presented at several conferences and workshops. These include the Annual Conference of the International Studies Association, March 2023; the "Exclusion, Integration, and Democracy GOODINT Workshop," May 2023, hosted by UiT—the Artic University of Norway; the "Political Theory of LGBTQ+ Refuge and Migration Workshop," March 2024, hosted by the University of Bergen, which included a manuscript workshop on a draft of the book; and an earlier manuscript workshop held at the European University Institute in June 2023. We would like to thank all those who engaged with our ideas at these workshops for their invaluable contributions, as well as the institutions that provided financial support in arranging these convenings.

We are deeply indebted to everyone who reviewed drafts of the full manuscript (some multiple times), including Bridget Anderson, Brent Drummond, Zach Fisch, Patti Lenard, Stephen Meili, Nishin Nathwani, Kalypso Nicolaïdis, Ryan Thompson, Mengia Tschalaer, and Annamari Vitikainen, as well as to others who gave feedback on specific chapters, including Luigi Achilli, Laurie Anderson, Megan Bradley, Natasha Bunzl, Benjamin Carver, Stephen Damianos, Ane Engelstad, Victoria Finn, Cyril Ghosh, Daniel Goldstein, Karolina Kocemba, Margaret Renata Neil, Stephanie Pope, Alyson Price, Ezgi Sertler, Salvador Vidal-Ortiz, Jasmine Ward, and Kerri Woods.

Rebecca would like to thank Ivan and Alba for their support. This book was completed during a period of illness, and, without them, it would not have been possible. Rebecca would also like to thank Samuel for being an incredibly kind, thoughtful, and inspiring coauthor and a wonderful friend. Their work has changed mine, for the better.

Samuel would like to thank Juan Camilo and Piera for their support. An additional heartfelt thanks to their mother, Rima, for being their biggest champion, as well as to the rest of their friends and family, who have filled their days with laughter, love, and gossip in the years it took to write this book. A deep thanks to all of Samuel's research colleagues and interlocutors in Colombia, who have grounded their work, inspired every word, and become family in the process. An additional thanks to Sonia for her sage wisdom that came at just the right time. And a final thanks to Rebecca, the best coauthor a kvetch could ask for. I am a better scholar, writer, and friend because of you!

Lastly, we want to acknowledge that we draw, with permissions granted under open access licenses, from previously published work in parts of chapters 2, 6, and 7. This work includes Rebecca Buxton, "What Is Wrong with Persecution," *Journal of Social Philosophy* 54, no. 2 (2023): 201–17; Samuel Ritholtz and Rebecca Buxton, "Sanctuary After Asylum: Addressing a Gap in the Political Theory of Refuge," *American Political Science Review* 117, no. 3 (2023): 1166–71; and Samuel Ritholtz and Rebecca Buxton, "Queer Kinship and the Rights of Refugee Families," *Migration Studies* 9, no. 3 (2021): 1075–95.

About the Cover

The cover photo of a calendula flower frozen in ice comes from the photo series and research project LIMPIA led by photographer Carlos Saavedra and anthropologist Sebastián Ramírez.

Here is more about the project in the words of Saavedra and Ramírez:

> Every year, thousands are selectively killed and displaced in social cleansing campaigns in Colombia announced in publicly posted pamphlets. The selective killings have become a hallmark of the country's poorest neighborhoods. Often perpetrated by neighbors, under the auspices of paramilitary groups and with the complicity or even participation of local police, these murders are touted as the necessary procedures of order in places where official justice cannot reach. Drug users; petty criminals; LGBTQ folk, and especially trans women, are the preeminent targets of such campaigns.
>
> LIMPIA is a multimedia project that invites a consideration of social cleansing through the experiences of those who stand in resistance against it. This project accompanies a group of trans women who, faced with the extra-legal and legal dismissal of their lives, take recourse to magic to protect themselves and to reassert a modicum of agency. Bringing together photojournalism, anthropology, and artistic representation, the multimedia series inhabits the magically real space created by these women, illuminating the powers they conjure in the worlds they create. The series showcases portraits of the witches, the staging of rituals, and images of frozen plants, opening a space to consider what transformation, cleansing, and resistance look like in spaces of precarious survival.
>
> LIMPIA is imagined to exist between disciplines and knowledges in an effort to expand the bounds of storytelling that are traditionally produced about violence. It builds a space in which those who struggle against structural violence can meet to

create new representations of themselves and together weave novel images of power and possibility.

As the authors of *The Way Out*, we love the photo and its meaning for our book cover because it symbolizes agency and resilience in the face of pervasive social prejudice and political violence. We see a parallel between the stories of the incredible trans women of LIMPIA and the queer and trans displaced documented throughout the book. Both set in temporary contexts of harm, queer and trans people take the actions necessary to be their own sources of safety. Whether through ritual or movement, these protagonists help us to reimagine what it means to persist during adversity.

ABOUT THE COVER PHOTOGRAPHER

Carlos Saavedra is a Colombian documentary photographer. He published his first book *Madres Terra* (Raya Editorial, 2022) with Sebastián Ramírez and *las Madres de los Falsos Positivos de Soacha y Bogotá*.

Notes

PREFACE

1. Hannah Arendt, *Men in Dark Times* (Harcourt Brace & Company, 1968), ix–x.

INTRODUCTION

1. Certain details of the hearing presented have been modified to protect the identities of those involved.

2. Judicial Division of the Council of State, Afdeling rechtspraak van de Raad van State, Rechtspraak Vreemdelingenrecht Gids Vreemdelingenrecht (oud) D12-51 (August 13, 1981).

3. Matter of Toboso-Alfonso, 20 I&N Dec. 819 (BIA 1990).

4. David Johnston, "Ruling Backs Homosexuals on Asylum," *The New York Times*, June 17, 1994, https://www.nytimes.com/1994/06/17/us/ruling-backs -homosexuals-on-asylum.html.

5. Connor Cory, "The LGBTQ Asylum Seeker: Particular Social Groups and Authentic Queer Identities," *Georgetown Journal of Gender and the Law* 20 (2018): 577.

6. Refugee Appeal No. 1312/93 Re GJ (30 August 1995), New Zealand Refugee Status Appeals Authority, [1998] INLR 387; Mandivavarira Mudarikwa

et al., *LGBTI+ Asylum Seekers in South Africa: A Review of Refugee Status Denials Involving Sexual Orientation and Gender Identity* (Lawyers for Human Rights, African Human Rights Network, and University of the Witwatersrand African Centre for Migration & Society, April 2021). For recent research on the refugee protection regime in South America, see Esteban Scuzarello Octavio, "Adjudicando protección: el proceso de refugio para personas LGBTQI+ en Sudamérica," *Relaciones Internacionales* 58 (2025): 58–78.

7. UK Lesbian & Gay Immigration Group (UKLGIG), "Failing the Grade" (Rainbow Migration, 2010), https://www.rainbowmigration.org.uk/publications/failing-the-grade/.

8. Eithne Luibhéid, *Entry Denied: Controlling Sexuality at the Border* (University of Minnesota Press, 2002), 21.

9. Luibhéid, *Entry Denied*, 23. Many countries still restrict entry and work permits for individuals living with HIV, including Bhutan, Brunei, Egypt, and Russia.

10. Ari Shaw and Namrata Verghese, *LGBTQI+ Refugees and Asylum Seekers: A Review of Research and Data Needs* (Williams Institute UCLA School of Law, June 2022).

11. For instance, Rainbow Railroad, an organization that helps LGBTIQ refugees to escape persecution, has a partnership with the Canadian Government.

12. As it relates to the law, Carlos Zelada argues that queering legal regimes requires recognizing the cisheteronormative biases embedded in their structures. A queer legal approach therefore has two objectives: "searching for how the law reveals its cisendoheteronormative genealogy and demanding a critical look at the hegemonic regimes of sexuality." Carlos J. Zelada, "Cuerpxs indisciplinadxs: Hacia una mirada cuir (Queer) (Cuy-r) de la regulación jurídica de las sexualidades disidentes," in *Repensando las reglas de juego: Caminos para evitar el colapso institucional y social*, edited by Ronnie Farfán, Santiago Mariani, and Cecilia O'Neill, 153–90 (Fondo Editorial Universidad del Pacífico, 2018), 181 (authors' translation).

13. Shaw and Verghese, *LGBTQI+ Refugees and Asylum Seekers*.

14. Henry Zeffman and Sam Francis, "Anti-Gay Discrimination Not Qualification for Asylum, Says Suella Braverman," BBC News, September 23, 2023, https://www.bbc.co.uk/news/uk-politics-66919416. Braverman's statement also reveals a misunderstanding of asylum law, which requires persecution (and not simply discrimination) *because of* gender identity or sexual orientation. Such exaggerations are common among those seeking to stir up fears of asylum-seekers "invading" countries of refuge. We thank Stephen Meili for this comment.

15. Glenn Thrush, "Under Trump, U.S. Prisons Offered Gender-Affirming Care," *The New York Times*, October 16, 2024, https://www.nytimes.com/2024/10/16/us/politics/trump-prisons-transgender-care-harris.html.

16. The White House, "Realigning the United States Refugee Admissions Program," Presidential actions, January 20, 2025, https://www.whitehouse.gov

/presidential-actions/2025/01/realigning-the-united-states-refugee-admissions
-program/.

17. Tom Phillips and Clavel Rangel, "'He Is Not a Gang Member': Outrage
as US Deports Makeup Artist to El Salvador Prison for Crown Tattoos," *The
Guardian*, April 1, 2025, https://www.theguardian.com/us-news/2025/apr/01/its
-a-tradition-outrage-in-venezuela-as-us-deports-makeup-artist-for-religious
-tattoos.

18. Jonathan Blitzer, "The Make Up Artist Donald Trump Deported Under The
Enemy Aliens Act" (*The New Yorker*, March 31, 2025), https://www.newyorker
.com/news/annals-of-immigration/the-makeup-artist-donald-trump-deported
-under-the-alien-enemies-act.

19. Phillips and Rangel, "'He Is Not a Gang Member.'"

20. The presiding immigration judge was also only made aware at the hearing that Andry had been deported by the US government. Responding to this
news from the ICE lawyer, the judge asked, "How can he be removed to El Salvador . . . if there's no removal order?" Jonathan Blitzer, "The Make Up Artist Donald Trump Deported."

21. Jamie Tabberer, "Trump administration deports gay make-up artist to
maximum security prison in El Salvador," *Attitude Magazine*, April 7, 2025,
https://www.attitude.co.uk/news/el-salvador-gay-makeup-artist-deported
-482195/.

22. Christopher Wiggins, "Gay Makeup Artist Andry Hernández Romero Describes Horrific Sexual & Physical Abuse at CECOT in El Salvador," *The Advocate*, July 26, 2025), https://www.advocate.com/news/andry-hernandez-romero
-cecot-torture.

23. Immigration Equality, "New Summary Report Details How Trump Administration Policies Endanger LGBTQI+ People at Risk of Persecution" (Immigration Equality, June 5, 2025), https://immigrationequality.org/press/press
-releases-2/new-summary-report-details-how-trump-administration-policies
-endanger-lgbtqi-people-at-risk-of-persecution/.

24. International Organization for Migration (IOM), "IOM Missing Migrants," 2024, https://missingmigrants.iom.int/region/mediterranean.

25. United Nations High Commission for Refugees (UNHCR), "Global
Trends: Forced Displacement in 2020," UNHCR, 2021, https://www.unhcr.org
/flagship-reports/globaltrends/; Ayelet Shachar, *The Shifting Border: Legal Cartographies of Migration and Mobility* (Manchester University Press, 2020).

26. David Scott FitzGerald, *Refuge Beyond Reach* (Oxford University Press,
2019).

27. A study conducted by the NGO Global Action for Trans Equality (GATE)
found that 56 percent of respondents felt that the human rights situation for
trans and gender-diverse individuals in their countries is worsening due to an-
tigender attacks. As a result, a significant number of trans and gender-diverse

human rights defenders have had to relocate globally, including board members, staff, and volunteers. GATE, *Impact of Anti-Gender Opposition on TGD and LGBTQI Movements: Global Report* (GATE, 2023).

28. Phillip M. Ayoub and Kristina Stoeckl, *The Global Fight Against LGBTI Rights: How Transnational Conservative Networks Target Sexual and Gender Minorities* (New York University Press, 2024).

29. Samuel Ritholtz and Margaret Neil, "LGBTQ+ Parents Are Being Removed from Their Children's Birth Certificates in Italy: Here's What's Behind This Disturbing Trend," *The Conversation*, June 28, 2023, https://theconversation.com/lgbtq-parents-are-being-removed-from-their-childrens-birth-certificates-in-italy-heres-whats-behind-this-disturbing-trend-208241.

30. Dean Cooper-Cunningham, "Security, Sexuality, and the Gay Clown Putin Meme: Queer Theory and International Responses to Russian Political Homophobia," *Security Dialogue* 53, no. 4 (2022): 302–23; Emil Edenborg, Queer on the Home Front: Russian LGBTIQ Activism and Queer Security in the Wake of Russia's War in Ukraine," *Security Dialogue* 56, no. 2 (2025): 170–87.

31. Graeme Reid, *Protection Against Violence and Discrimination Based on Sexual Orientation and Gender Identity in Relation to Forced Displacement* (Office of the High Commissioner for Human Rights, 2025), https://www.ohchr.org/en/documents/thematic-reports/ahrc5943-protection-against-violence-and-discrimination-based-sexual.

32. Paul J. Angelo and Will Freeman, "A Socially Conservative Left Is Gaining Traction in Latin America," *Americas Quarterly*, June 23, 2021.

33. J. F. S. Amaya, "La tormenta perfecta: Ideología de género y articulación de públicos," *Sexualidad, Salud y Sociedad (Rio de Janeiro)* (2017): 149–171; L. A. Payne, J. Zulver, and S. Escoffier, eds., *The Right Against Rights in Latin America* (Oxford University Press, 2023); Samuel Ritholtz and Miguel Mesquita, "The Transnational Force of Anti-LGBT+ Politics in Latin America," in *The Right Against Rights in Latin America*, edited by Leigh A. Payne, Julia Zulver, and Simón Escoffier (Oxford University Press, 2023): 98–111.

34. Stonewall, "New Data: Rise in Hate Crime Against LGBTQ+ People Continues, Stonewall Slams UK Gov. 'Inaction,'" Stonewall, October 2023, https://www.stonewall.org.uk/news/new-data-rise-hate-crime-against-lgbtq-people-continues-stonewall-slams-uk-gov-.

35. Yến Lê Espiritu, Lan Duong, Ma Vang, Victor Bascara, Khatharya Um, Lila Sharif, and Nigel Hatton, *Departures: An Introduction to Critical Refugee Studies*, vol. 3 (University of California Press, 2022).

36. Rahul Rao, *Out of Time: The Queer Politics of Postcoloniality* (Oxford University Press, 2020), 2.

37. Kath Browne and Catherine Nash, *Queer Methods and Methodologies: Intersecting Queer Theories and Social Science Research* (Routledge, 2010).

38. Browne and Nash, *Queer Methods and Methodologies*. Their use of "normative" here subtly differs from our use in the opening sentence of this paragraph.

We use "normative" to mean principally moral and ethical analysis, while Browne and Nash use it to mean relating to the standard or norm.

39. Eve Kosofsky Sedgwick, "Queer and Now," in *The Routledge Queer Studies Reader*, ed. Donald E. Hall and Annamarie Jagose (Routledge, 2012), 3–17.

40. Graeme Reid and Samuel Ritholtz, "A Queer Approach to Understanding LGBT Vulnerability During the COVID-19 Pandemic," *Politics & Gender* 16, no. 4 (2020): 1101–9, https://doi.org/10.1017/S1743923X20000707.

41. Columbia Law School, "Kimberlé Crenshaw on Intersectionality, More Than Two Decades Later," June 28, 2017, https://www.law.columbia.edu/news/archive/kimberle-crenshaw-intersectionality-more-two-decades-later; Kimberlé Crenshaw, "Mapping the Margins: Identity Politics, Intersectionality, and Violence Against Women," *Stanford Law Review* 43, no. 6 (1991): 1241–99; Kimberlé Crenshaw, "Demarginalizing the Intersection of Race and Sex: A Black De-marginalizing the Intersection of Race and Sex: A Black Feminist Critique of Antidiscrimination Doctrine, Feminist Theory and Antiracist Politics," *University of Chicago Legal Forum*, 139 (1989).

42. Patricia Hill Collins, *Black Feminist Thought: Knowledge, Consciousness and the Politics of Empowerment* (Routledge, 2000).

43. Momin Rahman, "Queer as Intersectionality: Theorizing Gay Muslim Identities," *Sociology* 44, no. 5 (October 1, 2010): 951–52, https://doi.org/10.1177/0038038510375733. In her 1989 text Crenshaw emphasizes the indispensability of intersectionality for feminist theory: "Because the intersectional experience is greater than the sum of racism and sexism, any analysis that does not take intersectionality into account cannot sufficiently address the particular manner in which Black women are subordinated. Thus, for feminist theory and antiracist policy discourse to embrace the experiences and concerns of Black women, the entire framework that has been used as a basis for translating 'women's experience' or 'the Black experience' into concrete policy demands must be rethought and recast." Crenshaw, "Demarginalizing the Intersection of Race and Sex," 140.

44. For more on how queer analysis challenges the binary between "forced" and "voluntary" migrants, see Davide Tomaselli, "'Forced' Refugees Versus 'Voluntary' Migrants: Deconstructing a Binary Through SOGIESC Claims of Asylum," *International Journal of Refugee Law* (2025).

45. Sarah Schulman, *Let the Record Show: A Political History of ACT UP New York, 1987–1993*, first edition (Farrar, Straus and Giroux, 2021).

46. Saidiya Hartman, *Wayward Lives, Beautiful Experiments: Intimate Histories of Riotous Black Girls, Troublesome Women, and Queer Radicals* (W. W. Norton, 2019).

47. R. K. Yin, *Case Study Research and Applications: Design and Methods*, 6th ed. (Sage, 2018).

48. Regarding LBQ (lesbian, bisexual, and queer) women and nonbinary people, this is changing. Chapter 2, on *persecution*, delves into some of the brilliant research being undertaken by scholars and activist organizations on the

subject matter. For more discussion on the research gap related to intersex lives during displacement, see the work of Organisation Intersex International Europe's Intersex Refugees and Asylum Seekers Project (https://www.oiieurope .org/programs/#refugees-asylum-seekers) and B Camminga, "Where are all the Intersex Asylum Seekers? Active Absenting or the Citational Chain of an Idea," *Feminist Formations* 36, no. 2 (2024): 189–202.

49. Bent Flyvbjerg, "Five Misunderstandings About Case-Study Research," *Qualitative Inquiry* 12, no. 2 (2006): 219–245; J. Seawright and J. Gerring, "Case Selection Techniques in Case Study Research: A Menu of Qualitative and Quantitative Options," *Political Research Quarterly* 61, no. 2 (2008): 294–308.

50. Robert E. Stake, *The Art of Case Study Research* (Sage, 1995).

51. Bhupinder S. Chimni, "The Birth of a 'Discipline': From Refugee to Forced Migration Studies," *Journal of Refugee Studies* 22, no. 1 (2009): 11–29.

52. Lucy Mayblin, *Asylum After Empire: Colonial Legacies in the Politics of Asylum Seeking* (Rowman & Littlefield, 2017); Lucy Mayblin and Joe Turner, *Migration Studies and Colonialism* (John Wiley, 2020).

53. Heaven Crawley, "Saving Brown Women from Brown Men? 'Refugee Women,' Gender and the Racialised Politics of Protection," *Refugee Survey Quarterly* 41, no. 3 (August 31, 2022): 355–80, https://doi.org/10.1093/rsq /hdac021; Meghana Nayak, *Who Is Worthy of Protection?: Gender-Based Asylum and US Immigration Politics* (Oxford University Press, 2015).

54. Matthew Gibney, *The Ethics and Politics of Asylum: Liberal Democracy and the Response to Refugees* (Cambridge University Press, 2004); David Owen, *What Do We Owe to Refugees?* (Polity, 2020); David Miller, *Strangers in Our Midst: The Political Philosophy of Immigration* (Harvard University Press, 2016); Serena Parekh, *No Refuge: Ethics and the Global Refugee Crisis* (Oxford University Press, 2020); Ashwini Vasanthakumar, *The Ethics of Exile: A Political Theory of Diaspora* (Oxford University Press, 2021).

55. Brandon A. Robinson, "Heteronormativity and Homonormativity," in *The Wiley Blackwell Encyclopedia of Gender and Sexuality Studies* (Wiley, 2016), 1–3.

56. International Commission of Jurists (ICJ), *Yogyakarta Principles: Principles on the Application of International Human Rights Law in Relation to Sexual Orientation and Gender Identity* (2007), https://www.refworld.org/legal /resolution/icjurists/2007/en/58135.

57. Judith Butler, "Critically Queer," *GLQ: A Journal of Lesbian and Gay Studies* 1, no. 1 (1993): 17–32.

58. The relationship between bodies, desires, identities, and gender expression is not necessarily linear or stable. Rather than conforming to binary logics and clear categorization, sexuality and gender often shift across time and context. Queer theorists have emphasized the fluid nature of sexualities, with scholars of sexual geography demonstrating that such identities are shaped through everyday practices, interpersonal encounters, and spatial arrangements. These dynamics

are particularly evident in specific localities, including those in the Global South, where sexuality is deeply embedded in social and material environments that might resist the "identity"-paradigm of conceptualizing sexual orientation and gender identity. Gavin Brown et al., "Sexualities in/of the Global South," *Geography Compass* 4, no. 10 (October 1, 2010): 1567–79, https://doi.org/10.1111/j.1749 -8198.2010.00382.x.

59. Giuseppe Campuzano, "Contemporary Travesti Encounters with Gender and Sexuality in Latin America," *Development* 52, no. 1 (March 2009): 75–83, https://doi.org/10.1057/dev.2008.90; Heather Love, "Queer," *Transgender Studies Quarterly* 1, no. 1–2 (2014): 172–76; Susan Stryker, *Transgender History: The Roots of Today's Revolution* (Seal Press, 2017); María-Amelia Viteri, *Desbordes* (SUNY Press, 2014), https://sunypress.edu/Books/D/Desbordes.

60. Annamari Vitikainen, "LGBT Rights and Refugees: A Case for Prioritizing LGBT Status in Refugee Admissions," *Ethics & Global Politics* 13, no. 1 (January 1, 2020): 64–78, https://doi.org/10.1080/16544951.2020.1735015.

61. Andrew Shacknove, "Who Is a Refugee?" *Ethics* 95, no. 2 (1985): 274–84; Owen, *What Do We Owe to Refugees?*; Chandran Kukathas, "Are Refugees Special?" in *Migration and Political Theory: The Ethics of Movement and Membership*, ed. Sarah Fine and Lea Ypi (Oxford University Press, 2016), 249–68.

62. It should be noted that not all LGBTIQ people with displacement backgrounds seek asylum in the same way, if at all. Florent Chossière argues that attending to how LGBTIQ people come to seek international protection can help reveal the limits of our understandings related to asylum processes as well as place asylum within a broader universe of migration outcomes for queer and trans people. Florent Chossière, "'I Knew About Political Asylum, but not About Asylum for Gay People': How Queer Exiles Come to Apply (or not) for SOGI Asylum in France," *Journal of Refugee Studies* (2025).

63. Nayak, *Who Is Worthy of Protection?*; Fatima El-Tayeb, *European Others: Queering Ethnicity in Postnational Europe* (University of Minnesota Press, 2011).

64. On a separate-but-related note, we deploy the term *displacement* without the adjective "forced" as we accept Abbey Steele's assertion that there is no such thing as "unforced" displacement. Abbey Steele, *Democracy and Displacement in Colombia's Civil War* (Cornell University Press, 2017).

65. American Civil Liberties Union, *Justice-Free Zones: U.S. Immigration Detention Under the Trump Administration* (ACLU 2020), https://www.aclu .org/publications/justice-free-zones-us-immigration-detention-under-trump -administration.

66. Crawley, "Saving Brown Women from Brown Men?" 368.

67. Some of the arguments in this chapter were previously published in Samuel Ritholtz and Rebecca Buxton, "Queer Kinship and the Rights of Refugee Families," *Migration Studies* 9, no. 3 (September 2021), 1075–95.

68. Some of the arguments in this chapter were previously published in Samuel Ritholtz and Rebecca Buxton, "Sanctuary after Asylum: Addressing a Gap in the Political Theory of Refuge," *American Political Science Review* 117, no. 3 (2023): 1166–1171.

CHAPTER 1. HOME

1. Rosie Pentreath, host, *OUTCast*, podcast, season 1, episode 3, "Meet the Gay Nigerian Refugee Who Sought Asylum in the UK to Escape Death Threats, Conversion Therapy and Violence," October 11, 2021, https://outcastpod.com/2021/10/11/gay-nigerian-refugee-asylum-uk-after-conversion-therapy/.

2. In some contexts, the mechanisms of conversion therapy may appear more "benign." For instance, it might involve talk therapy or exercises. This form of intervention is still undergirded by an attempt to "correct" the individual in question, and so still relies on the ideology of sexual brokenness. There is also no evidence that this form of conversion's therapy has any effect on the individual's sexual orientation or gender identity.

3. T. Jones, T. W. Jones, J. Power, M. Pallotta-Chiarolli, and N. Despott, "Mis-Education of Australian Youth: Exposure to LGBTQA+ Conversion Ideology and Practices," *Sex Education* 22, no. 5 (2021): 3, https://doi.org/10.1080/14681811.2021.1978964; Sarah Golightley, "'I'm Gay! I'm Gay! I'm Gay! I'm a Homosexual!': Overt and Covert Conversion Therapy Practices in Therapeutic Boarding Schools," *The British Journal of Social Work* 53, no. 3 (April 2023): 1426–44, https://doi.org/10.1093/bjsw/bcad049.

4. A review of evidence in 1991 found that conversion therapies were unethical, irresponsible, and constituted questionable and inadequate science. See Douglas Haldeman, "Sexual Orientation Conversion Therapy for Gay Men and Lesbians: A Scientific Study," in *Homosexuality: Research and Implications for Public Policy*, edited by John C. Gonsiorek and James D. Weinrich, 149–60 (Sage, 1991). https://web.archive.org/web/20180206023332/http://www.drdoughaldeman.com/doc/ScientificExamination.pdf.

5. Sarah Schulman, *Ties That Bind: Familial Homophobia and Its Consequences* (The New Press, 2009).

6. Rainbow Railroad, *2020 Annual Report* (Rainbow Railroad 2021), https://www.rainbowrailroad.org/2020-annual-report.

7. Not all of these countries have de jure criminalization. Some have de facto criminalization, in which authorities might use other broader laws, such as those relating to disorderly conduct or sex work, to crack down on queer and trans populations. Furthermore, many countries that criminalize same-sex relations—but make no mention of gender expression—still persecute trans people under the assumption that all trans people are homosexuals.

B Camminga, *Transgender Refugees and the Imagined South Africa* (Palgrave MacMillan, 2019).

8. Human Dignity Trust, "Map of Criminalization" (2024), https://www .humandignitytrust.org/lgbt-the-law/map-of-criminalisation. Alexander et al. also note that *state-enabled* killings occur in at least twenty-three countries. Christopher Alexander, Mai Sato, and Aleardo Zanghellini, "State-Enabled Killing of Same-Sex-Attracted People: A Legal Pluralist Account," *Law & Social Inquiry* 48, no. 3 (2023): 719–47, https://doi.org/10.1017/lsi.2022.48.

9. International Lesbian, Gay, Bisexual, Trans and Intersex Association (ILGA World), *In Relation to Forced Displacement: Submission to the UN Independent Expert on Protection Against Violence and Discrimination Based on Sexual Orientation and Gender Identity* (March 2025), https://ilga.org/resources /submissions-special-procedures-thematic-reports/; Rainbow Railroad, *Protection Against Violence and Discrimination Based on Sexual Orientation and Gender Identity in Relation to Forced Displacement, Submission to the UN Independent Expert on SOGI* (March 2025), https://www.rainbowrailroad.org/wp -content/uploads/2025/03/RR_SOGI-Report.pdf.

10. The United Nations Working Group on Arbitrary Detention has made it clear in multiple rulings that any detention based on one's sexual orientation and gender identity is a violation of international human rights law. See United Nations Human Rights Council Working Group on Arbitrary Detention, Opinion No. 14/2017 Concerning Cornelius Fonya (Cameroon), A/HRC/WGAD/2017/14, (United Nations, 2017); United Nations Human Rights Council Working Group on Arbitrary Detention, Opinion No. 20/2021 Concerning Douglas Tumuhimbise et al. (Uganda), A/HRC/WGAD/2021/20 (United Nations, 2021). We thank Priya Gopalan for helping us identify these opinions.

11. Rahul Rao has critiqued different ways of locating homophobia in space and time, especially discussing the debate around Uganda's Anti Homosexuality Act. Two dominant frames exist, one which frames homophobia as part of an African tradition, and one that views it as an import from Western actors. Instead, Rao argues that in such contexts homophobia "emerges as a transnational collaborative construction involving Ugandan and Western elites." Rahul Rao, *Out of Time*, 33.

12. Human Dignity Trust, "Nigeria" (2025), https://www.humandignitytrust .org/country-profile/nigeria/.

13. A similar point can be made here about states in which political leaders engage in hateful, divisive rhetoric against LGBTIQ populations and pass laws that prohibit "LGBT propaganda" or promote "family values," such as in Russia. While not necessarily engaging in direct persecutorial conduct against queer and trans populations, they are contributing to an environment that reinforces prejudice and legitimizes violence against them.

14. Indeed, much of the harm that drives queer and trans displacement and exacerbates the vulnerability of this population results from both the political

and legal context as well as social and cultural practices. In the wake of intra-familial harm, LGBTIQ populations seek to establish new networks of support (often with each other), which can be a source of joy and healing. But when crisis hits, whether resulting from climate change, war, or other "aberrations" of order, such as economic sanctions, these intimate informal networks of queer support can break down; they are not often the focus or on the radar of state or humanitarian actors and thus rarely receive key support. As a result, these populations are left out of aid provision, making them particularly vulnerable to crises, even if they are not intentionally targeted. John Marnell et al., eds., *East African Queer and Trans Displacements* (Bloomsbury Academic, 2025); OutRight International and Edge Effect, "'They Know What We Don't': Meaningful Inclusion of LGBTIQ People in Humanitarian Action" (OutRight International, 2024); Sima Shakhsari, "The Queer Time of Death: Temporality, Geopolitics, and Refugee Rights," *Sexualities* 17, no. 8 (2014): 998–1015.

15. Kate Manne discusses P. F. Strawson's conception of "interpersonal" reactive attitudes when outlining the naïve account of misogyny. See Kate Manne, *Ameliorating Misogyny in* Down Girl, (Oxford University Press, 2018), 58.

16. Kate Manne, *Ameliorating Misogyny*, 63.

17. Manne also conceptualizes this ameliorative shift as turning our focus "from misogyny's agents to its subjects." See *Ameliorating Misogyny*, 61.

18. M. T. Fullilove, "Psychiatric Implications of Displacement: Contributions from the Psychology of Place," *American Journal of Psychiatry* 153, no. 12 (1996): 1519.

19. Liisa H. Malkki, "Refugees and Exile: From 'Refugee Studies' to the National Order of Things," *Annual Review of Anthropology* 24 (1995): 515.

20. Helen Taylor, "Refugees, the State, and the Concept of Home," *Refugee Survey Quarterly* 32, no. 2 (2013): 130.

21. Danielle Roth et al., "Cycles of Displacement: Understanding Exclusion, Discrimination and Violence Against LGBTQI People in Humanitarian Contexts" (International Rescue Committee, 2021).

22. Rebecca Buxton and Lena Kainz, "All Refugees Want to Go Home, Right?" Open Democracy, October 18, 2017, https://www.opendemocracy.net/en/all-refugees-want-to-go-home-right/.

23. Sara Ahmed et al., "Introduction: Uprootings/Regroundings: Questions of Home and Migration," in *Uprootings/Regroundings Questions of Home and Migration*, edited by Sara Ahmed, Claudia Castañeda, Anne-Marie Fortier, and Mimi Sheller, 1–19 (Routledge, 2003).

24. Warsan Shire, "Home, and: Conversation about Home (At the Deportation Centre)," *Transition* 132, no. 1 (2021): 336–42.

25. Taylor, "Refugees, the State, and the Concept of Home," 132.

26. Shelley Mallett, "Understanding Home: A Critical Review of the Literature," *The Sociological Review* 52, no. 1 (2004): 62–89.

27. Doreen Massey, *Space, Place, and Gender* (University of Minnesota Press, 1994), 165.

28. Giulia Scalettaris, "Refugees and Mobility," *Forced Migration Review* 33 (2009).

29. Tara Polzer Ngwato, "Negotiating Belonging: The Integration of Mozambican Refugees in South Africa" (PhD thesis, London School of Economics, 2011).

30. Nicholas Van Hear, "Refugees in Diaspora," *Refuge: Canada's Journal on Refugees* 23, no. 1 (2006): 9–15.

31. Katy Long, *The Point of No Return* (Oxford University Press, 2013); Katy Long, "Permanent Crises? Unlocking the Protracted Displacement of Refugees and Internally Displaced Persons" (Refuge Studies Centre, 2011).

32. Jasna Čapo, "'Durable Solutions,' Transnationalism, and Homemaking Among Croatian and Bosnian Former Refugees," *Refuge: Canada's Journal on Refugees* 31, no. 1 (2015): 32.

33. Barry N. Stein, and Frederick C. Cuny, "Refugee Repatriation during Conflict: Protection and Post-Return Assistance," *Development in Practice* 4, no. 3 (January 1994): 186.

34. Megan Bradley, "Return in Dignity: A Neglected Refugee Protection Challenge," *Canadian Journal of Development Studies / Revue canadienne d'études du développement* 28, no. 3–4 (January 1, 2009): 371–82, https://doi.org/10.1080/02255189.2009.9669219.

35. Madan Sarup, "Home and Identity," in *Traveller's Tales: Narratives of Home and Displacement*, edited by Jon Bird, Barry Curtis, Melinda Mash, Tim Putnam, George Robertson, and Lisa Tickner (Routledge, 1994), 91.

36. H. Jones et al., *Go Home?: The Politics of Immigration Controversies* (Manchester University Press, 2017), 208.

37. Malkki, "Refugees and Exile: From 'Refugee Studies' to the National Order of Things," 516.

38. Emma Haddad, *The Refugee in International Society: Between Sovereigns* (Cambridge University Press, 2008).

39. Liisa Malkki, *Purity and Exile: Violence, Memory, and National Cosmology Among Hutu Refugees in Tanzania* (Chicago University Press, 1995), 15.

40. Betty Freidan, *The Feminine Mystique* (Penguin Modern Classics, 1963).

41. Simone De Beauvoir, *The Second Sex* (Routledge, 2014), 118.

42. Luce Irigaray, *An Ethics of Sexual Difference* (Cornell University Press, 1993).

43. Silvia Federici, *Caliban and the Witch: Women, the Body and Primitive Accumulation* (Penguin Modern Classics, 2004).

44. Biddy Martin and Chandra Talpade Mohanty, "Feminist Politics: What's Home Got to Do with It?" in *Feminist Studies/Critical Studies*, edited by Teresa de Lauretis (Springer, 1986), 196.

45. Martin and Mohanty, "Feminist Politics," 230.

46. bell hooks, "Homeplace: A Site of Resistance," in *Undoing Place? A Geographical Reader* (Routledge, 1997), 384.

47. Iris Marion Young, "House and Home: Feminist Variations on a Theme," in *Motherhood and Space: Configurations of the Maternal Through Politics, Home, and the Body,* edited by Sarah Hardy and Caroline Wiedmer (Palgrave Macmillan, 2005), 157.

48. Young, "House and Home," 149-50.

49. Young, 162.

50. Young, 162.

51. Young, 163.

52. Young, 164.

53. We, of course, do not mean to assert that this is a universal experience.

54. Anne-Marie Fortier, "'Coming Home': Queer Migrations and Multiple Evocations of Home," *European Journal of Cultural Studies* 4, no. 4 (2001): 647–65.

55. Schulman, *Let the Record Show.*

56. Nicole L. Asquith and Christopher A. Fox, "No Place Like Home: Intrafamilial Hate Crime Against Gay Men and Lesbians," in *Queering Criminology,* edited by Angela Dwyer, Matthew Ball, and Thomas Crofts (Palgrave Macmillan, 2016), 163–82; National Center for Lesbian Rights (NCLR), *The Challenges to Successful Lesbian Asylum Claims* (NCLR, 2006).

57. Pip McKnight, Jenny Phillimore, and Leila Zadeh, "Forced Migration and Sexual and Gender-Based Violence in Queer Communities: UK Findings from the SEREDA Project," Institute for Research into Superdiversity, University of Birmingham, June 2024, https://www.birmingham.ac.uk/documents/college-social-sciences/social-policy/publications/queer-sereda-web.pdf; Cynthia Cockburn, "The Continuum of Violence: A Gender Perspective on War and Peace," in *Sites of Violence* (University of California Press, 2004), 24–44.

58. Asquith and Fox, "No Place Like Home," 178.

59. Youngsook Choi, "The Meaning of Home for Transgendered People," in *Queer Presences and Absences,* ed. Yvette Taylor and Michelle Addison (Basingstoke: Palgrave Macmillan, 2013), 125–26.

60. Gloria González-López, *Family Secrets: Stories of Incest and Sexual Violence in Mexico,* volume 1 (New York University Press, 2015).

61. Judith Butler, *Gender Trouble* (Routledge, 2002).

62. María Mercedes Gómez, "Prejudice-Based Violence," in *Gender and Sexuality in Latin America: Cases and Decisions,* Ius Gentium: Comparative Perspectives on Law and Justice, ed. Cristina Motta and Macarena Saez (Springer 2013), 279–323, https://doi.org/10.1007/978-94-007-6199-5_8; Iris Marion Young, *Justice and the Politics of Difference* (Princeton University Press, 1990).

63. Young, *Justice and the Politics of Difference,* 60.

64. Eve Kosofsky Sedgwick, *Epistemology of the Closet* (University of California Press, 2008).

65. Owen Jones, "Can't Choose Your Family at Christmas? Those Rejected by Their Loved Ones Would Disagree," *The Guardian*, December 22, 2022, https://www.theguardian.com/commentisfree/2022/dec/22/family-christmas-lgbtq-relatives-friends.

66. Sean Rehaag, "Patrolling the Borders of Sexual Orientation: Bisexual Refugee Claims in Canada," *McGill Law Journal*, 53 (2008).

67. Galop, *LGBT+ Experiences of Abuse from Family Members* (Galop, April 1, 2022), https://www.ohchr.org/sites/default/files/documents/issues/lgbt/subm-protection-against-violence-aca-94-university-birmingham-research-in-ation.pdf.

68. Brandon Andrew Robinson, *Coming Out to the Streets: LGBTQ Youth Experiencing Homelessness* (University of California Press, 2020).

69. Samuel Ritholtz, "Is Queer-and-Trans Youth Homelessness a Form of Displacement? A Queer Epistemological Review of Refugee Studies' Theoretical Borders," *Ethnic and Racial Studies* 46, no. 9 (2022): 1–23, https://doi.org/10.1080/01419870.2022.2099747.

70. Cheshire Calhoun, *Feminism, the Family, and the Politics of the Closet: Lesbian and Gay Displacement* (Oxford University Press, 2000).

71. Jason Bryant, "The Meaning of Queer Home: Between Metaphor and Material," *Home Cultures* 12, no. 3 (2015): 261–89, https://doi.org/10.1080/17406315.2015.1084754; Andrew Gorman-Murray, "Queer Politics at Home: Gay Men's Management of the Public/Private Boundary; Queer Politics at Home," *New Zealand Geographer* 68, no. 2 (August 2012): 111–20, https://doi.org/10.1111/j.1745-7939.2012.01225.x; Youngsook Choi, "The Meaning of Home for Transgendered People."

72. Youngsook Choi, "The Meaning of Home for Transgendered People," 130.

73. Gorman-Murray, "Queer Politics at Home," 111.

74. Bryant, "The Meaning of Queer Home," 262.

75. Bryant, 263.

76. Bryant, 262.

77. Anne-Marie Fortier, "Re-Membering Places and the Performance of Belonging(s)," *Theory, Culture & Society* 16, no. 2 (1999): 41–64.

78. Fortier, "'Coming Home.'"

79. David Eng, "Out Here and Over There: Queerness and Diaspora in Asian American Studies," *Social Text* 52 no. 53 (1997): 32, https://www.jstor.org/stable/466733.

80. Kath Weston, "Get Thee to a Big City: Sexual Imaginary and the Great Gay Migration," *GLQ: A Journal of Lesbian and Gay Studies* 2, no. 3 (June 1995): 253–77, https://doi.org/10.1215/10642684-2-3-253.

81. José Esteban Muñoz et al., *Cruising Utopia: The Then and There of Queer Futurity* (New York University Press, 2019).

82. Alexander, Sato, and Zanghellini, "State-Enabled Killing of Same-Sex-Attracted People."

CHAPTER 2. PERSECUTION

1. Women for Refugee Women, "See Us, Believe Us, Stand with Us: The Experiences of Lesbian and Bisexual Women Seeking Asylum in the UK," 2023, https://www.refugeewomen.co.uk/see-us-believe-us-stand-with-us/. Anu was assisted by Women for Refugee Women, a UK-based charity.

2. This is not an absolute requirement. Past persecution alone is enough for asylum as long as relevant country conditions have not changed and internal relocation to a "safer" part of the country is not available. For example, female genital cutting is widely considered a basis for asylum, even though—in most cases—the asylum seeker would not be subject to the procedure again. We thank Stephen Meili for this comment.

3. House of Lords, Judgments - *Islam (A.P.) v. Secretary of State for the Home Department Regina v. Immigration Appeal Tribunal and Another Ex Parte Shah (A.P.)* (Conjoined Appeals) (March 25, 1999). See also UNHCR's 2002 guidance on gender-related persecution, which argues that the Geneva Convention should be seen as encompassing gender-based violence. UNHCR, "Guidelines on International Protection No. 1: Gender-Related Persecution Within the Context of Article 1A(2) of the 1951 Convention and/or Its 1967 Protocol Relating to the Status of Refugees" (UNHCR, 2002), https://www.refworld.org/policy/legalguidance/unhcr/2002/en/31754.

4. Moira Dustin, "Pathways to Refugee Protection for Women: Victims of Violence or Genuine Lesbians?" *Refugee Survey Quarterly* 41, no. 3 (September 2022): 399, https://doi.org/10.1093/rsq/hdac013.

5. European Union Agency for Asylum, *LGBTIQ Applicants in the EU+: Assessing Asylum Claims Based on Sexual Orientation, Gender Identity, Gender Expression, and Sex Characteristics* (European Union Agency for Asylum, 2023), https://euaa.europa.eu/sites/default/files/publications/2023-09/AR2023_factsheet20_LGBTIQ_applicants_EN.pdf.

6. Dustin, "Pathways to Refugee Protection for Women," 409.

7. The following discussion on the legal definitions of persecution was first published in Rebecca Buxton, "What's Wrong with Persecution," *Journal of Social Philosophy* 52, no. 4 (2022): 201–17.

8. Elena Fiddian-Qasmiyeh et al., "The International Law of Refugee Protection," in *The Oxford Handbook of Refugee and Forced Migration Studies*, ed. Elena Fiddian-Qasmiyeh et al. (Oxford University Press, 2014), https://doi.org/10.1093/oxfordhb/9780199652433.013.0021; Jane McAdam, "Rethinking the Origins of 'Persecution' in Refugee Law," *International Journal of Refugee Law*

25, no. 4 (December 2013): 667–92, https://doi.org/10.1093/ijrl/eet048; Scott Rempell, "Defining Persecution," *Utah Law Review* 2013, no. 1 (2013): 283–344; H. Storey, "What Constitutes Persecution? Towards a Working Definition," *International Journal of Refugee Law* 26, no. 2 (June 2014): 272–85; Atle Grahl-Madsen, *The Status of Refugees in International Law*, vol. 1, *Refugee Character* (A. W. Sijthoff, 1966); Francesco Maiani, "The Concept of 'Persecution' in Refugee Law: Indeterminacy, Context-Sensitivity, and the Quest for a Principled Approach" (*Les Dossiers du Grihl*, 2010), http://journals.openedition.org/dossiersgrihl/3896. Persecution is classified as a crime against humanity in both the Nuremberg Principles (1946) and The Rome Statute of the International Criminal Court (1998). See UN General Assembly, "Affirmation of the Principles of International Law Recognized by the Charter of the Nürnberg Tribunal," December 11, 1946, https://www.refworld.org/docid/3b00f1ee0.html; United Nations, Rome Statute of the International Criminal Court, 17 July 1998, in Force on 1 July 2002, United Nations, Treaty Series, Vol. 2187, No. 38544, Depositary: Secretary-General of the United Nations, Http://Treaties.Un.Org., 1998.

9. Atle Grahl-Madsen argues that this ambiguity might deliberately account for the fact that humans are always finding new ways to persecute one another: "It seems as if the drafters have wanted to introduce a flexible concept which might be applied to circumstances as they might arise; in other words, that they capitulated before the inventiveness of humanity to think up new ways of persecuting fellow men." Grahl-Madsen, *The Status of Refugees in International Law*, 193.

10. United Kingdom: *High Court, R v. Secretary of State for the Home Department, Ex parte Celal Yureki*, High Court: Queen's Bench Division, February 15, 1990.

11. In 2021, the Inter-American Court on Human Rights ruled that Honduras was responsible for the murder of Vicky Hernández, a transgender woman, in 2009. The landmark ruling found that the government's failure to adequately protect her (or make any effort to curb the high levels of violence against the trans community in the country) as well as properly investigate her killing (even after accusations of police involvement) amounted to responsibility for her death. The ruling is the first time that the regional court held a state responsible for the murder of a trans person, setting a precedent according to which the unwillingness or inability to protect a queer or trans person amounts to state culpability. Laura Paddison and Nina Lakhani, "Honduran State Responsible for Trans Woman's Murder – Court," *The Guardian*, June 29, 2021, https://www.theguardian.com/global-development/2021/jun/29/honduran-state-responsible-for-trans-womans-court.

12. Australian Government, Migration Act 1958 (Federal Register of Legislation, 2018), https://www.legislation.gov.au/Details/C2018C00337.

13. United Kingdom Home Office, "Asylum Policy Instruction: Sexual Orientation in Asylum Claims," UK Home Office, 2016.

14. Immigration Appeal Tribunal, *Mustafa Doymus v. Secretary of State for the Home Department*, no. HX/ 90112/99, July 19, 2000.

15. Deborah Anker, *Law of Asylum in the United States*, Immigration Law Library, Thomson Reuters, 2017, 184.

16. James Hathaway and Michelle Foster, *The Law of Refugee Status*, 2nd ed. (Cambridge University Press, 2014), 185.

17. European Union, "Directive 2011/95/EU of the European Parliament and of the Council of 13 December 2011 on Standards for the Qualification of Third-Country Nationals or Stateless Persons as Beneficiaries of International Protection, for a Uniform Status for Refugees or for Persons Eligible for Subsidiary Protection, and for the Content of the Protection Granted (Recast)," European Union: Council of the European Union, 2011.

18. Hélène Lambert, "The Conceptualisation of 'Persecution' by the House of Lords: *Horvath v. Secretary of State for the Home Department*," *International Journal of Refugee Law* 13, no. 1 (2001): 16–31.

19. It should also be noted that Nigeria criminalizes female same-sex relations. As such, Anu would not likely have been able to seek protection from the state for an act of intimate violence perpetrated in an effort to "correct" her sexuality. Human Dignity Trust, "Nigeria: Country Profile" (Human Dignity Trust, 2025).

20. This despite the fact that the EU qualification directive includes female genital cutting as an example of an act that should be given "due consideration" in establishing a well-founded fear of persecution. See consideration 30: https://eur-lex.europa.eu/eli/dir/2011/95/oj/eng.

21. Mengia Tschalaer, "Victimhood and Femininities in Black Lesbian Asylum Cases in Germany," *Journal of Ethnic and Migration Studies* 47, no. 15 (2020): 3531–48.

22. Mengia Tschalaer, "Black Lesbians Denied Asylum in Germany," Open Democracy, August 14, 2019, https://www.opendemocracy.net/en/beyond-trafficking-and-slavery/black-lesbians-denied-asylum-germany/, emphasis added.

23. Tschalaer, "Victimhood and Femininities." In the wake of sustained advocacy and a new government in Germany, refugee status determination processes were updated throughout Germany to be more responsible to the needs of LGBTIQ asylum seekers. Future research is needed to understand how this update protocol has affected the asylum claims of Black lesbians. Roshni Majumdar, "Germany Amends Asylum Rules in Favor of Queer Refugees" (Deutsche Welle, October 1, 2022), https://www.dw.com/en/germany-amends-asylum-rules-in-favor-of-queer-refugees/a-63303955.

24. This framing also reflects the "culture of disbelief" in many asylum determination systems. See, e.g., Diego García Rodríguez and Calogero Giametta, "Queer Asylum: Between Hostility and Incredibility," *International Migration*

62, no. 2 (2024): 232–6; Nuno Ferreira, "Utterly Unbelievable: The Discourse of 'Fake' SOGI Asylum Claims as a Form of Epistemic Injustice," *International Journal of Refugee Law* 34, no. 4 (February 2023): 303–26, https://doi.org/10.1093/ijrl/eeac041.

25. Nayak, *Who Is Worthy of Protection?*

26. See, e.g., Venice Choi, "Living Discreetly: A Catch 22 in Refugee Status Determinations on the Basis of Sexual Orientation," *Brooklyn Journal of International Law* 36, no. 1 (2010): 241–63; Giulia Cragnolini, "Lesbian, Gay, Bisexual and Transgender Refugees: Challenges in Refugee Status Determination and Living Conditions in Turkey," in *Fleeing Homophobia*, edited by Thomas Spijkerboer, 116–38 (Routledge, 2013); Carmelo Danisi et al., eds., *Queering Asylum in Europe*, IMISCOE Research Series (Springer International Publishing, 2021); Jenni Millbank, "Sexual Orientation and Refugee Status Determination over the Past 20 Years," *Fleeing Homophobia: Sexual Orientation, Gender Identity and Asylum* 32 (2013); Richard Mole, *Queer Migration and Asylum in Europe* (UCL Press, 2021); Massimo Prearo, "The Moral Politics of LGBTI Asylum: How the State Deals with the SOGI Framework," *Journal of Refugee Studies* 34, no. 2 (July 2020): 1277–2509, https://doi.org/10.1093/jrs/feaa047; Jana Wessels, "Sexual Orientation in Refugee Status Determination," *Refugee Studies Centre Working Paper Series* 74 (2011), https://www.refworld.org/reference/themreport/rsc/2011/en/106701l.

27. Notably, many of these acts of violence are recognized in international agreements such as the Istanbul Convention. However, they still fail to be treated as relevant acts of *persecution* in pursuit of refugee protection in many cases. We thank Mengia Tschalaer for this comment.

28. Samuel Ritholtz, "Is Queer-and-Trans Youth Homelessness a Form of Displacement?"

29. For some examples of LGBTIQ persecution see: Rebecca A. Hopkinson et al., "Persecution Experiences and Mental Health of LGBT Asylum Seekers," *Journal of Homosexuality* 64, no. 12 (October 15, 2017): 1650–66, https://doi.org/10.1080/00918369.2016.1253392; Sharalyn R. Jordan, "Un/Convention(al) Refugees: Contextualizing the Accounts of Refugees Facing Homophobic or Transphobic Persecution," *Refuge* 26, no. 2 (2009): 165–182; Dominic Scicchitano, "The 'Real' Chechen Man: Conceptions of Religion, Nature, and Gender and the Persecution of Sexual Minorities in Postwar Chechnya," *Journal of Homosexuality* 68, no. 9 (July 2021): 1545–62, https://doi.org/10.1080/00918369.2019.1701336; Aaron Sussman, "Expanding Asylum Law's Pattern-or-Practice-of-Persecution Framework to Better Protect LGBT Refugees," *University of Pennsylvania Journal of Law and Social Change* 16, no. 2 (2013): 111–32.

30. Melanie Judge, *Blackwashing Homophobia: Violence and the Politics of Sexuality, Gender and Race* (Routledge, 2017); Samuel Ritholtz, "Civil War and the Politics of Difference: Paramilitary Violence Against LGBT People in

Colombia" (PhD diss., Refugee Studies Centre, University of Oxford, 2022); Eric A. Stanley, *Atmospheres of Violence* (Duke University Press, 2021).

31. Lorena Fuentes, "'The Garbage of Society': Disposable Women and the Socio-Spatial Scripts of Femicide in Guatemala," *Antipode* 52, no. 6 (November 2020): 1667–87, https://doi.org/10.1111/anti.12669; Shatema Threadcraft, "North American Necropolitics and Gender: On #BlackLivesMatter and Black Femicide," *South Atlantic Quarterly* 116, no. 3 (July 2017): 553–79, https://doi.org/10.1215/00382876-3961483; Melissa W. Wright, "Necropolitics, Narcopolitics, and Femicide: Gendered Violence on the Mexico-U.S. Border," *Signs: Journal of Women in Culture and Society* 36, no. 3 (March 2011): 707–31, https://doi.org/10.1086/657496.

32. Rachel Lewis, "Deportable Subjects: Lesbians and Political Asylum," *Feminist Formations* 25, no. 2 (2013): 174–94, https://doi.org/10.1353/ff.2013.0027; Mia Liinason, "Challenging the Visibility Paradigm: Tracing Ambivalences in Lesbian Migrant Women's Negotiations of Sexual Identity," *Journal of Lesbian Studies* 24, no. 2 (2020): 110–25. Cheryl Llewellyn, "Erasing Violence: Lesbian Women Asylum Applicants in the United States," *Journal of Lesbian Studies* 25, no. 4 (2021): 339–55, https://doi.org/10.1080/10894160.2021.1889939.

33. Carol Bohmer and Amy Shuman, "Producing Epistemologies of Ignorance in the Political Asylum Application Process," *Identities* 14, no. 5 (December 2007): 603–29, https://doi.org/10.1080/10702890701662607.

34. Roxana Akbari and Stefan Vogler, "Intersectional Invisibility: Race, Gender, Sexuality, and the Erasure of Sexual Minority Women in US Asylum Law," *Law and Social Inquiry* 46, no. 4 (2021): 1062–91, https://doi.org/10.1017/lsi.2021.15; Bohmer and Shuman, "Producing Epistemologies of Ignorance"; Lewis, "Deportable Subjects."

35. Akbari and Vogler, "Intersectional Invisibility."

36. Wendy Isaack, "'No Choice But to Deny Who I Am': Violence and Discrimination Against LGBT People in Ghana" (Human Rights Watch, 2018). For work on how transmasculine individuals navigate the imposition of womanhood in a different context, see Nisrine Chaer's work in Lebanon: Nisrine Chaer, "*Fadh, Sharaf* and Respectable Passing as New Frameworks for Understanding Transmasculinity in the MENA Region: Case Studies of Transmasculine Refugees in Lebanon," *Journal of Refugee Studies*, 2023.

37. NCLR, *The Challenges to Successful Lesbian Asylum Claims.*

38. Gómez, "Prejudice-Based Violence."

39. Young also recognizes the anxiety-producing nature of homosexuality, explaining, "Homophobia is the paradigm of such border anxiety. The construction of the idea of race, its connection with physical attributes and lineage, still makes it possible for a white person to know that she is not Black or Asian. But as homosexuality has become increasingly deobjectified, no specific characteristics, no physical, genetic, mental, or moral 'character,' marks off homosexuals from heterosexuals. It thus becomes increasingly difficult to assert any difference

between homosexuals and heterosexuals except their choice of sexual partners. Homophobia is one of the deepest fears of difference precisely because the border between gay and straight is constructed as the most permeable; anyone at all can become gay, especially me, so the only way to defend my identity is to turn away with irrational disgust." Young, *Justice and the Politics of Difference*, 60.

40. Gómez, "Prejudice-Based Violence," 284.

41. José Fernando Serrano-Amaya, *Homophobic Violence in Armed Conflict and Political Transition* (Springer, 2017).

42. Young, *Justice and the Politics of Difference*, 60.

43. Butler, *Gender Trouble*.

44. Young, *Justice and the Politics of Difference*, 63.

45. Samuel Ritholtz, "Civil War and the Politics of Difference."

46. Rebecca Buxton, "What Is Wrong with Persecution."

47. Samuel Ritholtz, "Brutality on Display: Media Coverage and the Spectacle of Anti-LGBTQ Violence in the Colombian Civil War," *Third World Quarterly* 45, no. 5 (2024): 903–25.

48. Achille Mbembe, "Necropolitics," *Public Culture* 15, no. 1 (2003): 22.

49. Shatema Threadcraft, *Intimate Justice: The Black Female Body and the Body Politic* (Oxford University Press, 2016).

50. Wright, "Necropolitics, Narcopolitics, and Femicide."

51. Wright, "Necropolitics, Narcopolitics, and Femicide," 710.

52. Eric Stanley, "Near Life, Queer Death: Overkill and Ontological Capture," *Social Text* 29, no. 2 (2011): 14.

53. Stanley, "Near Life, Queer Death," 14.

54. Stephen Tomsen, *Violence, Prejudice and Sexuality* (Routledge, 2013).

55. Judith Butler, *Bodies That Matter: On the Discursive Limits of Sex* (Taylor & Francis, 2011).

56. Judge, *Blackwashing Homophobia*, 1.

57. Serrano-Amaya, *Homophobic Violence in Armed Conflict and Political Transition*.

58. Hathaway and Foster, *The Law of Refugee Status*.

59. Victoria Neilson, "Homosexual or Female-Applying Gender-Based Asylum Jurisprudence to Lesbian Asylum Claims," *Stanford Law & Policy Review* 16 (2005): 417–42.

60. Llewellyn, "Erasing Violence."

61. Tschalaer, "Victimhood and Femininities."

62. Stanley, *Atmospheres of Violence*.

63. Eithne Luibhéid, "Migrant and Refugee Lesbians: Lives That Resist the Telling," *Journal of Lesbian Studies* 24, no. 2 (April 2020): 57–76.

64. David Murray, "Real Queer: 'Authentic' LGBT Refugee Claimants and Homonationalism in the Canadian Refugee System," *Anthropologica* 56, no.1 (2014): 21–32.

65. Akbari and Vogler, "Intersectional Invisibility"; Sara L. McKinnon, *Gendered Asylum: Race and Violence in US Law and Politics* (University of Illinois Press, 2016); Lisa M. Diamond, "Female Bisexuality from Adolescence to Adulthood: Results from a 10-Year Longitudinal Study," *Developmental Psychology* 44, no. 1 (2008): 5.

66. Gauri van Gulik, "Fast-Tracked Unfairness: Detention and Denial of Women Asylum Seekers in the UK" (Human Rights Watch, 2010); Lewis, "Deportable Subjects."

67. Liinason, "Challenging the Visibility Paradigm"; Deborah A. Morgan, "Not Gay Enough for the Government: Racial and Sexual Stereotypes in Sexual Orientation Asylum Cases," *Law & Sexuality: A Review of Lesbian, Gay, Bisexual & Transgender Legal Issues* 15 (2006): 135–61.

68. Akbari and Vogler, "Intersectional Invisibility," 1062.

69. Erin Kilbride identifies lesbian, bisexual, and queer women as vulnerable to the following rights abuses: "forced and coerced marriage to men; labor rights and sexual violence at work; violence by security forces against masculine-presenting women; unequal property, inheritance, and land rights; legal restrictions on women's movement and violent attacks on LBQ+ couples in public; parental rights and access to fertility treatment; access to sexual, reproductive, and mental health services; sexual assault and follow-up care; barriers to asylum; access to justice; and attacks against LBQ+ human rights defenders." Erin Kilbride, "'This Is Why We Became Activists': Violence Against Lesbian, Bisexual, and Queer Woman and Non-Binary People," Human Rights Watch, February 14, 2023, https://www.hrw.org/report/2023/02/14/why-we-became-activists/violence-against-lesbian-bisexual-and-queer-women-and-non.

70. NCLR, *The Challenges to Successful Lesbian Asylum Claims.*

71. In an interview with Erin Kilbride of Human Rights Watch, an LBQ+ activist in Kyrgyzstan who married at nineteen explained, "There is no path to freedom if you don't get married [to a man]."

72. NCLR, *The Challenges to Successful Lesbian Asylum Claims*, 8–9.

73. For instance, some jurisdictions only criminalize specific sexual acts such as "sodomy" or "buggery." Other places, such as Malawi, explicitly prohibit men from "dressing as women." Many states still criminalize same-sex relations between women, and while some jurisdictions have repealed these laws in the last ten years, others—such as Chad and Brunei—have explicitly introduced new laws criminalizing same-sex activity between women. For an up-to-date map of different forms of criminalization see "#OUTLAWED: 'The Love That Dare Not Speak Its Name,'" Human Rights Watch, 2025, https://features.hrw.org/features/features/lgbt_laws/.

74. The NCLR documents at least seven ways that lesbian women can be persecuted tacitly by the state: "Countries refuse to prosecute male family members who seek to punish and control lesbian women through sexual and physical

violence. Countries provide no protection to lesbians who are raped by men in an attempt to 'fix' their lesbianism. Countries offer no protection to lesbians forced into heterosexual marriage, either through physical violence, economic and social coercion, or religious and cultural laws. Countries allow lesbians to be incarcerated in psychiatric institutions or forced to undergo 'treatment' because of their sexual orientation. Countries allow doctors and mental health professionals to punish lesbianism as a form of social and political deviance under the cover of medical or psychiatric care. Countries collaborate in the removal of children from lesbian mothers solely because of the mother's sexual orientation. Countries tolerate or promote severe discrimination against lesbians in education, employment, housing, health care, and social services." NCLR, *The Challenges to Successful Lesbian Asylum Claims*, 8.

75. This is despite the fact that Directive 2004/83/EC of the Council of the European Union identifies sexual and gender-based violence as forms of persecution. European courts often deny such forms of violence as not related to their membership in a particular social group. Tschalaer, "Victimhood and Femininities."

76. Citing a 2017 UNHCR report, Tschalaer notes "that asylum claims based on gender-specific violence (forced marriage, rape, forced pregnancies, marital and domestic violence, etc.) often go unrecognized within a system that was initially set out to protect persons (read: men) from political persecution." Tschalaer, "Victimhood and Femininities," 4; Lewis, "Deportable Subjects."

77. NCLR, *The Challenges to Successful Lesbian Asylum Claims*.

78. Lewis, "Deportable Subjects."

79. Bohmer and Shuman, "Producing Epistemologies of Ignorance."

80. Tschalaer, "Victimhood and Femininities," 13.

81. Elif Sari has documented how lesbian asylum seekers from non-Western contexts must navigate these sexual, gender, racial, and colonial logics to still be deemed "deserving" of protection by the global refugee regime. Elif Sari, "Lesbian Refugees in Transit: The Making of Authenticity and Legitimacy in Turkey," *Journal of Lesbian Studies* 24, no. 2 (2020): 140–58.

82. As will be articulated in later chapters, the socially situated nature of prejudice is not something specific to the state of origin. Relational harm means that homo/transphobia persist throughout the displacement process and facilitate new forms of persecution in new environments that result from a queer and displaced person's range of identities. In analyzing the experiences of LGBTIQ displaced populations in Nairobi, Hester Moore argues that although violence is a shared thread across queer and marginalized communities, its form and the actors who perpetrate it vary depending on a person's specific identity and positioning. This underscores the importance of rejecting one-dimensional framings of queer refugees in favor of more nuanced, situated understandings. Hester Moore, "'The Atmosphere Is Oppressive': Investigating the Intersection of Violence with the Cisgender Lesbian, Bisexual, and Queer Women Refugee

Community in Nairobi, Kenya," in *LGBTI Asylum Seekers and Refugees from a Legal and Political Perspective*, edited by Arzu Güler, Maryna Shevtsova, and Denise Venturi (Springer International, 2019).

83. Its relative intelligibility does not necessarily translate into success for the cases of GBQ+ men and nonbinary people, who often do not fit within this intelligible "ideal."

84. Efforts to make gender-based persecution a war crime as well as efforts to recognize witchcraft-related violence and domestic violence as forms of persecution must also contend with confronting this existing social imaginary of persecution. See, e.g., Sara Dehm and Jenni Millbank, "Witchcraft Accusations as Gendered Persecution in Refugee Law," *Social & Legal Studies* 28, no. 2 (April 2019): 202–26; Elena Fiddian-Qasmiyeh, "Gender and Forced Migration," in *The Oxford Handbook of Refugee and Forced Migration Studies*, edited by Elena Fiddian-Qasmiyeh et al., 395–408 (Oxford University Press, 2014); Rosemary Grey et al., "Gender-Based Persecution as a Crime Against Humanity: The Road Ahead," *Journal of International Criminal Justice* 17, no. 5 (2019): 957–79; Jenni Millbank and Anthea Vogl, "Adjudicating Fear of Witchcraft Claims in Refugee Law," *Journal of Law and Society* 45, no. 3 (2018): 370–97.

CHAPTER 3. FLIGHT

1. Lorenzo Tondo, "'I Will Not Be Held Prisoner': The Trans Women Turned Back at Ukraine's Borders," *The Guardian*, March 22, 2022, https://www.the guardian.com/global-development/2022/mar/22/i-will-not-be-held-prisoner -the-trans-women-turned-back-at-ukraines-borders.

2. LGBTIQ people were not the only group prevented from crossing the border safely. Many non-white Ukrainians or long-term residents were beaten, questioned, or pushed to the back of the queue for assistance. A group of visiting medical students from Nigeria were threatened at gunpoint when they asked why a pregnant Black woman had been prevented from boarding a train to safety. Border guards are also not the only "officials" who engage in exit denials at the border. Espinosa et al. discuss *extrajudicial border enforcement*, whereby airline officials act as "extended state agents" and prevent LGBTIQ people from boarding aircraft. Adriana Espinosa et al., "Extrajudicial Border Enforcement Against LGBTIQ+ Asylum Seekers," *Journal of Refugee Studies* (June 2024), https://doi.org/10.1093/jrs/feae031.

3. Julia Johnson, "CBS Blasted on Twitter for Including Transgender Rights in Ukrainian War Coverage," *Washington Examiner*, March 22, 2021, https:// www.washingtonexaminer.com/news/cbs-blasted-on-twitter-for-including -transgender-rights-in-ukraine-war-coverage.

4. Yvonne Su and Samuel Ritholtz, "How LGBT Refugees from Ukraine Are Highly Vulnerable," *The Washington Post*, April 13, 2022, https://www.washington post.com/politics/2022/04/13/lgbtq-trans-ukraine-asylum-human-rights/.

5. UNHCR, "Figures at a Glance, 2024," UNHCR, 2024, https://www.unhcr.org/uk/figures-glance.

6. For recent work in political philosophy on internal displacement, see Jamie Draper, "Justice and Internal Displacement," *Political Studies* 71, no. 2 (2021): 314–31, https://doi.org/10.1177/00323217211007641; Jamie Draper and David Owen, *The Political Philosophy of Internal Displacement* (Oxford University Press, 2024).

7. Internal Displacement Monitoring Centre / Norwegian Refugee Council, *GRID 2018: Global Report on Internal Displacement* (IDMC/NRC 2018), 81. IDPs do not have a distinct status under international law, but state authorities are responsible for their protection under existing international human rights, humanitarian, and refugee law. The guiding principles on internal displacement provide a framework for how the rights of internally displaced persons (IDPs) should be protected. While these principles constitute "soft" law, some argue that they are an important norm-generating mechanism. See Phil Orchard, "Protection of Internally Displaced Persons: Soft Law as a Norm-Generating Mechanism," *Review of International Studies* 36, no. 2 (2010): 281–303.

8. Ilaria Michelis, "Later Is a Cis-Hetero Patriarchal Time Zone: Narratives of Resistance to LGBTQI+ Inclusion amongst Humanitarian Practitioners," *Journal of Refugee Studies* (October 2023), https://doi.org/10.1093/jrs/feado72.

9. Sandra Smiley, "Out of Sight, out of Mind? Transgender People in Humanitarian Emergencies," Humanitarian Law and Policy Analysis, March 31, 2020, https://blogs.icrc.org/law-and-policy/2020/03/31/out-sight-mind-transgender-people-humanitarian-emergencies/.

10. Adeel Saeed, "Pakistan's Trans Community Is Especially Vulnerable to Climate Crises," *Global Health Now* (blog), September 27, 2024, https://globalhealthnow.org/2024-09/pakistans-trans-community-especially-vulnerable-climate-crises.

11. OutRight International, "Vulnerability Amplified: The Impact of the COVID-19 Pandemic on LGBTIQ People" (OutRight International, 2020); OutRight International and Edge Effect, "'They Know What We Don't'"; Reid and Ritholtz, "A Queer Approach to Understanding LGBT Vulnerability."

12. Marnell et al., *East African Queer and Trans Displacements*; OutRight International and Edge Effect, "'They Know What We Don't:'"; Shakhsari, "The Queer Time of Death."

13. Human Rights Watch, *'Even If You Go to the Skies, We'll Find You': LGBT People in Afghanistan After the Taliban Takeover*, 2022, https://www.hrw.org/report/2022/01/26/even-if-you-go-skies-well-find-you/lgbt-people-afghanistan-after-taliban-takeover.

14. Dylan Robertson, "Kenya Blocks LGBTQ+ Refugees from Resettling in Canada," 76Crimes, 2024, https://76crimes.com/2024/12/11/kenya-blocks-lgbtq-refugees-canada/; Sadiya Ansari, "'We've Lost So Many Lives': Why LGBTQ+ Refugees Are Giving Up on Kenya," Context by Thomson Reuters

Foundation, 2025, https://www.context.news/socioeconomic-inclusion/long-read /weve-lost-so-many-lives-lgbtq-refugees-are-giving-up-on-kenya.

15. Christopher Kyriakides et al., "Beyond Refuge: Contested Orientalism and Persons of Self-Rescue," *Canadian Ethnic Studies* 50, no. 2 (2018): 59–78.

16. Migrant Watch, "Nearly 90% of Those Crossing in Boats from Safe Countries Are Male," Migrant Watch, 2022, https://www.migrationwatchuk.org /press-release/668/nearly-90-of-those-crossing-in-boats-from-safe-countries -are-male.

17. Some scholars have adopted Cynthia Enloe's term "womenandchildren" to capture the ways in which these two groups are often described as if they were inseparable. Cynthia Enloe, "Womenandchildren: Propaganda Tools of Patriarchy," in *Mobilizing Democracy: Changing the U.S. Role in the Middle East*, edited by Greg Bates (Common Courage Press, 1991): 29-32.

18. FitzGerald, *Refuge Beyond Reach*.

19. Matthew Gibney, "Forced Migration, Engineered Regionalism and Justice Between States," in *New Regionalism and Asylum Seekers*, ed. Susan Kneebone and Felicity Rawlings-Sanaei (Berhahn Books, 2007).

20. The European Union has also reportedly lost over 150 million euros in a controversial migration deal with Tunisia. The money has been linked to human rights violations, including allegations that security services in receipt of EU funds raped migrant women. Mark Townsend, "EU Unable to Retrieve €150m Paid to Tunisia Despite Links to Rights Violations," *The Guardian*, October 11, 2024), https://www.theguardian.com/global-development/2024/oct/11/eu -funding-migrant-deal-tunisia-human-rights-violations-asylum-icc.

21. In practice, few refugees are returned to Turkey, as Greek courts acknowledge that is not a safe country to be returned to. For more information, see International Rescue Committee, "What Is the EU-Turkey Deal?" March 18, 2022, https://eu.rescue.org/article/what-eu-turkey-deal.

22. International Rescue Committee, "What Is the EU-Turkey Deal?"

23. Amnesty International, "Libya/EU: Conditions Remain 'Hellish' as EU Marks 5 Years of Cooperation Agreements" (Amnesty International, 2022), https://www.amnesty.org/en/latest/news/2022/01/libya-eu-conditions-remain -hellish-as-eu-marks-5-years-of-cooperation-agreements/.

24. IOM, "Missing Migrants Project," 2021, https://missingmigrants.iom.int/.

25. Roxanne Doty, "Bare Life: Border-Crossing Deaths and Spaces of Moral Alibi," *Environment and Planning D: Society and Space* 29, no. 4 (2011): 599–612.

26. Even when displaced people do reach the territories of other states they are often immobilized again in camps and detention centers, a fact to which we will turn in chapter 5, on *containment*. These often place extreme limits on refugees' freedom of movement. Jason De León, *The Land of Open Graves* (University of California Press, 2015).

27. Patel's top civil servant argued that there was not sufficient evidence of the policy's deterrence effect, which was key to the financial viability of the project;

although it would cost more to deport asylum seekers to Rwanda, these deportations would also supposedly result in fewer asylum applications altogether.

28. A host of states in the Global North have attempted to implement the "third country alternatives" in which asylum seekers can be sent to have their claims considered or in the case that their claims are denied. Many of these "third countries" are countries with de jure criminalization of LGBTIQ identity or recognized contexts of heightened anti-LGBTIQ violence and discrimination. As such, akin to the previous British government's Rwanda Plan, there has been little consideration for how these "safe country" agreements might introduce new harms to queer and trans asylum seekers. Rainbow Migration, "Rainbow Migration Submission to the UN Independent Expert on Protection Against Violence and Discrimination Based on Sexual Orientation and Gender Identity. London: Rainbow Migration." (Rainbow Migration, 2025), https://www.rainbowmigration.org.uk/publications/rainbow-migration-submission-to-the-un-independent-expert-on-protection-against-violence-and-discrimination-based-on-sogi/.

29. Martha Balaguera, "Trans-Migrations: Agency and Confinement at the Limits of Sovereignty," *Signs: Journal of Women in Culture and Society* 43, no. 3 (March 2018): 641–64, https://doi.org/10.1086/695302.

30. Weston, "Get Thee to a Big City." Héctor Carillo labels the phenomenon of cross-border movement primarily motivated by sexuality as "sexual migration." Héctor Carrillo, "Sexual Migration, Cross-Cultural Sexual Encounters, and Sexual Health," *Sexuality Research & Social Policy* 1, no. 3 (September 2004): 58–70.

31. Aren Aizura, *Mobile Subjects: Transnational Imaginaries of Gender Reassignment* (Duke University Press, 2018), 173.

32. Satvinder Juss, "Sexual Orientation and the Sexualisation of Refugee Law," *International Journal on Minority and Group Rights* 22, no. 1 (2015): 128–53.

33. B Camminga and John Marnell, "Introduction," in *Queer and Trans African Mobilities: Migration, Asylum and Diaspora* (Bloomsbury, 2022), 2.

34. Caio Simões Araújo, "Along the Pink Corridor: Histories of Queer Mobility Between Maputo and Johannesburg (ca. 1900–2020)," in *Queer and Trans African Mobilities: Migration, Asylum and Diaspora* (Bloomsbury, 2022).

35. Balaguera, "Trans-Migrations."

36. Arundhathi, "Gender-Based Spatial Segregation: Ladies' Compartments in the Mumbai Local Trains," *Gender, Place & Culture* 31, no. 2 (August 2022): 1–21, https://doi.org/10.1080/0966369X.2022.2115980.

37. Mimi Sheller, "Racialized Mobility Transitions in Philadelphia: Urban Sustain-Ability and the Problem of Transport Inequality," *City and Society* 27, no. 1 (2015): 70–91.

38. Kenji Yoshino, "Covering," *Yale Law Journal* 111, no. 4 (2002): 772. Passing need not always be purposeful. Many people pass not because they are actively trying to conceal their identity but because people perceive them to be straight or gender conforming.

39. Kenji Yoshino, "Covering."

40. Thank you to Kerri Woods for encouraging us to consider this point.

41. The so-called discretion requirement mandated that LGBTQ people should not receive refugee protection if they could continue living in their country of origin while "acting discretely." The United Kingdom Supreme Court in *HJ (Iran) and HT (Cameroon) v. Secretary of State for the Home Department* held that the discretion requirement was unlawful if the applicants in fact hid their sexuality due to a well-founded fear of persecution. In 2013, the Court of Justice of the European Union (CJEU) banned discretion reasoning. For a discussion of the history and persistence of discretion reasoning in asylum decisions, see Petra Sussner, "Addressing Heteronormativity: The Not-So-Lost Requirement of Discretion in (Austrian) Asylum Law," *International Journal of Refugee Law* 34, no. 1 (March 2022): 31–53, https://doi.org/10.1093/ijrl/eeac018.

42. Vanessa Yarwood et al., "LGBTQI + Migrants: A Systematic Review and Conceptual Framework of Health, Safety and Wellbeing during Migration," *International Journal of Environmental Research and Public Health* 19, no. 2 (January 2022), https://doi.org/10.3390/ijerph19020869.

43. Kerilyn Schewel, "Understanding Immobility: Moving Beyond the Mobility Bias in Migration Studies," *International Migration Review* 54, no. 2 (June 2020): 328–55, https://doi.org/10.1177/0197918319831952.

44. Stephen C. Lubkemann, "Migratory Coping in Wartime Mozambique: An Anthropology of Violence and Displacement in 'Fragmented Wars,'" *Journal of Peace Research* 42, no. 4 (July 2005): 455, https://doi.org/10.1177/0022343305054093.

45. These calls for renewed focus on immobility, or at least for looking beyond the usually legal category of refugeehood, hasn't sparked a general shift in the discipline; many still focus on people on the move rather than the denial of opportunities of movement. Serena Parekh, "Beyond the Ethics of Admission: Stateless People, Refugee Camps and Moral Obligations," *Philosophy & Social Criticism* 40, no. 7 (August 2013): 645–63, https://doi.org/10.1177/0191453713498254.

46. Jørgen Carling, "Migration in the Age of Involuntary Immobility: Theoretical Reflections and Cape Verdean Experiences," *Journal of Ethnic and Migration Studies* 28, no. 1 (January 2002): 5–42, https://doi.org/10.1080/13691830120103912.

47. *Voluntary immobility* occurs when an individual can move but has no aspiration to. *Involuntary immobility* is the opposite, occurring when an individual wishes to move but does not have the ability. A later category of "acquiescent immobility" has been introduced by Kerilyn Schewel. Kerilyn Schewel, "Understanding Immobility: Moving Beyond the Mobility Bias in Migration Studies," *International Migration Review* 54, no. 2 (June 2020): 328–55, https://doi.org/10.1177/0197918319831952. It was also later showcased in a paper on Filipino nurses and their shifting movement aspirations. Yasmin Y. Ortiga and Romeo Luis A.

Macabasag, "Understanding International Immobility Through Internal Migration: 'Left Behind' Nurses in the Philippines," *International Migration Review* 55, no. 2 (June 2021): 460–81, https://doi.org/10.1177/0197918320952042.

48. Naiara Rodriguez-Pena, "Moving Across (Im)Mobility Categories: The Importance of Values, Family and Adaptation for Migration," *Journal of Ethnic and Migration Studies* 49, no. 3 (May 2022): 1–18, https://doi.org/10.1080/1369183X.2022.2064839.

49. There has been a general shift from ability to "capability" language in mobility literature. See Schewel, "Understanding Immobility"; Hein de Haas, "Migration and Development in Southern Morocco," PhD diss., The Dutch Research School for International Development (CERES), 2003.

50. Tom Shakespeare, "The Social Model of Disability," in *The Disability Studies Reader*, ed. Lennard J. Davis (Psychology Press, 2006).

51. Nick Van Hear, "'I Went as Far as My Money Would Take Me': Conflict, Forced Migration and Class," in *Forced Migration and Global Processes: A View From Forced Migration Studies* (Rowman and Littlefield, 2006), 125–58.

52. Hawley G. Fogg-Davis. "Theorizing Black Lesbians Within Black Feminism: A Critique of Same-Race Street Harassment," *Politics & Gender* 2, no. 1 (2006): 57–76.

53. Gloria Anzaldúa, *Borderlands/La Frontera: The New Mestiza* (Aunt Lute Books, 1987), 25, quoted in Bina Fernandez, "Queer Border Crossers: Pragmatic Complicities, Indiscretions and Subversions," in *Queering International Law Possibilities, Alliances, Complicities, Risks*, ed. Dianne Otto (Routledge, 2017).

54. Emilie McDonnell, *Protecting the Right to Leave in an Era of Externalised Migration Control* (Bloomsbury Publishing, 2026).

55. For a discussion of the risks of prioritization discourse see Sarah Fine, "Refugees and the Limits of Political Philosophy," *Ethics & Global Politics* 13, no. 1 (January 2020): 6–20, https://doi.org/10.1080/16544951.2020.1735017.

56. It is also a risk, when thinking about induced immobility within the state, to assume that all is well once the border is crossed. Chapter 7 of this book, on *sanctuary*, demonstrates that this assumption is deeply mistaken. Immobility experienced while still *within* the sending state is just one further barrier faced by people on the move, and overcoming this inequality is far from enough.

57. International Committee of the Red Cross, "How Humanitarian Corridors Work to Help People in Conflict Zones" (2022), https://www.icrc.org/en/document/how-humanitarian-corridors-work.

58. Daniel Boffey and Lorenzo Tondo, "Russia Accused of Shelling Mariupol Humanitarian Corridor," *The Guardian*, April 26, 2022, https://www.theguardian.com/world/2022/apr/26/russia-accused-of-shelling-mariupol-humanitarian-corridor.

59. CARE International, "CARE Joins Statement Calling 'Humanitarian Corridor' Proposal Deeply Flawed" (CARE, 2015), https://www.care.org/news-and

-stories/press-releases/care-joins-statement-calling-humanitarian-corridor
-proposal-deeply-flawed/.

60. Private actors such as airline staff can also play a role in preventing mobility. See Espinosa et al., "Extrajudicial Border Enforcement against LGBTIQ+ Asylum Seekers."

61. This was the case even (or perhaps especially) within ideologies that sought to liberate minoritized groups. Serene Khader discusses "imperialist feminisms" and their commitment to a particular form of "enlightenment freedom" that we ought to reject. See Serene Khader, *Decolonizing Universalism: A Transnational Feminist Ethic* (Oxford University Press, 2019).

62. Chimni, "The Birth of a 'Discipline.'"

63. Kimberley Hutchings, "Cosmopolitan Just War and Coloniality," in *Empire, Race and Global Justice*, ed. Duncan Bell (Cambridge University Press, 2019), 212, https://doi.org/10.1017/9781108576307.010.

64. Red Regional por la Movilidad Humana LGBTIQ+ de Latinoamérica y el Caribe, "Llamado a aportes: Protección contra la violencia y la discriminación por orientación sexual e identidad de género en relación con el desplazamiento forzado" (Internal submission to the Office of the UN High Commissioner for Human Rights, 2024); Caribe Afirmativo, "Informe alternativo sobre la situación de derechos humanos de personas LGBTI desplazadas forzadamente en Colombia presentado al ACNUR" (Caribe Afirmativo, 2021), https://caribe afirmativo.lgbt/wp-content/uploads/2021/03/Informe-AcnurMar.pdf.

65. UNHCR does still often work with internally displaced people. For instance, in Ukraine, they have supported displaced transgender people through the local project T-ema.

66. Rainbow Railroad, *2023 Annual Report: Understanding the State of Global LGBTQI+ Persecution* (Rainbow Railroad, 2024), https://www.rainbow railroad.org/the-latest/annualreport.

67. Of course, it should not be left only to queer and trans people themselves to develop these remedial tools and secure their own security and protection, particularly when they must push back against the international order and its norms to do so.

CHAPTER 4. ASSESSMENT

1. The questions in this chapter were asked to real people in their asylum interviews. Some of the questions are direct quotes from transcripts and training materials, while others are adapted from retellings by the asylum seekers themselves. The questions in italics have been added by us for narrative coherence.

2. In some contexts, such as when the host state is not a signatory to the Refugee Convention, the refugee status determination process will be delegated

to UNHCR. In this case, it is not state officials but UN officers who undertake the interview procedure. The focus of this chapter is on state-led interview processes.

3. Bojana Asanovic, *Still Falling Short: The Standard of Home Office Decision-Making in Asylum Claims Based on Sexual Orientation and Gender Identity* (UK Lesbian and Gay Immigration Group, July 2018); Shaw and Verghese, *LGBTQI+ Refugees and Asylum Seekers*.

4. UN General Assembly, "Convention Relating to the Status of Refugees" (United Nations, July 28, 1951), https://www.refworld.org/docid/3be01b964.html.

5. Bernardo Zacka, *When the State Meets the Street* (Harvard University Press, 2018).

6. From as early as 2013, UNHCR guidance has given advice on how to interview an LGBTIQ person seeking asylum. This guidance asks staff, for instance, to ensure that they do not make judgements on the basis of pervasive stereotypes about LGBTIQ people and offers guidelines on how to conduct sensitive interviews when discussing sexual violence. However, many of the examples of questions given above have happened *after* such guidance was offered. For instance, in 2016, the Home Office also issued guidance on this topic, but the intrusive questions reported above continued well beyond that date. See UK Home Office, "Asylum Policy Instruction: Sexual Orientation in Asylum Claims," https://assets.publishing.service.gov.uk/media/5a804b17ed915d74e622d9dc/Sexual-orientation-in-asylum-claims-v6.pdf. The problem, then, is not a need for more guidance, but a need to translate that guidance into practice. For further guidance, see UNHCR, "UNHCR Guidance Note on Refugee Claims Relating to Sexual Orientation and Gender Identity" (United Nations High Commission for Refugees, November 21, 2008), https://www.refworld.org/docid/48abd5660.html; UK Home Office, "Asylum Interviews (Version 9.0)," 2022.

7. US Citizenship and Immigration Services, "USCIS Guidance for Adjudicating LGBTI Refugee and Asylum Claims," 2015, https://www.aila.org/library/uscis-guidance-adjudicating-lgbti-refugee-asylum.

8. At the same time as the improvements have been made in interviews for LGBTIQ asylum claims, there's been the development of another problematic state practice—namely, the blanket recognition of certain countries of origin as "safe." Many host states are starting to recognize countries as "safe" in order to justify refoulement, externalize their borders, and prevent asylum claims. These "safe" countries may be the countries of origin or third countries where host states are trying to send asylum seekers either during or after their claims are considered. However, in many contexts, recognized safe countries have de jure and de facto criminalization of LGBTIQ populations or high rates of violence against LGBTIQ people. For example, nine of the countries on Italy's safe country list have de jure criminalization and many others have documented histories of being unable or unwilling to protect their LGBTIQ populations, such as

Colombia. This issue is exacerbated by a second phenomenon—that of RSD adjudicators relying on outdated "country of origin" information reports, as well as reports that do not account for the experiences of LGBTIQ populations. Together, these two issues have resulted in the unfair denial of asylum claims for LGBTIQ populations and demonstrate the stakes of failing to adopt a just RSD process for the queer and trans displaced. Redazione, "Aggiornata la lista dei 'paesi sicuri,'" Il Grande Colibrì, May 12, 2024, https://www.ilgrandecolibri.com /lista-paesi-sicuri/; Rainbow Migration, "Rainbow Migration Submission to the UN Independent Expert."

9. Women for Refugee Women, "See Us, Believe Us, Stand With Us."

10. Rebecca Buxton, "Respect and Asylum," *Journal of Applied Philosophy* 41, no. 5 (November 2024): 909–24, https://doi.org/10.1111/japp.12750.

11. Much of this work has been undertaken by the ERC funded Sexual Orientation and Gender Identity Claims of Asylum (SOGICA) Project, https://www .sogica.org/en/publications/. See Danisi et al., *Queering Asylum in Europe*. See also, Choi, "Living Discreetly"; Cragnolini, "Lesbian, Gay, Bisexual and Transgender Refugees"; Jenni Millbank, "From Discretion to Disbelief: Recent Trends in Refugee Determinations on the Basis of Sexual Orientation in Australia and the United Kingdom," *The International Journal of Human Rights* 13, no. 2 (2009): 391–414; Millbank, "Sexual Orientation and Refugee Status Determination."

12. Ferreira, "Utterly Unbelievable"; Cailan Cordwell, "Not Queer Enough: Challenges of LGBT Credibility and Identity in US Asylum," Master diss., Arizona State University, ProQuest 30425647. Rodríguez and Giametta, "Queer Asylum."

13. This conceptual framework depends on the "Cass Identity Model" of homosexuality, first outlined in the 1970s, which posits a six-stage process of development of the "homosexual identity." Vivienne C. Cass, "Homosexual Identity Formation: A Theoretical Model," *Journal of Homosexuality* 4, no. 3 (April 1979): 219–35, https://doi.org/10.1300/J082v04n03_01. In *Entry Denied*, Eithne Luibhéid discusses that the broader ascription of identities in the process of border enforcement "contributed to constructing the very sexual categories and identities through which women's immigration possibility were then regulated." See Eithne Luibhéid, *Entry Denied*, xi.

14. Diego García Rodríguez, "Critiquing Trends and Identifying Gaps in the Literature on LGBTQ Refugees and Asylum-Seekers," *Refugee Survey Quarterly* 42, no. 4 (2023): 518–41; Alexander Dhoest, "Learning to Be Gay: LGBTQ Forced Migrant Identities and Narratives in Belgium," *Journal of Ethnic and Migration Studies* 45, no. 7 (2019): 1075–89; Calogero Giametta, "Narrativising One's Sexuality/Gender: Neo-Liberal Humanitarianism and the Right of Asylum," in *Sexuality, Citizenship, and Belonging*, 55–72 (Routledge, 2015); John Marnell, "Telling a Different Story: On the Politics of Representing African LGBTQ Migrants, Refugees and Asylum Seekers," in *Queer and Trans African Mobilities: Migration, Asylum and Diaspora*, ed. B Camminga and

John Marnell (Bloomsbury, 2022); David Murray, "The (Not So) Straight Story: Queering Migration Narratives of Sexual Orientation and Gendered Identity Refugee Claimants," *Sexualities* 17, no. 4 (June 2014): 451–71, https://doi.org/10.1177/1363460714524767; Nayak, *Who Is Worthy of Protection?*; Prearo, "The Moral Politics of LGBTI Asylum."

15. Karin Åberg, "A Requirement of Shame: On the Evolution of the Protection of LGB Refugees," *International Journal of Refugee Law* 35, no. 1 (March 2023): 37–57, https://doi.org/10.1093/ijrl/eead008.

16. Tschalaer, "Victimhood and Femininities"; Mengia Tschalaer, "Between Queer Liberalisms and Muslim Masculinities: LGBTQI+ Muslim Asylum Assessment in Germany," *Ethnic and Racial Studies* 43, no. 7 (2020): 1265–83.

17. Nina Held and Aderonke Apata, "Intersections of Gender, Sexuality and 'Race' in Queer Asylum Claims," in *Research Handbook on Refugee and Asylum Policy,* edited by Jane Freedman and Glenda Santana de Andrade (Elgar, 2024).

18. Thomson Reuters Foundation, "Nigerian LGBTQ Activist Granted Asylum in UK After 13-Year Legal Battle," NBC News, August 14, 2017, https://www.nbcnews.com/feature/nbc-out/nigerian-lgbtq-activist-granted-asylum-uk-after-13-year-legal-n792661.

19. Jack Ashton, "Nigerian Gay Rights Activist Who Judge Accused of 'Faking' Her Sexuality Wins 13-Year Legal Battle for Asylum in UK," *The Independent,* August 14, 2017, https://www.independent.co.uk/news/uk/home-news/nigeria-gay-rights-activist-aderonke-apata-uk-asylum-granted-high-court-fake-sexuaity-lesbian-lgbt-persecution-africa-a7888931.html.

20. Diane Taylor, "Barrister Says She Became Legal Expert While in Home Office Immigration Detention," *The Guardian,* October 22, 2022), https://www.theguardian.com/uk-news/2022/oct/22/barrister-says-she-became-legal-expert-while-in-home-office-immigration-detention.

21. All the substantive questions in this chapter come from the following sources: Meka Beresford, "The Home Office Quizzed a Bisexual Asylum Seeker on LGBT Terminology During His Interview Process," *PinkNews*, November 12, 2016, https://www.thepinknews.com/2016/11/12/the-home-office-quizzed-a-bisexual-asylum-seeker-on-lgbt-terminology-during-his-interview-process/; Kimberley Bond, "'You Need to Prove That You're Gay': LGBTQ+ Asylum Seekers in the UK," *Metro*, June 6, 2022, https://metro.co.uk/2022/06/06/asylum-seekers-in-the-uk-how-lgbtq-refugees-prove-their-sexuality-16744541/; Kirstie Brewer, "'How Do I Convince the Home Office I'm a Lesbian?'" BBC News, February 26, 2020, sec. Stories, https://www.bbc.com/news/stories-51636642; Government of Canada, "Applicants Persecuted for Their Diverse Sexual Orientation or Gender Identity or Expression (SOGIE)," Immigration, Refugees, and Citizenship, September 21, 2020, https://www.canada.ca/en/immigration-refugees-citizenship/corporate/publications-manuals/operational-bulletins-manuals/refugee-protection/resettlement/priority-special/sexual-orientation-gender

-identity.html; Rhuaridh Marr, "Australia Asked Gay Asylum Seekers If They 'Drink Cum,' Then Tried to Suppress the Interviews," *Metro Weekly*, July 16, 2019, https://www.metroweekly.com/2019/07/australia-asked-gay-asylum-seekers-if -they-liked-to-drink-cum-then-tried-to-suppress-the-interview/; Carl Morris for Morris, "Lesbian Asylum Seekers Asked Whether They Use Sex Toys," *Metro*, April 4, 2013, https://metro.co.uk/2013/04/04/lesbian-asylum-seekers-asked -have-you-read-oscar-wilde-do-you-use-sex-toys-where-do-you-go-clubbing -3582916/; Hannah Ryan, "These Are The 'Inappropriate' Questions Asylum-Seekers Were Asked By Australia To Prove They Were Gay," *BuzzFeed*, January 8, 2019, sec. AUNews, https://www.buzzfeed.com/hannahryan/two-men-seeking -australias-protection-from-lgbt-persecution; Mark Townsend and Diane Taylor, "'Home Office Wouldn't Believe I Was Gay: How Do You Prove It?'" *The Guardian*, February 8, 2014, sec. UK News, https://www.theguardian.com/uk -news/2014/feb/08/home-office-gay-asylum-seekers-questioning; Trixie Torres, "Asylum Interview Sample Questions: Shoreline Immigration," Shoreline Immigration, July 18, 2022, https://shorelineimmigration.com/asylum/asylum -interview-sample-questions/; Held and Apata, "Intersections of Gender, Sexuality and 'Race.'"

CHAPTER 5. CONTAINMENT

1. Human Rights Watch, "HIV/AIDS Services for Immigrants Detained by the United States," December 5, 2007, https://www.hrw.org/report/2007/12/05 /chronic-indifference/hiv/aids-services-immigrants-detained-united-states.
2. As of June 2025, over 56,000 people have been placed in immigration detention throughout the US. According to Human Rights Watch this is a 40 percent increase since June 2024 and constitutes the highest population of detained people in the history of US immigration detention. This situation reflects the Trump administration's renewed effort on immigration enforcement through ICE. This crackdown incorporates mass arrests and deportations, as well as the proliferation of ICE-run detention centers that have been accused of gross human rights violations. These abuses include infringements on the rights and safety of trans populations, who have been denied court-ordered protections while in detention. In line with the federal policy that no longer recognizes trans identity, ICE officials have increasingly placed trans individuals in single-gender accommodation that does not match their gender identity, at a severe risk to their safety, and has stopped reporting any data on transgender people in detention. Human Rights Watch, "'You Feel Like Your Life Is Over': Abusive Practices at Three Florida Immigration Detention Centers Since January 2025" (Human Rights Watch, 2025), https://www.hrw.org/report/2025/07/21/you-feel-like-your -life-is-over/abusive-practices-at-three-florida-immigration; Matt Sledge, "ICE

is Erasing Rules That Protect Trans Detainees" (The Intercept, March 27, 2025), https://theintercept.com/2025/03/27/ice-trans-immigrant-detainees; Vera, "ICE is Excluding Data on Transgender People in Detention," (June 30, 2025), https://www.vera.org/news/ice-is-excluding-data-on-transgender-people-in-detention

3. American Civil Liberties Union, "Justice-Free Zones."

4. Centre for American Progress, "ICE's Rejection of Its Own Rules Is Placing LGBT Immigrants at Severe Risk of Sexual Abuse," American Progress, May 30, 2018, https://www.americanprogress.org/article/ices-rejection-rules-placing-lgbt-immigrants-severe-risk-sexual-abuse/. Human Rights Watch also reported that shortly after her death, Victoria's fellow detainees who were witnesses of what had happened were relocated to different detention centers across the country, Human Rights Watch, "HIV/AIDS Services for Immigrants Detained by the United States."

5. Stefan Vogler and Rocío Rosales, "Classification and Coercion: The Gendered Punishment of Transgender Women in Immigration Detention," *Social Problems* 70, no. 3 (April 2022): 698–716.

6. The Black Diaspora Liberty Initiative et al. submission to the Independent Expert on SOGI details that Black trans women in US immigration detention face a combination of transphobic and racist abuses, including withholding of medical care, frequent solitary confinement, sexual and verbal abuse, and unsafe housing—driven by the profit motives of privately operated facilities and systemic discrimination. See also Physicians for Human Rights, "Endless Nightmare: Torture and Inhuman Treatment in Solitary Confinement in U.S. Immigration Detention" (Physicians for Human Rights, 2024).

7. Laura P. Minero et al. "Latinx Trans Immigrants' Survival of Torture in U.S. Detention: A Qualitative Investigation of the Psychological Impact of Abuse and Mistreatment," *International Journal of Transgender Health* 23, no. 1–2 (2021): 36–59.

8. Adrian Blomfield, "Can One of Africa's Largest Refugee Camps Evolve into a City?" AP News, April 7, 2025, https://apnews.com/article/kenya-refugees-kakuma-permanent-city-5ade4e335987ef0535fb7ea9e21ba183.

9. Anadolu Agency, "Kenya Gives UN 14-Day Deadline to Close Refugee Camps," AA News, March 24, 2021, https://www.aa.com.tr/en/africa/kenya-gives-un-14-day-deadline-to-close-refugee-camps/2186765#:~:text=%E2%80%9CThe%20UNHCR%20has%20been%20informed,the%20ongoing%20COVID%2D19%20pandemic.

10. Médecins Sans Frontières, "MSF Statement on June 2022 Deadline to Close Refugee Camps in Kenya," ReliefWeb, April 2021, https://reliefweb.int/report/kenya/msf-statement-june-2022-deadline-close-refugee-camps-kenya.

11. K. Pincock, "UNHCR and LGBTI Refugees in Kenya: The Limits of 'Protection.' *Disasters* 45, no. 4 (2021): 844–64. LGBTIQ asylum seekers must also navigate the complexities of transiting through (or waiting in) countries where

there is criminalization but where international protection is also possible. These "parallel legal regimes" trouble the possibility of local integration as a durable solution for displaced LGBTIQ people in many parts of the world. See B Camminga, "Encamped Within a Camp: Transgender Refugees and Kakuma Refugee Camp (Kenya)," in *Invisibility in African Displacements: From Structural Marginalization to Strategies of Avoidance*, ed. Jesper Bjarnesen and Simon Turner (Zed Books, 2020).

12. Jade Wilson, "Why LGBTQ+ Refugees Are Stuck in Limbo in Kenya," Context, 2025, https://www.context.news/socioeconomic-inclusion/why-lgbtq-refugees-are-stuck-in-limbo-in-kenya.

13. Marnell et al., *East African Queer and Trans Displacements*.

14. Camminga, "Encamped Within a Camp."

15. Rainbow Railroad, "Rainbow Railroad and ORAM Release Report on LGBTQI+ Refugees in Kakuma Refugee Camp, Kenya" (Rainbow Railroad, 2021), https://www.rainbowrailroad.org/news/rainbow-railroad-and-oram-release-report-on-lgbtqi-refugees-in-kakuma-refugee-camp-kenya.

16. Rainbow Railroad, "Rainbow Railroad and ORAM."

17. UNHCR, "UNHCR Statement on the Situation of LGBTIQ+ Refugees in Kakuma Camp," March 25, 2021, https://www.unhcr.org/ke/19859-unhcr-statement-on-the-situation-of-lgbtiq-refugees-in-kakuma-camp.html. It should be noted that in 2018, the UNHCR had moved LGBTIQ refugees in Kakuma to Nairobi in order to provide greater protection. The changing nature of LGBTIQ and refugee politics in Kenya makes such an effort today challenging. Nita Bhalla, "U.N. Moves LGBT+ Refugees to Safe Houses after Kenya Camp Attacks," Reuters, December 13, 2018, https://www.reuters.com/article/us-kenya-lgbt-refugees-idUSKBN1OC1Y9/.

18. Amnesty International, "Kenya: Homophobic Attack Leaves Man Dead At Kakuma Refugee Camp; UN Safety Measures Review Needed" (Amnesty International, 2021), https://www.amnesty.org.au/kenya-homophobic-attack-leaves-man-dead-at-kakuma-refugee-camp-un-safety-measures-review-needed/.

19. Some detainees submit asylum applications while in detention centers, as a way to oppose their deportation. International law allows for the detention of asylum seekers in cases in which the detainee is perceived as a threat to public safety.

20. Bail for Immigration Detainees (BiD), "Hidden Histories: Yarl's Wood and Its Captive Women," BiD, 2019, https://www.biduk.org/articles/437-hidden-histories-yarl-s-wood-and-its-captive-women.

21. Jamie Grierson, "Legal Action Launched Against Plan to House Asylum Seekers at Yarl's Wood," *The Guardian*, 2021, https://www.theguardian.com/uk-news/2021/jan/16/legal-action-launched-against-plan-to-house-asylum-seekers-at-yarls-wood.

22. Giorgio Agamben, *Homo Sacer: Sovereign Power and Bare Life* (Stanford University Press, 1998); Michael Agier, *Managing the Undesirables: Refugee*

Camps and Humanitarian Government (Cambridge: Polity Press, 2011). Patricia Owens has argued against Agamben's framing of the refugee camp as a space of "bare life" by interrogating political action, such as refugee lip-sewing, to highlight forms of resistance. See Patricia Owens, "Reclaiming 'Bare Life'?: Against Agamben on Refugees," *International Relations* 23, no. 4 (2009): 567–82.

23. In this sense, the sovereignty present in state containment practices reflects John Torpey's argument in *The Invention of the Passport* in which he claims that modern states hold a monopoly on "the legitimate means of movement." John Torpey, *The Invention of the Passport* (Cambridge University Press, 2000).

24. Gemma Bird, "Constructing Vulnerability and Victimhood at the EU Border," *Polity* 54, no. 4 (October 2022): 874–81, https://doi.org/10.1086/721564.

25. American Civil Liberties Union, "Unchecked Growth."

26. Article 9 (1) of the International Covenant on Civil and Political Rights (ICCPR) states, "Everyone has the right to liberty and security of person. No one shall be subjected to arbitrary arrest or detention. No one shall be deprived of his liberty except on such grounds and in accordance with such procedure as are established by law."

27. Immigration detention is part of the process for creating subjects that are deportable. Lewis, "Deportable Subjects."

28. Jonathan Blitzer, *Everyone Who Is Gone Is Here: The United States, Central America, and the Making of a Crisis* (Penguin, 2024); Tina Vasquez, "Trump's Border Policy Tore Apart Many Families: Nobody Knows What Happens to Them Now," *The Guardian*, January 17, 2025, https://www.theguardian.com/us-news/ng-interactive/2025/jan/17/trump-policy-family-separation-future.

29. Ian Urbina, "The Secretive Prisons That Keep Migrants Out of Europe," *The New Yorker*, November 28, 2021, https://www.newyorker.com/magazine/2021/12/06/the-secretive-libyan-prisons-that-keep-migrants-out-of-europe.

30. Eithne Luibhéid, "Treated Neither with Respect nor with Dignity: Contextualizing Queer and Trans Migrant 'Illegalization' in Detention and Deportation," in *Queer and Trans Migrations: Dynamics of Illegalization, Detention, and Deportation*, edited by Eithne Luidhéid and Karma Chávez (University of Illinois Press, 2020).

31. Ryan Thoreson, "Trump Administration Moves to Reject Transgender Identity, Rights" (Human Rights Watch, 2025), https://www.hrw.org/news/2025/01/23/trump-administration-moves-reject-transgender-identity-rights.

32. Shana Tabak and Rachel Levitan, "LGBTI Migrants in Immigration Detention: A Global Perspective," *Harvard Journal of Law & Gender* 37 (2014): 20–23.

33. Vogler and Rosales, "Classification and Coercion."

34. Centre for American Progress, "ICE's Rejection of Its Own Rules."

35. Liza Doubossarskaia et al. *No Human Being Should Be Held There: The Mistreatment of LGBTQ and HIV-Positive People in U.S. Federal Immigration*

Jails (Immigration Equality, National Immigrant Justice Center, and Human Rights First, June 2024), https://immigrationequality.org/no-human-being -should-be-held-there-the-mistreatment-of-lgbtq-and-hiv-positive-people-in-u -s-federal-immigration-jails-june-2024/; Laura Harvey, *LGBTQI+ People's Experiences of Immigration Detention: A Pilot Study* (Rainbow Migration and University of Brighton, February 2023), https://www.rainbowmigration.org.uk /wp-content/uploads/2023/02/LGBTQI-peoples-experiences-of-immigration -detention-Report.pdf.

36. Physicians for Human Rights, "Endless Nightmare."

37. Tabak and Levitan, "LGBTI Migrants," 14.

38. There are similar threats to LGBTIQ populations in nonimmigration prison settings.

39. Gay Express, "Gay Asylum Seekers Attacked In German Refugee Camp," July 19, 2017, https://gayexpress.co.nz/2017/07/gay-asylum-seekers-attacked -german-refugee-camp/.

40. Thibault Spirlet, "Russian LGBTQ+ Asylum Seekers Face Uphill Battle to Make Claims in EU," *The Parliament Magazine*, April 15, 2024, https://www .theparliamentmagazine.eu/news/article/russian-lgbtq-asylum-seekers-face -uphill-battle-to-make-claims-in-eu.

41. McCullouch, Gerald, dir. *Stuck in Greece: An LGBT Refugee Crisis*, 2022 (Hard G Productions, 2023), www.stuckingreecethefilm.com.

42. Julia Caroline Morris, *Asylum and Extraction in the Republic of Nauru* (Cornell University Press, 2023); Anna Talbot, Anthea Vogl, and Sara Dehm, "The Gender- and Sexuality-Based Harms of Refugee Externalization: A Role for Human Rights Due Diligence," *International Journal of Refugee Law* 36, no. 1–2 (March 2024): 60–76, https://doi.org/10.1093/ijrl/eeae010.

43. Oliver Laughland, "Gay Asylum Seekers on Manus Island Write of Fear of Persecution in PNG," *The Guardian*, September 24, 2014, https://www .theguardian.com/world/2014/sep/24/gay-asylum-seekers-manus-island-fear -persecution-png.

44. Camminga, "Encamped Within a Camp."

45. Camminga, 42.

46. Camminga, 48.

47. Camminga notes that LGBTIQ residents of Kakuma were also attacked by local community members when housed outside of the official camp.

48. Juss, "Sexual Orientation and the Sexualisation of Refugee Law." As El-Tayeb notes, this problematic logic can also be extended to racialized communities in Europe, who are often framed as being sources of homo/transphobia, reflecting a "less tolerant, non-European" culture. El-Tayeb rejects this framing, noting the range of queer and feminist political activism and cultural production that results from these communities, who develop their own spaces of resistance against racism, homo/transphobia, nationalism, and classism in Europe. El-Tayeb, *European Others*.

49. Jasbir Puar, *Terrorist Assemblages: Homonationalism in Queer Times* (Duke University Press, 2007); Cheryl Llewellyn, "Homonationalism and Sexual Orientation-Based Asylum Cases in the United States," *Sexualities* 20, no. 5–6 (2016), 682–98.

50. Crawley, "Saving Brown Women from Brown Men?" 356.

51. This is similar to the argument that we made in chapter 3, on *flight*—namely, that LGBTIQ refugees are not inherently "immobile." They are *immobilized* by a set of norms and practices that makes their movement difficult.

52. Chan Tov McNamarah, "Silent, Spoken, Written, and Enforced: The Role of Law in the Construction of the Post-Colonial Queerphobic State," *Cornell International Law Journal* 51, no. 2 (2018): 495.

53. McNamarah, "Silent, Spoken, Written, and Enforced."

54. Rahul Rao, *Out of Time.*

55. Chapter 7, on *sanctuary*, takes head-on the idea that once queer and trans refugees have been offered asylum they are safe.

56. John Ndiritu, The Challenges Facing LGBTQI+ Refugees in Kakuma Refugee Camp, Kenya (Organization for Refuge, Asylum and Migration [ORAM] and Rainbow Railroad, 2021).

57. Balaguera, "Trans-Migrations."

58. Kath Weston, *Families We Choose: Lesbians, Gays, Kinship* (Columbia University Press, 1997).

59. Camminga, "Encamped Within a Camp."

60. Sharry Aiken and Stephanie J. Silverman, "Decarceral Futures: Bridging Immigration and Prison Justice Towards an Abolitionist Future," *Citizenship Studies* 25, no. 2 (February 2021): 147, https://doi.org/10.1080/13621025.2021.1890405.

61. Eric A. Stanley, Dean Spade, and Queer (In)Justice, "Queering Prison Abolition, Now?" *American Quarterly* 64, no. 1 (2012): 123, https://doi.org/10.1353/aq.2012.0003. Also quoted in Aiken and Silverman, "Decarceral Futures."

62. Ayten Gündoğdu, *Rightlessness in an Age of Rights* (Oxford University Press, 2015), 120.

63. Aiken and Silverman, "Decarceral Futures," 141.

64. Cetta Mainwaring and Stephanie J. Silverman, "Detention-as-Spectacle," *International Political Sociology* 11, no. 1 (March 2017): 21–38, https://doi.org/10.1093/ips/olw016.

65. Mainwaring and Silverman, "Detention-as-Spectacle."

66. Aiken and Silverman, "Decarceral Futures," 141.

67. Zein Murib, *Terms of Exclusion: Rightful Citizenship Claims and the Construction of LGBT Political Identity* (Oxford University Press, 2023).

68. For instance, End Trans Detention.

69. Raquel Willis, "Six LGBTQ+ Activists on What We Should Abolish and Legalize by 2069," *Out*, June 10, 2019, https://www.out.com/out-exclusives/2019/6/10/six-lgbtq-activists-what-we-should-abolish-and-legalize-2069.

70. Stanley, Spade, and Queer (In)Justice, "Queering Prison Abolition, Now?" 124.

71. Davis, *Are Prisons Obsolete?*, 2003.

72. Mainwaring and Silverman, "Detention-as-Spectacle."

73. Tommie Shelby has offered an argument against prison abolition, claiming that prisons are not inherently racist but rather reflect a deeply racist and unequal social world. The "crime control" function of prisons can therefore be rescued with radical reform rather than abolition. Tommie Shelby, *The Idea of Prison Abolition* (Princeton University Press, 2022).

74. UNHCR, "Policy on Alternatives to Camps" (UNHCR, 2009), https://www.unhcr.org/uk/media/unhcr-policy-alternatives-camps.

75. A/HRC/13/30/Add.1 at para. 58: The Working Group on Arbitrary Detention "considers that administrative detention as such of migrants in an irregular situation, that is to say migrants crossing the border of a country in an irregular manner or without proper documentation, or having overstayed a permit of stay, and hence being liable for removal, is not in contravention of international human rights instruments. The Working Group is fully aware of the sovereign right of States to regulate migration. However, it considers that immigration detention should gradually be abolished. Migrants in an irregular situation have not committed any crime. The criminalization of irregular migration exceeds the legitimate interests of States in protecting its territories and regulating irregular migration flows."

76. The UNWGAD has previously articulated its concern for the treatment of LGBTIQ asylum seekers in Kakuma Camp after an attack on the population in 2018. See UN Working Group on Arbitrary Detention et al., *Communication to the Government of Kenya Alleging Violence, Arbitrary Detention, and Ill-Treatment of LGBT Refugees in Kakuma Camp*, Reference AL KEN 9/2018, September 21, 2018.

CHAPTER 6. REUNION

1. Amnesty International, "Key Facts About the Migrant and Refugee Caravans Making Their Way to the USA," Amnesty International, November 16, 2018, https://www.amnesty.org/en/latest/news/2018/11/key-facts-about-the-migrant-and-refugee-caravans-making-their-way-to-the-usa/; Adolfo Flores, "LGBT Members of the Caravan Went Ahead First to Dodge Danger and Discrimination," Buzzfeed News, November 14, 2018, https://www.buzzfeednews.com/article/adolfoflores/this-is-how-lgbt-members-of-the-caravan-made-it-to-the.

2. Adolfo Flores, "LGBT Members of the Caravan."

3. William N. Eskridge Jr., "Beyond Lesbian and Gay 'Families We Choose,'" *Sex, Preference and Family: Essays on Law and Nature* 277 (1997): 286.

4. Wendy Fry and Molly Hennessy-Fiske, "Vulnerable LGBTQ Migrants Left to Wait in Mexico," *The San Diego Union-Tribune*, November 3, 2019, https://www.sandiegouniontribune.com/news/border-baja-california/story/2019-11-03/trump-administration-leaving-vulnerable-lgbt-migrants-to-wait-in-mexico.

5. Kate Smith, "10 Transgender Women Seeking Asylum Just Won Their Immigration Cases After Months of Violence and Discrimination," CBS News, 2019, https://www.cbsnews.com/news/lgbt-rights-ten-lgbt-asylum-seekers-are-winning-theirimmigration-cases-after-months-of-violence-and-discrimination/.

6. US Citizenship and Immigration Services, "Obtaining Derivative Refugee/Asylee Status for a Spouse," US Citizenship and Immigration Services, 2019, https://my.uscis.gov/exploremyoptions/obtain_refugee_asylum_status_for_spouse.

7. Anna Miller, "How the U.S. Immigration System Nearly Tore This LGBTQ Couple Apart," *The Week*, January 1, 2020, https://www.unhcr.org/uk/what-we-do/respond-emergencies/shelter/alternatives-camps.

8. US Citizenship and Immigration Services, "Obtaining Derivative Refugee/Asylee Status for a Spouse."

9. Notably, the need for such documentation is also highly Western-centric, as couples from countries that do not share the same registration practices are also potentially excluded.

10. Beyond this denial of equality before the law, it should also be noted that LGBTIQ asylum seekers within the US immigration detention system also experience disproportionate amounts of abuse and violence from state and non-state actors. As noted by Luibhéid and Chávez, "In detention, LGBTI migrants often get placed in solitary confinement, allegedly for their own protection, and are at increased risk of sexual and physical violence at the hands of detention officials and other detainees and a higher risk of illness and medical neglect." *Queer and Trans Migrations: Dynamics of Illegalization, Detention, and Deportation* (University of Illinois Press, 2020), 3; Tabak and Levitan, "LGBTI Migrants in Immigration Detention: A Global Perspective," *Harvard Journal of Law & Gender* 37 (2014): 45.

11. United Nations, "United Nations Conference of Plenipotentiaries on the Status of Refugees and Stateless Persons" (Geneva, July 25, 1951), https://www.unhcr.org/protection/travaux/40a8a7394/final-act-united-nations-conference-plenipotentiaries-status-refugees-stateless.html.

12. UNHCR, "Background Note for the Agenda Item: Family Reunification in the Context of Resettlement and Integration" (UNHCR, 2001), https://www.unhcr.org/3b30baa04.pdf.

13. Sarah Song, *Immigration and Democracy* (Oxford University Press, 2019), 132.

14. Martha Nussbaum, "Human Capabilities, Female Human Beings," in *Women, Culture, and Development: A Study of Human Capabilities*, ed. Martha Nussbaum and Jonathan Glover, 61–104 (Oxford University Press, 1995).

15. Iseult Honohan, "Reconsidering the Claim to Family Reunification in Migration," *Political Studies* 57, no. 4 (2009): 768–87.

16. Gibney, *The Ethics and Politics of Asylum*, 14.

17. UNHCR, "Background Note," 2.

18. See "Indefinite Leave to Remain (permission to stay as a refugee, humanitarian protection, Discretionary or Section 67 Leave)," 2025, https://www.gov.uk/settlement-refugee-or-humanitarian-protection/family-reunion.

19. See Home Office, "Appendix family reunion (sponsors with protection)," 2025, https://www.gov.uk/government/publications/family-reunion-instruction/family-reunion-accessible#Evidence-1.

20. See US Citizenship and Immigration Services, "Relative Petitions: Eligibility Requirements," UCIS Policy Manual, vol. 4, part c, chapter 2 (2025), https://www.uscis.gov/policy-manual/volume-4-part-c-chapter-2.

21. Guy Goodwin-Gill and Jane McAdam, *The Refugee in International Law* (Oxford University Press, 2007), 318–19.

22. *Boyle v. UK*, No. 16580/90 (European Court of Human Rights May 15, 1992); Case of *Marckx v. Belgium*, No. 6833/74 (European Court of Human Rights June 13, 1979).

23. UK Home Office, "Family Reunion: For Refugees and Those with Humanitarian Protection Version 4.0," January 9, 2020, https://assets.publishing.service.gov.uk/government/uploads/system/uploads/attachment_data/file/856915/family-reunion-guidance-v4.0-ext.pdf.

24. Inter-American Court of Human Rights, *Advisory Opinion on Gender Identity, Equality, and Non-Discrimination of Same-Sex Couples* (2017), OC-24/17, 2017, https://www.escr-net.org/caselaw/2018/advisory-opinion-gender-identity-equality-and-non-discrimination-same-sex-couples-2017.

25. This advisory note was also radical because it confirmed that the American Convention on Human Rights (ACHR) obliges states "to guarantee the right to alteration of public records—including name, image, and sex/gender marker—to reflect an individual's self-perceived gender identity. Such rectifications of public records must be complete; confidential; cheap; and based solely on the free and informed consent of the requestor, not requiring medical interventions, such as surgical or hormonal treatments."

26. G. W. F. Hegel, *Elements of the Philosophy of Right*, Cambridge Texts in the History of Political Thought, ed. Allen. W. Wood (Cambridge University Press [1991] 1820).

27. Friedrich Engels, *The Origin of the Family, Private Property, and the State* (Hottingen-Zurich, 1884).

28. Song, *Immigration and Democracy*, 143.

29. Song, 150.

30. Honohan, "Reconsidering the Claim," 775.

31. Song, *Immigration and Democracy*, 139.

32. Honohan, "Reconsidering the Claim," 775.

33. Sedgewick, "Queer and Now," 10.

34. Sedgewick, *Epistemology of the Closet*, 81.

35. Judith Butler, "Is Kinship Always Already Heterosexual?" *Differences: A Journal of Feminist Cultural Studies* 13, no. 1 (2002): 14–44; Phillip M. Ayoub and Kristina Stoeckl, *The Global Fight Against LGBTI Rights: How Transnational Conservative Networks Target Sexual and Gender Minorities* (New York University Press, 2024); Ritholtz and Mesquita, "The Transnational Force of Anti-LGBT+ Politics."

36. Butler, "Is Kinship Always Already Heterosexual?"; Lee Edelman, *No Future: Queer Theory and the Death Drive* (Duke University Press, 2004); Eskridge Jr., "Beyond Lesbian and Gay 'Families We Choose'"; Sedgwick, "Queer and Now"; Weston, *Families We Choose*.

37. Butler, "Is Kinship Always Already Heterosexual?" 16.

38. In recent years, efforts have been undertaken to prevent queer couples from being recognized as parents even through surrogacy. When Giorgia Meloni came to power in Italy, she orchestrated an effort to prohibit the use of assistive reproductive technology for all Italians, including while abroad. As a result of this law, the state will not recognize the nongenetic parent of a same-sex couple from the birth certificate of a child born abroad from surrogacy. The effects of this effort are particularly concerning in cases where the nongenetic parent is the only Italian citizen, as it in effect removes the citizenship right of the child to be Italian. This effort therefore effectively bans queer people from being parents in Italy. Samuel Ritholtz and Margaret Neil, "LGBTQ+ Parents Are Being Removed from Their Children's Birth Certificates in Italy: Here's What's Behind This Disturbing Trend," *The Conversation*, June 28, 2023, https://theconversation.com/lgbtq-parents-are-being-removed-from-their-childrens-birth-certificates-in-italy-heres-whats-behind-this-disturbing-trend-208241.

39. Sedgewick, "Queer and Now," 5.

40. Butler, "Is Kinship Always Already Heterosexual?" 21.

41. Kath Weston, *Families We Choose*, 27.

42. Butler "Is Kinship Always Already Heterosexual?"

43. Edelman, *No Future*, 30.

44. Sedgewick, "Queer and Now." Queer theorists have debated the merits of social constructions associated with reproductive futurism, which lead queer and trans people to be considered as "a people without a future." While scholars disagree on the implications of "queer non-futurity," in the given discussion, its associated assumptions risk denying queer families recognition as family units. Leo Bersani, *Homos* (Harvard University Press, 1996); Edelman, *No Future*; José Esteban Muñoz et al., *Cruising Utopia: The Then and There of Queer Futurity* (New York University Press, 2019).

45. Butler, "Is Kinship Always Already Heterosexual?" 14.

46. Butler, 15.

47. Butler, 37.

48. Butler, "Critically Queer."

49. Eskridge Jr. "Beyond Lesbian and Gay 'Families We Choose,'" 877.

50. Weston, *Families We Choose*.

51. David Murray Schneider and Raymond Thomas Smith, *Class Differences in American Kinship* (University Microfilms International, 1978).

52. Weston, *Families We Choose*, 31.

53. Emily A. Arnold and Marlon M. Bailey, "Constructing Home and Family: How the Ballroom Community Supports African American GLBTQ Youth in the Face of HIV/AIDS," *Journal of Gay & Lesbian Social Services* 21, no. 2–3 (May 2009): 171–88, https://doi.org/10.1080/10538720902772006.

54. Arnold and Bailey, "Constructing Home and Family," 174.

55. Voguing comes from ball culture.

56. Butler, "Critically Queer," 28.

57. Campuzano, "Contemporary Travesti Encounters with Gender and Sexuality in Latin America," *Development* 52, no. 1 (March 2009): 75–83; Fernanda Cardozo, "Performatividades de gênero, performatividades de parentesco: Notas de um estudo com travestis e suas famílias na cidade de Florianópolis/SC," 2012; Cristian Alejandro Darouiche, "Formas de sociabilidad y vínculos de parentesco entre mujeres trans que realizan sexo comercial en la Ciudad de Mar Del Plata," *Ponencia presentada en las XXVI jornadas de jóvenes investigadores AUGM, Mendoza*, 2018; Patricia Fogelman, "Travestis migrantes, arte y religiosidad en la cultura queer de Buenos Aires," *Revista brasileira de história das religiões* XII, no. 36 (April 2020): 9–34; Julieta Vartabedian Cabral, "Geografía travesti: Cuerpos, sexualidad y migraciones de travestis brasileñas (Rio de Janeiro-Barcelona)" (PhD diss., Universitat de Barcelona, 2012), https://www.tdx.cat/handle/10803/95889#page=81; Katrin Vogel, "The Mother, the Daughter, and the Cow: Venezuelan Transformistas' Migration to Europe," *Mobilities* 4, no. 3 (2009): 367–87.

58. Cabral, "Geografía travesti."

59. Juliana Martínez and Salvador Vidal-Ortiz, eds., *Traver el Saber* (Editorial de la Universidad Nacional de la Plata [EDULP], 2018), 59–60.

60. Vogel, "The Mother, the Daughter, and the Cow," 368–69. This dynamic has appeared frequently as well in many of Samuel's interviews with trans Venezuelan migrants in Colombia.

61. Campuzano, "Contemporary Travesti Encounters"; Marlene Wayar, *Travesti: Una Teoría lo suficientemente buena* (Editorial Muchas Nueces, 2018).

62. Elif Sari, "Unsafe Present, Uncertain Futures: LGBTI Asylum in Turkey," in *Queer and Trans Migrations: Dynamics of Illegalization, Detention, and Deportation*, ed. Eithne Luibhéid and Karma R. Chávez (University of Illinois Press, 2020), 99.

63. Edward Siddons, "'We're Brothers, Sisters and Activists': The Greek Collective of Gay and Trans Refugees," *The Guardian*, September 16, 2018,

https://www.theguardian.com/world/2018/sep/16/we-are-brothers-sisters-and
-activists-greek-gay-trans-collective-of-refugees.

64. Tracy Morison, Ingrid Lynch, and Vasu Reddy, *Queer Kinship: South African Perspectives on the Sexual Politics of Family-Making and Belonging* (Routledge, 2019); Daniel Wesangula, "On the Run from Persecution: How Kenya Became a Haven for LGBT Refugees," *The Guardian*, February 23, 2017, https://www.theguardian.com/global-development-professionals-network/2017/feb/23/on-the-run-from-persecution-how-kenya-became-a-haven-for-lgbt-refugees; B Camminga and John Marnell, *Queer and Trans African Mobilities: Migration, Asylum and Diaspora,* (Zed Books, 2022).

65. Sari, "Unsafe Present, Uncertain Futures," 99–100.

66. Flores, "LGBT Members of the Caravan."

67. In January 2025, the Trump administration effectively ended the possibility of seeking asylum at the US Southern border. As they are unable to return home, many people still wait in the North of Mexico in the hope that the policy might change or in preparation for travel via irregular routes. Thomas Graham, "US asylum seekers in despair after Trump cancels CBP One app: 'Start from zero again,'" *The Guardian*, January 23, 2025, https://www.theguardian.com/us-news/2025/jan/23/trump-cbp-one-app-cancelled-mexico.

68. Balaguera, "Trans-Migrations"; Ana Paula Castro Garcés and Pablo Castro Domingo, "La 72, Hogar-refugio para personas migrantes: La sociedad civil organizada en la atención de la agenda de los transmigrantes en la frontera México-Guatemala," *Revista pueblos y fronteras digital* 15 (2020): 33. The risks to LGBTIQ migrants associated with waiting in Mexican border towns could be another moral claim for expedited determination through group consideration.

69. Fry and Hennessy-Fiske, "Vulnerable LGBTQ Migrants." In the final section of chapter 3, *on flight*, we discuss the safe house networks that have been developed in response to forms of induced immobility.

70. As highlighted by Mahtab's tragic story in chapter 7, on *sanctuary*, for many LGBTIQ refugees, resettlement in a new country does not promise the end of their struggles. Sima Shakhsari, "Killing Me Softly With Your Rights," in *Queer Necropolitics*, edited by Jin Haritaworn, Adi Kuntsman, and Silvia Posocco (Routledge, 2014), 93–110. Like any other person, they require a community in their new country to support them through a difficult transition. But that is not guaranteed for LGBTIQ refugees, as many discriminatory cultural or societal norms persist among diaspora communities. Unconditional love, emotional and physical support, and guidance are what's needed and what "families," chosen or not, can provide.

CHAPTER 7. SANCTUARY

1. Lily Wakefield, "Gay Asylum Seeker Flees Persecution in Morocco, Only to Endure More Homophobia When Arriving in the UK," *PinkNews*, February 6,

2021, https://www.pinknews.co.uk/2021/02/06/morocco-gay-asylum-seeker
-cardiff-wales-housing-homophobia-abderrahim-el-habachi/.

2. The United Nations Independent Expert on Sexual Orientation and Gender Identity has echoed Abderrahim's call for improved accommodation for queer and trans displaced populations, recommending that states in his recent report on queer and trans displacement "develop and maintain more inclusive strategies to ensure safe housing." United Nations Independent Expert on Sexual Orientation and Gender Identity, *Protection Against Violence and Discrimination Based on Sexual Orientation and Gender Identity in Relation to Forced Displacement*, Reference A/HRC/59/43, 17 April 2025, para 89(a), https://www.ohchr.org/en/documents/thematic-reports/ahrc5943-protection-against-violence-and-discrimination-based-sexual.

3. Emphasis added.

4. Vitikainen, "LGBT Rights and Refugees."

5. Parekh, "Beyond the Ethics of Admission: Stateless People, Refugee Camps and Moral Obligations."

6. Michael Walzer, *Spheres of Justice* (New York: Basic Books, 1983), 49.

7. Song, *Immigration and Democracy*.

8. Christopher Heath Wellman, "Immigration," Stanford Encyclopedia of Philosophy, 2019, https://plato.stanford.edu/entries/immigration/.

9. Joseph Carens, *The Ethics of Immigration* (Oxford University Press, 2013); Mollie Gerver, "Must Refugees Return?" *Critical Review of International Social and Political Philosophy* 24, no. 4 (2019), https://doi.org/10.1080/13698230.2019.1573347; Gibney, *The Ethics and Politics of Asylum*; Miller, *Strangers in Our Midst*, 2016; Song, *Immigration and Democracy*; Kieran Oberman, "Enough Spurious Distinctions: Refugees Are Just People in Need of Refuge," *Law and Philosophy* 32, no. 5 (January 2025), https://doi.org/10.1007/s10982-024-09516-1. Those who defend the focus on persecution include Max Cherem, "Refugee Rights: Against Expanding the Definition of a 'Refugee' and Unilateral Protection Elsewhere," *Journal of Political Philosophy* 24, no. 2 (2016): 183–205; and Matthew Price, *Rethinking Asylum: History, Purpose, and Limits* (Cambridge University Press, 2009).

10. Gibney, *The Ethics and Politics of Asylum*; Gillian Brock, *Justice for People on The Move* (Cambridge University Press, 2020); David Owen, *What Do We Owe to Refugees?* (Polity, 2020); James Souter, "Towards a Theory of Asylum as Reparation for Past Injustice," *Political Studies* 62, no. 2 (June 1, 2014): 326–42, https://doi.org/10.1111/1467-9248.12019.

11. Walzer, *Spheres of Justice*; Cherem, "Refugee Rights: Against Expanding the Definition."

12. Parekh, "Beyond the Ethics of Admission."

13. The Refugee Convention includes several substantive rights to which people are entitled after receiving asylum. These include housing, healthcare,

and access to employment. However, receiving states often fail to ensure that these rights are met.

14. Miller, *Strangers in Our Midst*; Michael Dummett, *On Immigration and Refugees* (Routledge, 2001).

15. David Owen, "Differentiating Refugees: Asylum, Sanctuary and Refuge," in *The Political Philosophy of Refuge*, ed. David Miller and Christine Straehle (Cambridge University Press, 2020), 19–38.

16. As such, queer and trans displacement *from* states in the Global South *to* other states in the Global South remains remarkably undertheorized in the literature. This critique of the Eurocentric frameworks of queer and trans asylum is well articulated in B Camminga, *Transgender Refugees and the Imagined South Africa*.

17. Vitikainen, "LGBT Rights and Refugees."

18. See also Gottfried Schweiger, "Should States Prioritize Child Refugees?" *Ethics & Global Politics* 12, no. 2 (December 2019): 46–61, https://doi.org/10.1080/16544951.2019.1649958; David Miller, "Selecting Refugees," in *The Political Philosophy of Refuge*, ed. Christine Straehle and David Miller (Cambridge University Press, 2019), 97–113; Fine, "Refugees and the Limits of Political Philosophy."

19. We use the term *postasylum* to pick out this specific concern.

20. Eithne Luibhéid, "QUEER/MIGRATION: An Unruly Body of Scholarship," *GLQ: A Journal of Lesbian and Gay Studies* 14, no. 2–3 (January 2008): 169–90, https://doi.org/10.1215/10642684-2007-029; Ritholtz, "Is Queer-and-Trans Youth Homelessness a Form of Displacement?"

21. Tschalaer, "Between Queer Liberalisms and Muslim Masculinities"; Millbank, "From Discretion to Disbelief"; Prearo, "The Moral Politics of LGBTI Asylum."

22. Rebecca A. Hopkinson et al., "Persecution Experiences and Mental Health of LGBT Asylum Seekers," *Journal of Homosexuality* 64, no. 12 (2017): 1650–66; Michael Kareff, "Constructing Sexuality and Gender Identity for Asylum Through a Western Gaze: The Oversimplification of Global Sexual and Gender Variation and Its Practical Effect on LGBT Asylum Determinations," *Georgetown Immigration Law Journal* 35, no. 615 (2020).

23. Cragnolini, "Lesbian, Gay, Bisexual and Transgender Refugees."

24. Nayak, *Who Is Worthy of Protection?*

25. Juss, "Sexual Orientation and the Sexualisation of Refugee Law," 129.

26. El-Tayeb, *European Others*.

27. Jasbir Puar, *Terrorist Assemblages*.

28. Patti Tamara Lenard, *Democracy and Exclusion* (Oxford University Press, 2023), 133.

29. Lenard, *Democracy and Exclusion*, 150.

30. Ritholtz and Buxton, "Queer Kinship."

31. Laura Sjoberg, *Gendering Global Conflict: Toward a Feminist Theory of War* (Columbia University Press, 2013).

32. Su and Ritholtz, "How LGBT Refugees from Ukraine Are Highly Vulnerable."

33. Phillip M. Ayoub and Douglas Page, "When Do Opponents of Gay Rights Mobilize? Explaining Political Participation in Times of Backlash Against Liberalism," *Political Research Quarterly* 73, no. 3 (September 2020): 696–713, https://doi.org/10.1177/1065912919853377. Note that Hungary does not currently process asylum claims on their territory at all.

34. Alicia Roth Weigel, *Inverse Cowgirl : A Memoir* (HarperOne, 2023).

35. For more information on endosexism (prejudice based on sex characteristics) in asylum processes, see the work of the Organisation Intersex International Europe's Intersex Refugees and Asylum Seekers Project (https://www.oiieurope.org/programs/#refugees-asylum-seekers) as well as B Cimminga, "Where are all the Intersex Asylum Seekers? Active Absenting or the Citational Chain of an Idea," *Feminist Formations* 36, no. 2 (2024): 189–202.

36. Reid and Ritholtz, "A Queer Approach to Understanding LGBT Vulnerability."

37. Karin Wachter, Laurie Cook Heffron, and Jessica Dalpe, "'Back Home You Just Go Talk to the Family': The Role of Family Among Women Who Seek Help for Intimate Partner Violence Pre- and Postresettlement to the United States," *Journal of Interpersonal Violence* 36, no. 15–16 (August 2021): 7574–98.

38. Danisi et al., *Queering Asylum in Europe*; Sabine Jansen, "Introduction," in *Fleeing Homophobia*, ed. Thomas Spijkerboer, 19–49 (Routledge, 2013); Richard C. M. Mole, *Queer Migration and Asylum in Europe* (UCL Press, 2021); Thomas Wimark, "Housing Policy with Violent Outcomes: The Domestication of Queer Asylum Seekers in a Heteronormative Society," *Journal of Ethnic and Migration Studies* 47, no. 3 (2021): 703–22; Yarwood et al., "LGBTQI + Migrants."

39. Francesca Bentley, "Coming to America: It's Not Like the Movie," Pulitzer Center, November 12, 2020, https://pulitzercenter.org/reporting/coming-america-its-not-movie.

40. BBC News, "Roman Protasevich: Belarus Dissident Seized from Ryanair Plane," June 25, 2021, https://www.bbc.co.uk/news/world-europe-57229635.

41. Pentreath, "Meet the Gay Nigerian Refugee Who Sought Asylum in the UK to Escape Death Threats, Conversion Therapy and Violence."

42. Micro Rainbow, "Held Back: Poverty of LGBTQI Refugees in the UK: An Insight into the Lived Experiences of LGBTQI Refugees in the UK" (Micro Rainbow, 2023).

43. Shakhsari, "Killing Me Softly."

44. For more on the "dangerization" of particular zones in the Global South, see Ruben Andersson, "Here Be Dragons: Mapping an Ethnography of Global Danger," *Current Anthropology* 57, no. 6 (December 2016): 707–31.

45. Inés Valdez, "Association, Reciprocity, and Emancipation: A Transnational Account of the Politics of Global Justice," in *Empire, Race and Global*

Justice, ed. Duncan Bell (Cambridge University Press, 2019), 128, https://doi.org /10.1017/9781108576307.006.

46. Alex Sager, "Methodological Nationalism, Migration and Political Theory," *Political Studies* 64, no. 1 (October 2014): 42–59, https://doi.org/10.1111/1467 -9248.12167.

47. As discussed in our introduction, LGBTIQ displaced people sit at the center of this Venn diagram, thus facing a kind of double backlash.

48. See our discussion of these networks, as well as Rainbow Railroad, in chapter 3, on *flight*.

49. This is not always the case. B Camminga has noted that LGBTIQ organizations in South Africa sometimes exclude LGBTIQ migrants and refugees due to the belief that resources are scarce and that working with such groups might open them up to backlash. See B Camminga, "Competing Marginalities and Precarious Politics: A South African Case Study of NGO Representation of Transgender Refugees," *Gender, Place & Culture* 31, no. 9 (September 2024): 1293–310, https://doi.org/10.1080/0966369X.2022.2137473. Information on the No Pride in Detention Campaign is available here: https://www.rainbowmigration.org.uk /no-pride-in-detention/.

50. Canada's private sponsorship scheme has recently been thrown into question. In November 2024, the Canadian Government announced a pause on new community sponsorship applications, to last until at least December 2025. See Government of Canada, "Temporary Pause on Intake of Refugee Sponsorship Applications from Groups of Five and Community Sponsors" (Government of Canada, 2024), https://www.canada.ca/en/immigration-refugees-citizenship /news/notices/temporary-pause-intake-refugee-sponsorship-applications -groups-five-community-sponsors.html.

51. For a discussion of solidarity and diaspora politics, see Ashwini Vasanthakumar, "Exiles as Solidary Intermediaries," in *The Ethics of Exile: A Political Theory of Diaspora*, ed. Ashwini Vasanthakumar (Oxford University Press, 2021), https://doi.org/10.1093/oso/9780198828938.003.0004.

52. Andrea Sangiovanni, and Juri Viehoff, "Solidarity in Social and Political Philosophy," *The Stanford Encyclopedia of Philosophy*, 2023, https://plato .stanford.edu/entries/solidarity/.

53. Mattxiv, "Say no to pinkwashing, say no to Bill Maher," Instagram, October 21, 2024, https://www.instagram.com/p/DBZz86_BHZu/?img_index=6& igsh=azduNmE1bngzbmgw.

54. Sa'ed Atshan, *Queer Palestine and The Empire of Critique* (Stanford University Press, 2020). Homosexuality has been decriminalized in The West Bank— which follows the Jordanian penal code—since the 1950s, having been originally introduced by British colonial influence.

55. Critics of the solidarity shown between LGBTIQ groups and Palestinian causes often fail to note that there are several important organizations in Palestine advocating for LGBTIQ rights, including Aswat and alQaws.

56. Lydia Polgreen and Vishakha Darbha, "An Interview with Sarah Schulman: 'They're Coming After All of Us. So You Might as Well Tell the Truth,'" *The New York Times*, April 10, 2025, https://www.nytimes.com/2025/04/10/opinion/sarah-schulman-solidarity.html.

57. The legal and political system can also play a role in this production of new meanings, especially when trying to understand contexts of adversity. Seyla Benhabib outlines the concept of *jurisgenesis*, which she defines as ". . . the law's capacity to create a normative universe of meaning, which can often escape the provenance of formal lawmaking." See Seyla Benhabib, *Dignity in Adversity: Human Rights in Turbulent Times* (Polity, 2021), 15.

58. Polgreen and Darbha, "An Interview with Sarah Schulman."

59. Sarah Schulman, *The Fantasy and Necessity of Solidarity* (Thesis, 2025).

CONCLUSION

1. The interview with Sebastián (pseudonym) took place in Colombia on September 16, 2024. Research approval provided by the Department of Politics and International Relations (University of Oxford), Research Ethics Committee, Ref No: SSH/DPIR_C1A_24_023.

2. IOM, UN Migration, "Update on IOM Operations Amid Budget Cuts" (IOM, UN Migration, March 2025), https://www.iom.int/news/update-iom-operations-amid-budget-cuts; Agence France-Presse, "UN migration agency laying off around 20% of HQ staff amid US aid cuts: sources," *France24*, March 14, 2025, https://www.france24.com/en/live-news/20250314-un-migration-agency-laying-off-around-20-of-hq-staff-amid-us-aid-cuts-sources.

3. As of June 2025, universities have responded in different ways to this federal government repression, with some kowtowing. Still our point is that under such pressure the rigorous defense of LGBTIQ+ rights and their connection to the rights of migrants and asylum seekers becomes much more contentious and difficult to sustain, particularly in the United States.

4. Lee Badgett. *The Economic Case for LGBT Equality: Why Fair and Equal Treatment Benefits Us All* (Beacon Press, 2020).

5. Christopher Heath Wellman, "Immigration and Freedom of Association," *Ethics* 119, no. 1 (2008): 109–41, https://doi.org/10.1086/592311; Miller, *Strangers in Our Midst*; David Miller, "Our Responsibility to Refugees," in Proceedings of the 2018 ZiF Workshop "Studying Migration Policies at the Interface between Empirical Research and Normative Analysis," ULB Münster, ed. M. Hoesch and L. Laube (2018), https://doi.org/10.17879/95189441435; Gibney, *The Ethics and Politics of Asylum*; Owen, *What Do We Owe to Refugees?*; Oberman, "Enough Spurious Distinctions."

6. Phil Cole, "Framing the Refugee," E-International Relations, November 25, 2016, https://www.e-ir.info/2016/11/25/framing-the-refugee/.

7. Jamie Draper, "Domination and Misframing in the Refugee Regime," *Critical Review of International Social and Political Philosophy* 25, no. 7 (2020): 939–62; Rufaida Al Hashmi, "Historical Injustice in Immigration Policy," *Political Studies* 71, no. 4 (November 1, 2023): 1261–76, https://doi.org/10 .1177/00323217211065557; Hallvard Sandven, "The Practice and Legitimacy of Border Control," *American Journal of Political Science* 68, no. 2 (August 2022), https://doi.org/10.1111/ajps.12736; Hallvard Sandven and Antoinette Scherz, "Rescue Missions in the Mediterranean and the Legitimacy of the EU's Border Regime," *Res Publica*, April 1, 2022, https://doi.org/10.1007/s11158-022-09550 -7; T. Alexander Aleinikoff and David Owen, "Refugee Protection: 'Here' or 'There'?" *Migration Studies* 10, no. 3 (September 2022): 464–83, https://doi .org/10.1093/migration/mnac002; Matthew J. Gibney, "Should Citizenship Be Conditional? The Ethics of Denationalization," *The Journal of Politics* 75, no. 3 (2013): 646–58; Buxton, "Respect and Asylum"; Rebecca Buxton and Matthew J. Gibney, "Must Refugees Be Grateful?" *Political Studies* 73, no. 1 (March 2024): 287–304, https://doi.org/10.1177/00323217241238124; Jamie Draper, "Climate Change and Displacement: Towards a Pluralist Approach," *European Journal of Political Theory* 23, no. 1 (May 2022): 3–28, https://doi.org/10.1177 /14748851221093446; Ayelet Shachar, *The Shifting Border* (Manchester University Press, 2020).

8. Buxton and Gibney, "Must Refugees Be Grateful?"

9. Robert E. Goodin, "Duties of Charity, Duties of Justice," *Political Studies* 65, no. 2 (June 2017): 268, https://doi.org/10.1177/0032321716647402. This is classically interpreted as a distinction between "perfect" and "imperfect" duties. Though, as Goodin demonstrates, perfect duties do not always trump imperfect ones. Therefore the "moral *importance* of the duties does not necessarily map onto the *form* of the duties."

10. Joel Feinberg, *The Moral Limits of Criminal Law*, vol. 1, *Harm to Others* (Oxford University Press, 1984); Rebecca Buxton, "Justice in Waiting: The Harms and Wrongs of Temporary Refugee Protection," *European Journal of Political Theory* 22, no. 1 (January 2023): 51–72, https://doi.org/10.1177/1474885120973578.

11. Draper, "Climate Change and Displacement."

12. On this point, Tina Nina Dixson argues for better inclusion of LGBTIQ refugees and refugee-led organizations (RLOs) into decision-making positions within the global refugee regime. As a scholar and activist with a displacement background, Dixson argues against shallow efforts of representation premised on visibility and for a more significant form of recognition premised on resources and redistribution. At the conclusion of her piece on this subject, Dixson declares, "A key step towards achieving this [inclusion] is recognizing LGBTIQ+ RLOs as experts equal to other humanitarian actors—not only valuing their expertise beyond storytelling but also ensuring equitable access to resources for their sustainability. The alternative queer future I envision here is one where we have rights without needing to fight for something as basic and fundamental as

your recognition of our existence. Now that you hopefully recognize us, we can work towards building collective solutions to address LGBTIQ+ displacement." Tina Nina Dixson, "Queer Refugees and Human Rights: On the Limits of Recognition," *Journal of Refugee Studies* (2024): 14.

13. Bohmer and Shuman. "Producing Epistemologies of Ignorance."

Works Cited

Åberg, Karin. "A Requirement of Shame: On the Evolution of the Protection of LGB Refugees." *International Journal of Refugee Law* 35, no. 1 (March 2023): 37–57. https://doi.org/10.1093/ijrl/eead008.

Agamben, Giorgio. *Homo Sacer: Sovereign Power and Bare Life.* Stanford University Press, 1998.

Agence France-Presse, "UN migration agency laying off around 20% of HQ staff amid US aid cuts: sources." *France24,* March 14, 2025. https://www.france24 .com/en/live-news/20250314-un-migration-agency-laying-off-around-20-of -hq-staff-amid-us-aid-cuts-sources.

Agier, Michael. *Managing the Undesirables: Refugee Camps and Humanitarian Government.* Polity Press, 2011.

Ahmed, Sara, Claudia Castañeda, Anne-Marie Fortier, and Mimi Sheller. "Introduction: Uprootings/Regroundings: Questions of Home and Migration." In *Uprootings/Regroundings Questions of Home and Migration.* Routledge, 2020: 1–19.

Aiken, Sharry, and Stephanie J. Silverman. "Decarceral Futures: Bridging Immigration and Prison Justice Towards an Abolitionist Future." *Citizenship Studies* 25, no. 2 (February 2021): 141–61. https://doi.org/10.1080/13621025 .2021.1890405.

Aizura, Aren. *Mobile Subjects: Transnational Imaginaries of Gender Reassignment.* Duke University Press, 2018.

Akbari, Roxana, and Stefan Vogler. "Intersectional Invisibility: Race, Gender, Sexuality, and the Erasure of Sexual Minority Women in US Asylum Law." *Law and Social Inquiry* 46, no. 4 (November 2021): 1062–91. https://doi.org/10.1017/lsi.2021.15.

Al Hashmi, Rufaida. "Historical Injustice in Immigration Policy." *Political Studies* 71, no. 4 (November 2023): 1261–76. https://doi.org/10.1177/00323217211065557.

Aleinikoff, T. Alexander, and David Owen. "Refugee Protection: 'Here' or 'There'?" *Migration Studies* 10, no. 3 (September 2022): 464–83. https://doi.org/10.1093/migration/mnac002.

Alexander, Christopher, Mai Sato, and Aleardo Zanghellini. "State-Enabled Killing of Same-Sex-Attracted People: A Legal Pluralist Account." *Law & Social Inquiry* 48, no. 3 (2023): 719–47. https://doi.org/10.1017/lsi.2022.48.

American Civil Liberties Union. "Justice-Free Zones: U.S. Immigration Detention Under the Trump Administration," ACLU, 2020. https://www.aclu.org/publications/justice-free-zones-us-immigration-detention-under-trump-administration.

———. "Unchecked Growth: Private Prison Corporations and Immigration Detention, Three Years Into the Biden Administration." ACLU, 2023. https://www.aclu.org/news/immigrants-rights/unchecked-growth-private-prison-corporations-and-immigration-detention-three-years-into-the-biden-administration.

Amnesty International. "Kenya: Homophobic Attack Leaves Man Dead at Kakuma Refugee Camp; UN Safety Measures Review Needed." Amnesty International, 2021. https://www.amnesty.org.au/kenya-homophobic-attack-leaves-man-dead-at-kakuma-refugee-camp-un-safety-measures-review-needed/.

———. "Key Facts About the Migrant and Refugee Caravans Making Their Way to the USA." Amnesty International, November 16, 2018. https://www.amnesty.org/en/latest/news/2018/11/key-facts-about-the-migrant-and-refugee-caravans-making-their-way-to-the-usa/.

———. "Libya/EU: Conditions Remain 'Hellish' as EU Marks 5 Years of Cooperation Agreements." Amnesty International, 2022. https://www.amnesty.org/en/latest/news/2022/01/libya-eu-conditions-remain-hellish-as-eu-marks-5-years-of-cooperation-agreements/.

Anadolu Agency. "Kenya Gives UN 14-Day Deadline to Close Refugee Camps." AA News, 2021. https://www.aa.com.tr/en/africa/kenya-gives-un-14-day-deadline-to-close-refugee-camps/2186765.

Andersson, Ruben. "Here Be Dragons: Mapping an Ethnography of Global Danger." *Current Anthropology* 57, no. 6 (December 1, 2016): 707–31.

Angelo, Paul J., and Will Freeman. "A Socially Conservative Left Is Gaining Traction in Latin America." *Americas Quarterly*, June 23, 2021. https://www.americasquarterly.org/article/a-socially-conservative-left-is-gaining-traction-in-latin-america/.

Anker, Deborah. *Law of Asylum in the United States*. Immigration Law Library. Thomson Reuters, 2017.

Ansari, Sadiya. "'We've Lost So Many Lives': Why LGBTQ+ Refugees Are Giving Up on Kenya." Context by Thomson Reuters Foundation, 2025. https://www.context.news/socioeconomic-inclusion/long-read/weve-lost-so-many-lives-lgbtq-refugees-are-giving-up-on-kenya.

Anzaldúa, Gloria. *Borderlands/La Frontera: The New Mestiza*. Aunt Lute Books, 1987.

Araújo, Caio Simões. "Along the Pink Corridor: Histories of Queer Mobility Between Maputo and Johannesburg (ca. 1900–2020)." In *Queer and Trans African Mobilities: Migration, Asylum and Diaspora*. Bloomsbury, 2022.

Arendt, Hannah. *Men in Dark Times*. Harcourt Brace & Company, 1968.

Arnold, Emily A., and Marlon M. Bailey. "Constructing Home and Family: How the Ballroom Community Supports African American GLBTQ Youth in the Face of HIV/AIDS." *Journal of Gay & Lesbian Social Services* 21, no. 2–3 (May 2009): 171–88. https://doi.org/10.1080/10538720902772006.

Arundhathi. "Gender-Based Spatial Segregation: Ladies' Compartments in the Mumbai Local Trains." *Gender, Place & Culture* 31, no. 2 (August 2022): 1–21. https://doi.org/10.1080/0966369X.2022.2115980.

Asanovic, Bojana. *Still Falling Short: The Standard of Home Office Decision-Making in Asylum Claims Based on Sexual Orientation and Gender Identity*. UK Lesbian and Gay Immigration Group, July 2018.

Ashton, Jack. "Nigerian Gay Rights Activist Who Judge Accused of 'Faking' Her Sexuality Wins 13-year Legal Battle for Asylum in UK." *The Independent*, August 14, 2017. https://www.independent.co.uk/news/uk/home-news/nigeria-gay-rights-activist-aderonke-apata-uk-asylum-granted-high-court-fake-sexulaity-lesbian-lgbt-persecution-africa-a7888931.html.

Asquith, Nicole L., and Christopher A. Fox. "No Place Like Home: Intrafamilial Hate Crime Against Gay Men and Lesbians." In *Queering Criminology*, edited by Angela Dwyer, Matthew Ball, and Thomas Crofts. Palgrave Macmillan, 2016: 163–82.

Atshan, Sa'ed. *Queer Palestine and The Empire of Critique*. Stanford University Press, 2020.

Australian Government. Migration Act 1958. Federal Register of Legislation, 2018. https://www.legislation.gov.au/Details/C2018C00337.

Ayoub, Phillip M., and Douglas Page. "When Do Opponents of Gay Rights Mobilize? Explaining Political Participation in Times of Backlash against Liberalism." *Political Research Quarterly* 73, no. 3 (September 1, 2020): 696–713. https://doi.org/10.1177/1065912919853377.

Ayoub, Phillip M., and Kristina Stoeckl. *The Global Fight Against LGBTI Rights: How Transnational Conservative Networks Target Sexual and Gender Minorities*. New York University Press, 2024.

Badgett, Lee. *The Economic Case for LGBT Equality: Why Fair and Equal Treatment Benefits Us All*. Beacon Press, 2020.

Bail for Immigration Detainees (BiD). "Hidden Histories: Yarl's Wood and Its Captive Women." BiD, 2019. https://www.biduk.org/articles/437-hidden-histories-yarl-s-wood-and-its-captive-women.

Balaguera, Martha. "Trans-Migrations: Agency and Confinement at the Limits of Sovereignty." *Signs: Journal of Women in Culture and Society* 43, no. 3 (March 2018): 641–64.

BBC News. "Roman Protasevich: Belarus Dissident Seized from Ryanair Plane." June 25, 2021. https://www.bbc.co.uk/news/world-europe-57229635.

Benhabib, Seyla. *Dignity in Adversity: Human Rights in Turbulent Times*. Polity, 2021.

Bentley, Francesca. "Coming to America: It's Not Like the Movie." Pulitzer Center, November 12, 2020. https://pulitzercenter.org/reporting/coming-america-its-not-movie.

Beresford, Meka. "The Home Office Quizzed a Bisexual Asylum Seeker on LGBT Terminology During His Interview Process." *PinkNews*, November 12, 2016. https://www.thepinknews.com/2016/11/12/the-home-office-quizzed-a-bisexual-asylum-seeker-on-lgbt-terminology-during-his-interview-process/.

Bersani, Leo. *Homos*. Harvard University Press, 1996.

Bhalla, Nita. "U.N. Moves LGBT+ Refugees to Safe Houses After Kenya Camp Attacks." Reuters, 2018. https://www.reuters.com/article/us-kenya-lgbt-refugees-idUSKBN1OC1Y9/.

Bird, Gemma. "Constructing Vulnerability and Victimhood at the EU Border." *Polity* 54, no. 4 (October 2022): 874–81.

Boffey, Daniel, and Lorenzo Tondo. "Russia Accused of Shelling Mariupol Humanitarian Corridor." *The Guardian*, April 26, 2022. https://www.theguardian.com/world/2022/apr/26/russia-accused-of-shelling-mariupol-humanitarian-corridor.

Blitzer, Jonathan. *Everyone Who Is Gone Is Here: The United States, Central America, and the Making of a Crisis*. Penguin, 2024.

———. "The Make Up Artist Donald Trump Deported Under The Enemy Aliens Act." *The New Yorker*, March 31, 2025. https://www.newyorker.com/news/annals-of-immigration/the-makeup-artist-donald-trump-deported-under-the-alien-enemies-act.

Blomfield, Adrian. "Can One of Africa's Largest Refugee Camps Evolve into a City?" AP News, April 7, 2025. https://apnews.com/article/kenya-refugees-kakuma-permanent-city-5ade4e335987ef0535fb7ea9e21ba183.

Bohmer, Carol, and Amy Shuman. "Producing Epistemologies of Ignorance in the Political Asylum Application Process." *Identities* 14, no. 5 (December 2007): 603–29.

Bond, Kimberley. "'You Need to Prove That You're Gay': LGBTQ+ Asylum Seekers in the UK." *Metro*, June 6, 2022. https://metro.co.uk/2022/06/06

/asylum-seekers-in-the-uk-how-lgbtq-refugees-prove-their-sexuality
-16744541/.

Bradley, Megan. "Return in Dignity: A Neglected Refugee Protection Challenge." *Canadian Journal of Development Studies / Revue canadienne
d'études du développement* 28, no. 3–4 (January 1, 2009): 371–82. https://doi
.org/10.1080/02255189.2009.9669219.

Brewer, Kirstie. "'How Do I Convince the Home Office I'm a Lesbian?'" BBC
News, February 26, 2020. https://www.bbc.com/news/stories-51636642.

Brock, Gillian. *Justice for People on The Move.* Cambridge University Press, 2020.

Brown, Gavin, Kath Browne, Rebecca Elmhirst, and Simon Hutta. "Sexualities
in/of the Global South." *Geography Compass* 4, no. 10 (October 1, 2010):
1567–79.

Browne, Kath, and Catherine Nash. *Queer Methods and Methodologies:
Intersecting Queer Theories and Social Science Research.* Routledge, 2010.

Bryant, Jason. "The Meaning of Queer Home: Between Metaphor and Material." *Home Cultures* 12, no. 3 (2015): 261–89. https://doi.org/10.1080/17406315
.2015.1084754.

Butler, Judith. *Bodies That Matter: On the Discursive Limits of Sex.* Taylor &
Francis, 2011.

———. "Critically Queer." *GLQ: A Journal of Lesbian and Gay Studies* 1, no. 1
(1993): 17–32.

———. *Gender Trouble.* Routledge, 2002.

———. "Is Kinship Always Already Heterosexual?" *Differences: A Journal of
Feminist Cultural Studies* 13, no. 1 (2002): 14–44.

Buxton, Rebecca. "Justice in Waiting: The Harms and Wrongs of Temporary
Refugee Protection." *European Journal of Political Theory* 22, no. 1 (January
2023): 51–72.

———. "Respect and Asylum." *Journal of Applied Philosophy* 41, no. 5 (November 2024): 909–24.

———. "What Is Wrong with Persecution." *Journal of Social Philosophy* 54, no. 2
(2023): 201–17.

Buxton, Rebecca, and Matthew J. Gibney. "Must Refugees Be Grateful?"
Political Studies 73, no. 1 (March 2024): 287–304.

Buxton, Rebecca, and Lena Kainz. "All Refugees Want to Go Home, Right?"
Open Democracy, October 18, 2017. https://www.opendemocracy.net/en/all
-refugees-want-to-go-home-right/.

Calhoun, Cheshire. *Feminism, the Family, and the Politics of the Closet: Lesbian
and Gay Displacement.* Oxford University Press, 2000.

Camminga, B. "Competing Marginalities and Precarious Politics: A South
African Case Study of NGO Representation of Transgender Refugees." *Gender,
Place & Culture* 31, no. 9 (September 2024): 1293–310.

———. "Encamped Within a Camp: Transgender Refugees and Kakuma Refugee
Camp (Kenya)." In *Invisibility in African Displacements: From Structural*

Marginalization to Strategies of Avoidance, edited by Jesper Bjarnesen and Simon Turner. Zed Books, 2020.

———. *Transgender Refugees and the Imagined South Africa*. Palgrave MacMillan, 2019.

———. "Where are all the Intersex Asylum Seekers? Active Absenting or the Citational Chain of an Idea." *Feminist Formations* 36, no. 2 (2024): 189–202.

Camminga, B, and John Marnell. "Introduction." In *Queer and Trans African Mobilities: Migration, Asylum and Diaspora*, 1–25. Bloomsbury, 2022.

Campuzano, Giuseppe. "Contemporary Travesti Encounters with Gender and Sexuality in Latin America." *Development* 52, no. 1 (March 2009): 75–83.

Čapo, Jasna. "'Durable Solutions,' Transnationalism, and Homemaking Among Croatian and Bosnian Former Refugees." *Refuge: Canada's Journal on Refugees* 31, no. 1 (2015).

Cardozo, Fernanda. "Performatividades de gênero, performatividades de parentesco: Notas de um estudo com travestis e suas famílias na Cidade de Florianópolis/SC," 2012.

CARE International. "CARE Joins Statement Calling 'Humanitarian Corridor' Proposal Deeply Flawed." CARE, 2015. https://www.care.org/news-and-stories/press-releases/care-joins-statement-calling-humanitarian-corridor-proposal-deeply-flawed/.

Carens, Joseph. *The Ethics of Immigration*. Oxford University Press, 2013.

Carrillo, Héctor. "Sexual Migration, Cross-Cultural Sexual Encounters, and Sexual Health." *Sexuality Research & Social Policy* 1, no. 3 (September 2004): 58–70.

Caribe Afirmativo. "Informe alternativo sobre la situación de derechos humanos de personas LGBTI desplazadas forzadamente en Colombia presentado al ACNUR." Caribe Afirmativo, 2021. https://caribeafirmativo.lgbt/wp-content/uploads/2021/03/Informe-AcnurMar.pdf.

Carling, Jørgen. "Migration in the Age of Involuntary Immobility: Theoretical Reflections and Cape Verdean Experiences." *Journal of Ethnic and Migration Studies* 28, no. 1 (January 2002): 5–42. https://doi.org/10.1080/13691830120103912.

Cass, Vivienne C. "Homosexual Identity Formation: A Theoretical Model." *Journal of Homosexuality* 4, no. 3 (April 1979): 219–35. https://doi.org/10.1300/J082v04n03_01.

Castro Garcés, Ana Paula, and Pablo Castro Domingo. "La 72, Hogar-refugio para personas migrantes: La sociedad civil organizada en la atención de la agenda de los transmigrantes en la frontera México-Guatemala." *Revista pueblos y fronteras digital* 15 (2020): 33.

Center for American Progress. "ICE's Rejection of Its Own Rules Is Placing LGBT Immigrants at Severe Risk of Sexual Abuse." American Progress,

2018. https://www.americanprogress.org/article/ices-rejection-rules-placing
-lgbt-immigrants-severe-risk-sexual-abuse/.

Chaer, Nisrine. *Fadh, Sharaf* and Respectable Passing as New Frameworks for
Understanding Transmasculinity in the MENA Region: Case Studies of
Transmasculine Refugees in Lebanon. *Journal of Refugee Studies*, 2023.

Cherem, Max. "Refugee Rights: Against Expanding the Definition of a 'Refugee'
and Unilateral Protection Elsewhere." *Journal of Political Philosophy* 24,
no. 2 (2016): 183–205.

Chossière, Florent. "'I Knew About Political Asylum, but not About Asylum for
Gay People': How Queer Exiles Come to Apply (or not) for SOGI Asylum in
France," *Journal of Refugee Studies*, 2025.

Chimni, Bhupinder S. "The Birth of a 'Discipline': From Refugee to Forced
Migration Studies." *Journal of Refugee Studies* 22, no. 1 (2009): 11–29.

Choi, Venice. "Living Discreetly: A Catch 22 in Refugee Status Determinations
on the Basis of Sexual Orientation." *Brooklyn Journal of International Law*
(2010): 241–63.

Cockburn, Cynthia. "The Continuum of Violence: A Gender Perspective on War
and Peace." In *Sites of Violence*, 24–44. University of California Press, 2004.

Cole, Phil. "Framing the Refugee," E-International Relations, November 25,
2016. https://www.e-ir.info/2016/11/25/framing-the-refugee/.

Collins, Patricia Hill, *Black Feminist Thought: Knowledge, Consciousness, and
the Politics of Empowerment*, Routledge, 2000.

Columbia Law School. "Kimberlé Crenshaw on Intersectionality, More Than
Two Decades Later." June 28, 2017. https://www.law.columbia.edu/news
/archive/kimberle-crenshaw-intersectionality-more-two-decades-later.

Cooper-Cunningham, Dean. "Security, Sexuality, and the Gay Clown Putin
Meme: Queer Theory and International Responses to Russian Political
Homophobia." *Security Dialogue* 53, no. 4 (2022): 302–23.

Cordwell, Cailan. "Not Queer Enough: Challenges of LGBT Credibility and
Identity in US Asylum." Master diss., Arizona State University. ProQuest
30425647.

Cory, Connor. "The LGBTQ Asylum Seeker: Particular Social Groups and
Authentic Queer Identities." *Georgetown Journal of Gender and the Law* 20
(2018): 577–600.

Cragnolini, Giulia. "Lesbian, Gay, Bisexual and Transgender Refugees: Challenges in Refugee Status Determination and Living Conditions in Turkey." In
Fleeing Homophobia, edited by Thomas Spijkerboer, 116–38. Routledge, 2013.

Crawley, Heaven. "Saving Brown Women from Brown Men? 'Refugee Women,'
Gender and the Racialised Politics of Protection." *Refugee Survey Quarterly*
41, no. 3 (August 31, 2022): 355–80.

Crenshaw, Kimberlé. "Demarginalizing the Intersection of Race and Sex: A
Black Demarginalizing the Intersection of Race and Sex: A Black Feminist

Critique of Antidiscrimination Doctrine, Feminist Theory and Antiracist Politics." *University of Chicago Legal Forum* (1989): 139–67.

———. "Mapping the Margins: Identity Politics, Intersectionality, and Violence Against Women." *Stanford Law Review* 43, no. 6 (1991): 1241–99.

Danisi, Carmelo, Moira Dustin, Nuno Ferreira, and Nina Held, eds. *Queering Asylum in Europe.* IMISCOE Research Series. Springer International, 2021.

Darouiche, Cristian Alejandro. "Formas de sociabilidad y vínculos de parentesco entre mujeres trans que realizan sexo comercial en la Ciudad de Mar Del Plata." *Ponencia presentada en las XXVI jornadas de jóvenes investigadores AUGM, Mendoza,* 2018.

Davis, Angela. *Are Prisons Obsolete?* Seven Stories Press, 2003.

De Beauvoir, Simone. *The Second Sex.* Routledge, 2014.

De León, Jason. *The Land of Open Graves.* University of California Press, 2015.

Dehm, Sara, and Jenni Millbank. "Witchcraft Accusations as Gendered Persecution in Refugee Law." *Social & Legal Studies* 28, no. 2 (April 2019): 202–26.

Dhoest, Alexander. "Learning to Be Gay: LGBTQ Forced Migrant Identities and Narratives in Belgium." *Journal of Ethnic and Migration Studies* 45, no. 7 (2019): 1075–89.

Diamond, Lisa M. "Female Bisexuality from Adolescence to Adulthood: Results from a 10-Year Longitudinal Study." *Developmental Psychology* 44, no. 1 (2008): 5–14.

Dixson, Tina Nina. "Queer Refugees and Human Rights: On the Limits of Recognition." *Journal of Refugee Studies* (2024): 1–17.

Draper, Jamie. "Climate Change and Displacement: Towards a Pluralist Approach." *European Journal of Political Theory* 23, no. 1 (May 2022): 3–28.

———. "Domination and Misframing in the Refugee Regime." *Critical Review of International Social and Political Philosophy* 25 no. 7 (2020): 939–62.

———. "Justice and Internal Displacement." *Political Studies* 71, no. 2 (2021): 314–31.

Draper, Jamie, and David Owen. *The Political Philosophy of Internal Displacement.* Oxford University Press, 2024.

Doty, Roxanne. "Bare Life: Border-Crossing Deaths and Spaces of Moral Alibi." *Environment and Planning D: Society and Space* 29, no. 4 (2011): 599–612.

Doubossarskaia, Liza, Bridget Crawford, Azadeh Erfani, Heidi Altman, Becky Gendelman, Christina Asencio, and Robyn Barnard. *No Human Being Should Be Held There: The Mistreatment of LGBTQ and HIV-Positive People in U.S. Federal Immigration Jails.* Immigration Equality, National Immigrant Justice Center, and Human Rights First, June 2024. https://immigrationequality.org/no-human-being-should-be-held-there-the-mistreatment-of-lgbtq-and-hiv-positive-people-in-u-s-federal-immigration-jails-june-2024/.

Dummett, Michael. *On Immigration and Refugees.* Routledge, 2001.

Dustin, Moira. "Pathways to Refugee Protection for Women: Victims of Violence or Genuine Lesbians?" *Refugee Survey Quarterly* 41, no. 3 (September 2022): 393–419. https://doi.org/10.1093/rsq/hdac013.

Edelman, Lee. *No Future: Queer Theory and the Death Drive*. Duke University Press, 2004.

Edenborg, Emil. "Queer on the Home Front: Russian LGBTIQ Activism and Queer Security in the Wake of Russia's War in Ukraine." *Security Dialogue* 56, no. 2 (2025): 170–87.

El-Tayeb, Fatima. *European Others: Queering Ethnicity in Postnational Europe*. University of Minnesota Press, 2011.

Eng, David. "Out Here and Over There: Queerness and Diaspora in Asian American Studies." *Social Text* 52 no. 53 (1997): 31–52. https://www.jstor.org/stable/466733.

Engels, Friedrich. *The Origin of the Family, Private Property, and the State*. Hottingen-Zurich, 1884.

Enloe, Cynthia. "Womenandchildren: Propaganda Tools of Patriarchy." In *Mobilizing Democracy: Changing the U.S. Role in the Middle East*, edited by Greg Bates, 29–32. Common Courage Press, 1991.

Eskridge, William N., Jr. "Beyond Lesbian and Gay 'Families We Choose.'" In *Sex, Preference and Family: Essays on Law and Nature*, edited by David M. Estlund and Martha C. Nussbaum, 277–89. Oxford University Press, 1997.

Espinosa, Adriana, Kathryn Hampton, Nishin Nathwani, Kimahli Powell, Monique Sereneo, and Curtis Wackett. "Extrajudicial Border Enforcement Against LGBTIQ+ Asylum Seekers." *Journal of Refugee Studies* (June 2024). https://doi.org/10.1093/jrs/feae031.

European Union. "Directive 2011/95/EU of the European Parliament and of the Council of 13 December 2011 on Standards for the Qualification of Third-Country Nationals or Stateless Persons as Beneficiaries of International Protection, for a Uniform Status for Refugees or for Persons Eligible for Subsidiary Protection, and for the Content of the Protection Granted (Recast)." European Union: Council of the European Union, 2011.

European Union Agency for Asylum. *LGBTIQ Applicants in the EU+: Assessing Asylum Claims Based on Sexual Orientation, Gender Identity, Gender Expression, and Sex Characteristics*. European Union Agency for Asylum, 2023. https://euaa.europa.eu/sites/default/files/publications/2023-09/AR2023_factsheet20_LGBTIQ_applicants_EN.pdf.

Federici, Silvia. *Caliban and the Witch: Women, the Body and Primitive Accumulation*. Penguin Modern Classics, 2004.

Feinberg, Joel. *The Moral Limits of Criminal Law*, volume 1, *Harm to Others*. Oxford University Press, 1984.

Fernandez, Bina. "Queer Border Crossers: Pragmatic Complicities, Indiscretions and Subversions." In *Queering International Law Possibilities, Alliances, Complicities, Risks*, edited by Dianne Otto. Routledge, 2017.

Ferreira, Nuno. "Utterly Unbelievable: The Discourse of 'Fake' SOGI Asylum Claims as a Form of Epistemic Injustice." *International Journal of Refugee Law* 34, no. 4 (February 2023): 303–26. https://doi.org/10.1093/ijrleeac041.

Fiddian-Qasmiyeh, Elena. "Gender and Forced Migration," In *The Oxford Handbook of Refugee and Forced Migration Studies*, edited by Elena Fiddian-Qasmiyeh, Gil Loescher, Katy Long, and Nando Sigona, 395–408. Oxford University Press, 2014.

Fiddian-Qasmiyeh, Elena, Gil Loescher, Katy Long, Nando Sigona, and Guy S. Goodwin-Gill. "The International Law of Refugee Protection." In *The Oxford Handbook of Refugee and Forced Migration Studies*, edited by Elena Fiddian-Qasmiyeh, Gil Loescher, Katy Long, and Nando Sigona. Oxford University Press, 2014.

Fine, Sarah. "Refugees and the Limits of Political Philosophy." *Ethics & Global Politics* 13, no. 1 (January 2020): 6–20. https://doi.org/10.1080/16544951.2020.1735017.

FitzGerald, David Scott. *Refuge Beyond Reach*. Oxford University Press, 2019.

Flores, Adolfo. "LGBT Members of the Caravan Went Ahead First to Dodge Danger and Discrimination." Buzzfeed News, November 14, 2018. https://www.buzzfeednews.com/article/adolfoflores/this-is-how-lgbt-members-of-the-caravan-made-it-to-the.

Flyvbjerg, Ben, "Five Misunderstandings About Case-Study Research." *Qualitative Inquiry* 12, no. 2 (2006): 219–245.

Fogelman, Patricia. "Travestis migrantes, arte y religiosidad en la cultura queer de Buenos Aires." *Revista brasileira de história das religiões* XII, no. 36 (April 2020): 9–34.

Fogg-Davis, Hawley G. "Theorizing Black Lesbians Within Black Feminism: A Critique of Same-Race Street Harassment." *Politics & Gender* 2, no. 1 (2006): 57–76.

Fortier, Anne-Marie. "'Coming Home': Queer Migrations and Multiple Evocations of Home." *European Journal of Cultural Studies* 4, no. 4 (2001): 405–24.

———. "Re-Membering Places and the Performance of Belonging(s)." *Theory, Culture & Society* 16, no. 2 (1999): 41–64.

Freidan, Betty. *The Feminine Mystique*. Penguin Modern Classics, 1963.

Fry, Wendy, and Molly Hennessy-Fiske. "Vulnerable LGBTQ Migrants Left to Wait in Mexico." *The San Diego Union-Tribune*, November 3, 2019. https://www.sandiegouniontribune.com/news/border-baja-california/story/2019-11-03/trump-administration-leaving-vulnerable-lgbt-migrants-to-wait-in-mexico.

Fuentes, Lorena. "'The Garbage of Society': Disposable Women and the Socio-Spatial Scripts of Femicide in Guatemala." *Antipode* 52, no. 6 (November 2020): 1667–87. https://doi.org/10.1111/anti.12669.

Fullilove, M. T. "Psychiatric Implications of Displacement: Contributions from the Psychology of Place." *American Journal of Psychiatry* 153, no. 12 (1996): 1516–23.

Galop. "LGBT+ Experiences of Abuse from Family Members." Galop, April 1, 2022. https://galop.org.uk/resource/lgbt-experiences-of-abuse-from-family-members/.

García Rodríguez, Diego. "Critiquing Trends and Identifying Gaps in the Literature on LGBTQ Refugees and Asylum-Seekers." *Refugee Survey Quarterly* 42, no. 4 (2023): 518–41.

García Rodríguez, Diego, and Calogero Giametta. "Queer Asylum: Between Hostility and Incredibility." *International Migration* 62, no. 2 (2024): 232–36.

GATE. "Impact of Anti-Gender Opposition on TGD and LGBTQI Movements: Global Report." GATE, 2023.

Gay Express. "Gay Asylum Seekers Attacked In German Refugee Camp." July 19, 2017. https://gayexpress.co.nz/2017/07/gay-asylum-seekers-attacked-german-refugee-camp/.

Gerver, Mollie. "Must Refugees Return?" *Critical Review of International Social and Political Philosophy*, 24, no. 4 (2021): 415–36.

Giametta, Calogero. "Narrativising One's Sexuality/Gender: Neo-Liberal Humanitarianism and the Right of Asylum." In *Sexuality, Citizenship, and Belonging*, 55–72. Routledge, 2015.

Gibney, Matthew. "Forced Migration, Engineered Regionalism and Justice Between States." In *New Regionalism and Asylum Seekers*, edited by Susan Kneebone and Felicity Rawlings-Sanaei. Berhahn Books, 2007.

———. *The Ethics and Politics of Asylum: Liberal Democracy and the Response to Refugees*. Cambridge University Press, 2004.

———. "Should Citizenship Be Conditional? The Ethics of Denationalization." *The Journal of Politics* 75, no. 3 (2013): 646–58.

Gómez, María Mercedes. "Prejudice-Based Violence." In *Gender and Sexuality in Latin America: Cases and Decisions*, Ius Gentium: Comparative Perspectives on Law and Justice, edited by Cristina Motta and Macarena Saez, 279–323. Springer, 2013. https://doi.org/10.1007/978-94-007-6199-5_8.

González-López, Gloria. *Family Secrets: Stories of Incest and Sexual Violence in Mexico*, volume 1. New York University Press, 2015.

Goodin, Robert E. "Duties of Charity, Duties of Justice." *Political Studies* 65, no. 2 (June 1, 2017): 268–83. https://doi.org/10.1177/0032321716647402.

Goodwin-Gill, Guy, and Jane McAdam. *The Refugee in International Law*. Oxford University Press, 2007.

Gorman-Murray, Andrew. "Queer Politics at Home: Gay Men's Management of the Public/Private Boundary; Queer Politics at Home." *New Zealand Geographer* 68, no. 2 (August 2012): 111–20. https://doi.org/10.1111/j.1745-7939.2012.01225.x.

Government of Canada. "Temporary Pause on Intake of Refugee Sponsorship Applications from Groups of Five and Community Sponsors." Government of Canada, 2024. https://www.canada.ca/en/immigration-refugees-citizenship /news/notices/temporary-pause-intake-refugee-sponsorship-applications -groups-five-community-sponsors.html.

Graham, Thomas. "US Asylum Seekers in Despair After Trump Cancels CBP One App: 'Start from Zero Again.'" *The Guardian*, January 23, 2025. https:// www.theguardian.com/us-news/2025/jan/23/trump-cbp-one-app-cancelled -mexico.

Grahl-Madsen, Atle. *The Status of Refugees in International Law*, volume 1: *Refugee Character*. A. W. Sijthoff, 1966.

Grey, Rosemary, Dianne Otto, and Judith Gardam. "Gender-Based Persecution as a Crime Against Humanity: The Road Ahead." *Journal of International Criminal Justice* 17, no. 5 (2019): 957–79.

Grierson, Jamie. "Legal Action Launched Against Plan to House Asylum Seekers at Yarl's Wood." *The Guardian*, January 16, 2021. https://www.the guardian.com/uk-news/2021/jan/16/legal-action-launched-against-plan-to -house-asylum-seekers-at-yarls-wood.

Golightley, Sarah. "'I'm Gay! I'm Gay! I'm Gay! I'm a Homosexual!': Overt and Covert Conversion Therapy Practices in Therapeutic Boarding Schools." *The British Journal of Social Work* 53, no. 3 (April 2023): 1426–44. https://doi .org/10.1093/bjsw/bcad049.

Gündoğdu, Ayten. *Rightlessness in an Age of Rights*. Oxford University Press, 2015.

Gulik, Gauri van. "Fast-Tracked Unfairness: Detention and Denial of Women Asylum Seekers in the UK." Human Rights Watch, 2010.

Haas, Hein de. "Migration and Development in Southern Morocco." PhD diss., The Dutch Research School for International Development (CERES), 2003.

Haddad, Emma. *The Refugee in International Society: Between Sovereigns*. Cambridge University Press, 2008.

Haldeman, Douglas. "Sexual Orientation Conversion Therapy for Gay Men and Lesbians: A Scientific Study." In *Homosexuality: Research and Implications for Public Policy*, edited by John C. Gonsiorek and James D. Weinrich, 149–60. Sage, 1991. https://web.archive.org/web/20180206023332/http:// www.drdoughaldeman.com/doc/ScientificExamination.pdf.

Hartman, Saidiya, *Wayward Lives, Beautiful Experiments: Intimate Histories of Riotous Black Girls, Troublesome Women, and Queer Radicals*. W. W. Norton, 2019.

Harvey, Laura. *LGBTQI+ People's Experiences of Immigration Detention: A Pilot Study*. Rainbow Migration and University of Brighton. February 2023. https://www.rainbowmigration.org.uk/wp-content/uploads/2023/02 /LGBTQI-peoples-experiences-of-immigration-detention-Report.pdf.

Hathaway, James C. *The Rights of Refugees Under International Law*. Cambridge University Press, 2014. https://doi.org/10.1017/9781108863537.

Hegel, G. W. F. *Elements of the Philosophy of Right*, Cambridge Texts in the History of Political Thought, edited by Allen. W. Wood. Cambridge University Press (1991), 1820.

Held, Nina, and Aderonke Apata. "Intersections of Gender, Sexuality and 'Race' in Queer Asylum Claims." In *Research Handbook on Refugee and Asylum Policy*, edited by Jane Freedman and Glenda Santana de Andrade. Cheltenham: Edward Elgar Publishing, 2024.

Hill Collins, Patricia. *Black Feminist Thought: Knowledge, Consciousness and the Politics of Empowerment*. Routledge, 2000.

Honohan, Iseult. "Reconsidering the Claim to Family Reunification in Migration." *Political Studies* 57, no. 4 (2009): 768–87.

hooks, bell. "Homeplace: A Site of Resistance." In *Undoing Place? A Geographical Reader*, 33–38. Routledge, 1997.

Hopkinson, Rebecca A., Eva Keatley, Elizabeth Glaeser, Laura Erickson-Schroth, Omar Fattal, and Melba Nicholson Sullivan. "Persecution Experiences and Mental Health of LGBT Asylum Seekers." *Journal of Homosexuality* 64, no. 12 (2017): 1650–66. https://doi.org/10.1080/00918369.2016.1253392.

Human Dignity Trust. "Map of Criminalization." 2024. https://www.humandignitytrust.org/lgbt-the-law/map-of-criminalisation.

———. "Nigeria: Country Profile." 2025. https://www.humandignitytrust.org/country-profile/nigeria/.

Human Rights Watch. *'Even If You Go to the Skies, We'll Find You': LGBT People in Afghanistan After the Taliban Takeover*. 2022. https://www.hrw.org/report/2022/01/26/even-if-you-go-skies-well-find-you/lgbt-people-afghanistan-after-taliban-takeover.

———. "HIV/AIDS Services for Immigrants Detained by the United States." December 5, 2007. https://www.hrw.org/report/2007/12/05/chronic-indifference/hiv/aids-services-immigrants-detained-united-states.

———. "'You Feel Like Your Life Is Over': Abusive Practices at Three Florida Immigration Detention Centers Since January 2025." July 21, 2025. https://www.hrw.org/report/2025/07/21/you-feel-like-your-life-is-over/abusive-practices-at-three-florida-immigration.

Hutchings, Kimberley. "Cosmopolitan Just War and Coloniality." In *Empire, Race and Global Justice*, edited by Duncan Bell, 211–27. Cambridge University Press, 2019. https://doi.org/10.1017/9781108576307.010.

Immigration Equality, "New Summary Report Details How Trump Administration Policies Endanger LGBTQI+ People at Risk of Persecution." Immigration Equality, June 5, 2025. https://immigrationequality.org/press/press-releases-2/new-summary-report-details-how-trump-administration-policies-endanger-lgbtqi-people-at-risk-of-persecution/.

Inter-American Court of Human Rights. "Advisory Opinion on Gender Identity, Equality, and Non-Discrimination of Same-Sex Couples, (2017), OC-24 / 17." 2017. https://www.escr-net.org/caselaw/2018/advisory-opinion-gender -identity-equality-and-non-discrimination-same-sex-couples-2017.

International Commission of Jurists. "Yogyakarta Principles: Principles on the Application of International Human Rights Law in Relation to Sexual Orientation and Gender Identity." 2007. https://www.refworld.org/legal /resolution/icjurists/2007/en/58135.

International Committee of the Red Cross. "How Humanitarian Corridors Work to Help People in Conflict Zones." 2022. https://www.icrc.org/en/document /how-humanitarian-corridors-work.

International Lesbian, Gay, Bisexual, Trans and Intersex Association (ILGA World). "In Relation to Forced Displacement: Submission to the UN Independent Expert on Protection Against Violence and Discrimination Based on Sexual Orientation and Gender Identity." March 2025. https://ilga .org/resources/submissions-special-procedures-thematic-reports/.

International Rescue Committee. "What Is the EU-Turkey Deal?" March 18, 2022. https://eu.rescue.org/article/what-eu-turkey-deal.

International Organization for Migration (IOM). "IOM Missing Migrants." 2024. https://missingmigrants.iom.int/region/mediterranean.

———. "Missing Migrants Project." 2021. https://missingmigrants.iom.int/.

International Organization for Migration (IOM) and UN Migration. "Update on IOM Operations Amid Budget Cuts." IOM, UN Migration, March 2025. https://www.iom.int/news/update-iom-operations-amid-budget-cuts.

Irigaray, Luce. *An Ethics of Sexual Difference*. Cornell University Press, 1993.

Isaack, Wendy. "'No Choice But to Deny Who I Am': Violence and Discrimina- tion Against LGBT People in Ghana." Human Rights Watch, 2018.

Jansen, Sabine. "Introduction." In *Fleeing Homophobia*, edited by Thomas Spijkerboer, 19–49. Routledge, 2013.

Johnson, Julia. "CBS Blasted on Twitter for Including Transgender Rights in Ukrainian War Coverage." *Washington Examiner*, March 22, 2021. https:// www.washingtonexaminer.com/news/cbs-blasted-on-twitter-for-including -transgender-rights-in-ukrainian-war-coverage.

Johnston, David. "Ruling Backs Homosexuals on Asylum." *The New York Times*, June 17, 1994. https://www.nytimes.com/1994/06/17/us/ruling-backs -homosexuals-on-asylum.html.

Jones, Owen. "Can't Choose Your Family at Christmas? Those Rejected by Their Loved Ones Would Disagree." *The Guardian*, December 12, 2022. https:// www.theguardian.com/commentisfree/2022/dec/22/family-christmas-lgbtq -relatives-friends.

Jones, Tiffany, Timothy W. Jones, Jennifer Power, Maria Pallotta-Chiarolli, and Nathan Despott. "Mis-Education of Australian Youth: Exposure to

LGBTQA+ Conversion Ideology and Practices." *Sex Education* 22, no. 5 (2021): 595–610.

Jordan, Sharalyn R. "Un/Convention(al) Refugees: Contextualizing the Accounts of Refugees Facing Homophobic or Transphobic Persecution." *Refuge* 26, no. 2 (2011): 165–82.

Judicial Division of the Council of State. Afdeling rechtspraak van de Raad van State, Rechtspraak Vreemdelingenrecht Gids Vreemdelingenrecht (oud) D12-51. August 13, 1981.

Judge, Melanie. *Blackwashing Homophobia: Violence and the Politics of Sexuality, Gender and Race.* Routledge, 2017.

Juss, Satvinder. "Sexual Orientation and the Sexualisation of Refugee Law." *International Journal on Minority and Group Rights* 22, no. 1 (2015): 128–53.

Kareff, Michael. "Constructing Sexuality and Gender Identity for Asylum Through a Western Gaze: The Oversimplification of Global Sexual and Gender Variation and Its Practical Effect on LGBT Asylum Determinations." *Georgetown: Immigration Law Journal* 35 (2020): 615-630.

Khader, Serene. *Decolonizing Universalism: A Transnational Feminist Ethic.* Oxford University Press, 2019.

Kilbride, Erin. "'This Is Why We Became Activists': Violence Against Lesbian, Bisexual, and Queer Woman and Non-Binary People." Human Rights Watch, February 14, 2023. https://www.hrw.org/report/2023/02/14/why-we-became -activists/violence-against-lesbian-bisexual-and-queer-women-and-non.

Kukathas, Chandran. "Are Refugees Special?" In *Migration and Political Theory: The Ethics of Movement and Membership*, ed. Sarah Fine and Lea Ypi, 249–68. Oxford University Press, 2016.

Kyriakides, Christopher, Lubna Bajjali, Arthur McLuhan, and Karen Anderson. "Beyond Refuge: Contested Orientalism and Persons of Self-Rescue." *Canadian Ethnic Studies* 50, no. 2 (2018): 59–78.

Lambert, Hélène. "The Conceptualisation of 'Persecution' by the House of Lords: Horvath v. Secretary of State for the Home Department." *International Journal of Refugee Law* 13, no. 1 (2001): 16–31.

Laughland, Oliver. "Gay Asylum Seekers on Manus Island Write of Fear of Persecution in PNG." *The Guardian*, September 24, 2014. https://www.the guardian.com/world/2014/sep/24/gay-asylum-seekers-manus-island-fear -persecution-png.

Lê Espiritu, Yên, Lan Duong, Ma Vang, Victor Bascara, Khatharya Um, Lila Sharif, and Nigel Hatton. *Departures: An Introduction to Critical Refugee Studies.* University of California Press, 2022.

Lenard, Patti Tamara. *Democracy and Exclusion.* Oxford University Press, 2023.

Lewis, Rachel. "Deportable Subjects: Lesbians and Political Asylum." *Feminist Formations* 25, no. 2 (2013): 174–94. https://doi.org/10.1353/ff.2013.0027.

Liinason, Mia. "Challenging the Visibility Paradigm: Tracing Ambivalences in Lesbian Migrant Women's Negotiations of Sexual Identity." *Journal of Lesbian Studies* 24, no. 2 (2020): 110–25.

Llewellyn, Cheryl. "Erasing Violence: Lesbian Women Asylum Applicants in the United States." *Journal of Lesbian Studies* 25, no. 4 (2021): 339–55.

———. "Homonationalism and Sexual Orientation-Based Asylum Cases in the United States." *Sexualities*, 20, no. 5–6 (2016), 682–98.

Long, Katy. "Permanent Crises? Unlocking the Protracted Displacement of Refugees and Internally Displaced Persons." Refuge Studies Centre, 2011.

———. *The Point of No Return*. Oxford University Press, 2013.

Love, Heather. "Queer." *Transgender Studies Quarterly* 1, no. 1–2 (2014): 172–76.

Luibhéid, Eithne. *Entry Denied: Controlling Sexuality at the Border*. University of Minnesota Press, 2002.

———. "Migrant and Refugee Lesbians: Lives That Resist the Telling," *Journal of Lesbian Studies* 24, no. 2 (April 2020): 57–76.

———. "QUEER/MIGRATION: An Unruly Body of Scholarship." *GLQ: A Journal of Lesbian and Gay Studies* 14, no. 2–3 (January 1, 2008): 169–90.

———. "Treated Neither with Respect nor with Dignity: Contextualizing Queer and Trans Migrant 'Illegalization' in Detention and Deportation." In *Queer and Trans Migrations: Dynamics of Illegalization, Detention, and Deportation*, edited by Eithne Luidhéid and Karma Chávez. University of Illinois Press, 2020.

Lubkemann, Stephen C. "Migratory Coping in Wartime Mozambique: An Anthropology of Violence and Displacement in 'Fragmented Wars.'" *Journal of Peace Research* 42, no. 4 (July 2005): 493–508. https://doi.org/10.1177/0022 343305054093.

Maiani, Francesco. "The Concept of 'Persecution' in Refugee Law: Indeterminacy, Context-Sensitivity, and the Quest for a Principled Approach." *Les Dossiers du Grihl*, 2010. http://journals.openedition.org/dossiersgrihl/3896.

Mainwaring, Cetta, and Stephanie J. Silverman. "Detention-as-Spectacle." *International Political Sociology* 11, no. 1 (March 2017): 21–38. https://doi.org /10.1093/ips/olw016.

Majumdar, Roshni. "Germany Amends Asylum Rules in Favor of Queer Refugees." Deutsche Welle, October 1, 2022. https://www.dw.com/en /germany-amends-asylum-rules-in-favor-of-queer-refugees/a-63303955.

Malkki, Liisa. *Purity and Exile: Violence, Memory, and National Cosmology among Hutu Refugees in Tanzania*. Chicago: Chicago University Press, 1995.

Malkki, Liisa H. "Refugees and Exile: From 'Refugee Studies' to the National Order of Things." *Annual Review of Anthropology* 24 (1995): 495–523.

Mallett, Shelley. "Understanding Home: A Critical Review of the Literature." *The Sociological Review* 52, no. 1 (2004): 62–89. https://doi.org/10.1111/j.1467 -954X.2004.00442.x.

Mandivavarira Mudarikwa, Miriam Gleckman-Krut, Amy-Leigh Payne, B Camminga, and John Marnell. *LGBTI+ Asylum Seekers in South Africa: A Review of Refugee Status Denials Involving Sexual Orientation and Gender Identity*. Lawyers for Human Rights, African Human Rights Network, and University of the Witwatersrand African Centre for Migration & Society. April 2021. https://lrc.org.za/wp-content/uploads/LGBTI-ASYLUM -REPORT-RFS.pdf.

Manne, Kate. *Down Girl: The Logic of Misogyny*. Oxford University Press, 2018.

Marnell, John. "Telling a Different Story: On the Politics of Representing African LGBTQ Migrants, Refugees and Asylum Seekers." In *Queer and Trans African Mobilities: Migration, Asylum and Diaspora*, edited by Teresa de Lauretis, B Camminga, and John Marnell. Bloomsbury Academic, 2022.

Marnell, John, B Camminga, Barbara Bompani, and Kamau Wairuri, eds. *East African Queer and Trans Displacements*. Bloomsbury Academic, 2025.

Marr, Rhuaridh. "Australia Asked Gay Asylum Seekers If They 'Drink Cum,' Then Tried to Suppress the Interviews." *Metro Weekly*, July 16, 2019. https:// www.metroweekly.com/2019/07/australia-asked-gay-asylum-seekers-if-they -liked-to-drink-cum-then-tried-to-suppress-the-interview/.

Martin, Biddy, and Chandra Talpade Mohanty. "Feminist Politics: What's Home Got to Do with It?" In *Feminist Studies/Critical Studies*, edited by Teresa de Laurentis, 191–212. Springer, 1986.

Martínez, Juliana, and Salvador Vidal-Ortiz, eds. *Traver el Saber*. Editorial de la Universidad Nacional de la Plata (EDULP), 2018.

Massey, Doreen. *Space, Place, and Gender*. University of Minnesota Press, 1994.

Mayblin, Lucy. *Asylum After Empire: Colonial Legacies in the Politics of Asylum Seeking*. Rowman & Littlefield, 2017.

Mayblin, Lucy, and Joe Turner. *Migration Studies and Colonialism*. John Wiley, 2020.

Mbembe, Achille. "Necropolitics." *Public Culture* 15, no. 1 (2003): 11–40.

McAdam, Jane. "Rethinking the Origins of 'Persecution' in Refugee Law." *International Journal of Refugee Law* 25, no. 4 (December 2013): 667–92. https://doi.org/10.1093/ijrl/eet048.

McCullouch, Gerald, dir. *Stuck in Greece: An LGBT Refugee Crisis*, 2022. Hard G Productions, 2023. www.stuckingreecethefilm.com.

McDonnell, Emilie. *Protecting the Right to Leave in an Era of Externalised Migration Control*. Bloomsbury Publishing, 2026 (forthcoming).

McKnight, Pip, Jenny Phillimore, and Leila Zadeh. "Forced Migration and Sexual and Gender-Based Violence in Queer Communities: UK Findings from the SEREDA Project." Institute for Research Into Superdiversity, University of Birmingham, June 2024. https://www.birmingham.ac.uk /documents/college-social-sciences/social-policy/publications/queer-sereda -web.pdf.

McKinnon, Sara L. *Gendered Asylum: Race and Violence in US Law and Politics*. University of Illinois Press, 2016.

McNamarah, Chan Tov. "Silent, Spoken, Written, and Enforced: The Role of Law in the Construction of the Post-Colonial Queerphobic State." *Cornell International Law Journal* 51, no. 2 (2018): 495–532.

Médecins Sans Frontières. "MSF Statement on June 2022 Deadline to Close Refugee Camps in Kenya." ReliefWeb, April 2021. https://reliefweb.int/report /kenya/msf-statement-june-2022-deadline-close-refugee-camps-kenya.

Michelis, Ilaria. "Later Is a Cis-Hetero Patriarchal Time Zone: Narratives of Resistance to LGBTQI+ Inclusion Amongst Humanitarian Practitioners." *Journal of Refugee Studies* (October 2023). https://doi.org/10.093/jrs/fead072.

Micro Rainbow. "Held Back: Poverty of LGBTQI Refugees in the UK; An Insight into the Lived Experiences of LGBTQI Refugees in the UK." Micro Rainbow, 2023.

Migrant Watch. "Nearly 90% of Those Crossing in Boats from Safe Countries Are Male." Migrant Watch, 2022. https://www.migrationwatchuk.org/press -release/668/nearly-90-of-those-crossing-in-boats-from-safe-countries -are-male.

Millbank, Jenni. "From Discretion to Disbelief: Recent Trends in Refugee Determinations on the Basis of Sexual Orientation in Australia and the United Kingdom." *The International Journal of Human Rights* 13, no. 2 (2009): 391–414.

———. "Sexual Orientation and Refugee Status Determination over the Past 20 Years." *Fleeing Homophobia: Sexual Orientation, Gender Identity and Asylum* 32 (2013).

Millbank, Jenni and Anthea Vogl. "Adjudicating Fear of Witchcraft Claims in Refugee Law." *Journal of Law and Society* 45, no. 3 (2018): 370–97.

Miller, Anna. "How the U.S. Immigration System Nearly Tore This LGBTQ Couple Apart." *The Week*, January 1, 2020. https://theweek.com/articles /884955/how-immigration-system-nearly-tore-lgbtq-couple-apart.

Miller, David. "Our Responsibility to Refugees." In Proceedings of the 2018 ZiF Workshop "Studying Migration Policies at the Interface between Empirical Research and Normative Analysis." ULB Münster, edited by Matthias Hoesch and Lena Laube, 2018. https://doi.org/10.17879/95189441435.

———. "Selecting Refugees." In *The Political Philosophy of Refuge*, edited by Christine Straehle and David Miller, 97–113. Cambridge University Press, 2019. https://www.cambridge.org/core/books/political-philosophy-of-refuge /selecting-refugees/C28BD2C94ACE32D7FD7F1AEF8B3BC6F4.

———. *Strangers in Our Midst: The Political Philosophy of Immigration*. Harvard University Press, 2016.

Minero, Laura P., Sergio Domínguez Jr., Stephanie L. Budge, and Bamby Salcedo. "Latinx Trans Immigrants' Survival of Torture in U.S. Detention:

A Qualitative Investigation of the Psychological Impact of Abuse and Mistreatment." *International Journal of Transgender Health* 23, no. 1–2: (2021) 36–59.

Mole, Richard C. M. *Queer Migration and Asylum in Europe*. UCL Press, 2021.

Moore, Hester. "'The Atmosphere Is Oppressive': Investigating the Intersection
of Violence with the Cisgender Lesbian, Bisexual, and Queer Women Refugee
Community in Nairobi, Kenya." In *LGBTI Asylum Seekers and Refugees from
a Legal and Political Perspective*, edited by Arzu Güler, Maryna Shevtsova,
and Denince Venturi. Springer International Publishing, 2019.

Morgan, Deborah A. "Not Gay Enough for the Government: Racial and Sexual
Stereotypes in Sexual Orientation Asylum Cases." *Law & Sexuality:
A Review of Lesbian, Gay, Bisexual & Transgender Legal Issues* 15 (2006):
135–61.

Morison, Tracy, Ingrid Lynch, and Vasu Reddy. *Queer Kinship: South African
Perspectives on the Sexual Politics of Family-Making and Belonging*.
Routledge, 2019.

Morris, Carl. "Lesbian Asylum Seekers Asked Whether They Use Sex Toys."
Metro, April 4, 2013. https://metro.co.uk/2013/04/04/lesbian-asylum-seekers
-asked-have-you-read-oscar-wilde-do-you-use-sex-toys-where-do-you-go
-clubbing-3582916/.

Morris, Julia Caroline. *Asylum and Extraction in the Republic of Nauru*. Cornell
University Press, 2023.

Muñoz, José Esteban, Joshua Chambers-Letson, Tavia Nyong'o, and Ann
Pellegrini. *Cruising Utopia: The Then and There of Queer Futurity*. New
York University Press, 2019.

Murib, Zein. *Terms of Exclusion: Rightful Citizenship Claims and the Construction of LGBT Political Identity*. Oxford University Press, 2023.

Murray, David. "Real Queer: 'Authentic' LGBT Refugee Claimants and Homonationalism in the Canadian Refugee System." *Anthropologica* 56, no. 1
(2014): 21–32.

———. "The (Not So) Straight Story: Queering Migration Narratives of Sexual
Orientation and Gendered Identity Refugee Claimants." *Sexualities* 17, no. 4
(June 2014): 451–71.

Nayak, Meghana. *Who Is Worthy of Protection?: Gender-Based Asylum and
US Immigration Politics*. Oxford University Press, 2015.

National Center for Lesbian Rights (NCLR). *The Challenges to Successful
Lesbian Asylum Claims*. NCLR, 2006.

Ndiritu, John. *The Challenges Facing LGBTQI+ Refugees in Kakuma Refugee
Camp, Kenya*. Organization for Refuge, Asylum and Migration (ORAM) and
Rainbow Railroad, 2021.

Neilson, Victoria. "Homosexual or Female-Applying Gender-Based Asylum
Jurisprudence to Lesbian Asylum Claims." *Stanford Law & Policy Review* 16
(2005): 417–42.

Nussbaum, Martha. "Human Capabilities, Female Human Beings." In *Women, Culture, and Development: A Study of Human Capabilities*, edited by Martha Nussbaum and Jonathan Glover, 61–104. Oxford University Press, 1995.

Oberman, Kieran. "Enough Spurious Distinctions: Refugees Are Just People in Need of Refuge." *Law and Philosophy*, January 7, 2025.

Orchard, Phil. "Protection of Internally Displaced Persons: Soft Law as a Norm-Generating Mechanism." *Review of International Studies* 36, no. 2 (2010): 281–303.

Ortiga, Yasmin Y., and Romeo Luis A. Macabasag. "Understanding International Immobility Through Internal Migration: 'Left Behind' Nurses in the Philippines." *International Migration Review* 55, no. 2 (June 2021): 460–81.

OutRight International. "Vulnerability Amplified: The Impact of the COVID-19 Pandemic on LGBTIQ People." OutRight International, 2020.

OutRight International, and Edge Effect. "'They Know What We Don't': Meaningful Inclusion of LGBTIQ People in Humanitarian Action." OutRight International, 2024.

Owen, David. "Differentiating Refugees: Asylum, Sanctuary and Refuge." In *The Political Philosophy of Refuge*, edited by David Miller and Christine Straehle, 19–38. Cambridge: Cambridge University Press, 2020.

———. *What Do We Owe to Refugees?* Polity, 2020.

Owens, Patricia. "Reclaiming 'Bare Life'?: Against Agamben on Refugees." *International Relations* 23, no. 4 (2009): 567–82.

Parekh, Serena. "Beyond the Ethics of Admission: Stateless People, Refugee Camps and Moral Obligations." *Philosophy & Social Criticism* 40, no. 7 (August 2013): 645–63. https://doi.org/10.1177/0191453713498254.

———. *No Refuge: Ethics and the Global Refugee Crisis*. Oxford University Press, 2020.

Paddison, Laura and Nina Lakhani, "Honduran State Responsible for Trans Woman's Murder–Court." *The Guardian*, June 29, 2021. https://www.theguardian.com/global-development/2021/jun/29/honduran-state-responsible-for-trans-womans-court.

Pentreath, Rosie, host. *OUTCast* podcast, season 1, episode 3, "Meet the Gay Nigerian Refugee Who Sought Asylum in the UK to Escape Death Threats, Conversion Therapy and Violence." October 11, 2021. https://outcastpod.com/2021/10/11/gay-nigerian-refugee-asylum-uk-after-conversion-therapy/.

Phillips, Tom, and Clavel Rangel. "'He Is Not a Gang Member': Outrage as US Deports Makeup Artist to El Salvador Prison for Crown Tattoos." *The Guardian*, April 1, 2025. https://www.theguardian.com/us-news/2025/apr/01/its-a-tradition-outrage-in-venezuela-as-us-deports-makeup-artist-for-religious-tattoos.

Physicians for Human Rights. "Endless Nightmare: Torture and Inhuman Treatment in Solitary Confinement in U.S. Immigration Detention." Physicians for Human Rights, 2024.

Pincock, K. "UNHCR and LGBTI Refugees in Kenya: The Limits of 'Protection.'" *Disasters* 45, no. 4 (2021): 844–64.

Polgreen, Lydia, and Vishakha Darbha. "An Interview with Sarah Schulman: 'They're Coming After All of Us. So You Might as Well Tell the Truth.'" *The New York Times*, April 10, 2025. https://www.nytimes.com/2025/04/10/opinion/sarah-schulman-solidarity.html.

Polzer Ngwato, Tara. "Negotiating Belonging: The Integration of Mozambican Refugees in South Africa." PhD diss., London School of Economics, 2011.

Prearo, Massimo. "The Moral Politics of LGBTI Asylum: How the State Deals with the SOGI Framework." *Journal of Refugee Studies* 34, no. 2 (July 2020): 1277–2509. https://doi.org/10.1093/jrs/feaa047.

Price, Matthew. *Rethinking Asylum: History, Purpose, and Limits*. Cambridge University Press, 2009.

Puar, Jasbir. *Terrorist Assemblages: Homonationalism in Queer Times*. Duke University Press, 2007.

Rahman, Momin. "Queer as Intersectionality: Theorizing Gay Muslim Identities." *Sociology* 44, no. 5 (October 1, 2010): 944–61. https://doi.org/10.1177/0038038510375733.

Rahul Rao. *Out of Time: The Queer Politics of Postcoloniality*. Oxford University Press, 2020.

Rainbow Migration. "Rainbow Migration Submission to the UN Independent Expert on Protection Against Violence and Discrimination Based on Sexual Orientation and Gender Identity. London: Rainbow Migration." Rainbow Migration, 2025. https://www.rainbowmigration.org.uk/publications/rainbow-migration-submission-to-the-un-independent-expert-on-protection-against-violence-and-discrimination-based-on-sogi/.

———. "No Pride in Detention." Rainbow Migration, 2025. https://www.rainbowmigration.org.uk/no-pride-in-detention.

Rainbow Railroad. *2020 Annual Report*. Rainbow Railroad, 2021. https://www.rainbowrailroad.org/2020-annual-report.

———. *2023 Annual Report: Understanding the State of Global LGBTQI+ Persecution*. Rainbow Railroad, 2024. https://www.rainbowrailroad.org/the-latest/annualreport.

———. *Protection Against Violence and Discrimination Based on Sexual Orientation and Gender Identity in Relation to Forced Displacement, Submission to the UN Independent Expert on SOGI*. March 2025. https://www.rainbowrailroad.org/wp-content/uploads/2025/03/RR_SOGI-Report.pdf.

———. "Rainbow Railroad and ORAM Release Report on LGBTQI+ Refugees in Kakuma Refugee Camp, Kenya." Rainbow Railroad, 2021. https://www.rainbowrailroad.org/news/rainbow-railroad-and-oram-release-report-on-lgbtqi-refugees-in-kakuma-refugee-camp-kenya.

Red Regional por la Movilidad Humana LGBTIQ+ de Latinoamérica y el Caribe. "Llamado a aportes: Protección contra la violencia y la discriminación por orientación sexual e identidad de género en relación con el desplazamiento forzado." Internal submission to the Office of the UN High Commissioner for Human Rights, 2024.

Redazione. "Aggiornata la lista dei 'paesi sicuri.'" *Il Grande Colibrì*, May 12, 2024. https://www.ilgrandecolibri.com/lista-paesi-sicuri/.

Rehaag, Sean. "Patrolling the Borders of Sexual Orientation: Bisexual Refugee Claims in Canada." *McGill Law Journal* 53 (2008).

Reid, Graeme, and Samuel Ritholtz. "A Queer Approach to Understanding LGBT Vulnerability During the COVID-19 Pandemic." *Politics & Gender* 16, no. 4 (2020): 1101–9. https://doi.org/10.1017/S1743923X20000707.

Rempell, Scott. "Defining Persecution." *Utah Law Review* 2013, no. 1 (2013): 283–344.

Ritholtz, Samuel. "Brutality on Display: Media Coverage and the Spectacle of Anti-LGBTQ Violence in the Colombian Civil War." *Third World Quarterly* 45, no. 5 (2024): 903–25.

———. "Civil War and the Politics of Difference: Paramilitary Violence Against LGBT People in Colombia." PhD diss., Refugee Studies Centre, University of Oxford, 2022.

———. "Is Queer-and-Trans Youth Homelessness a Form of Displacement? A Queer Epistemological Review of Refugee Studies' Theoretical Borders." *Ethnic and Racial Studies* 46, no. 9 (2022): 1–23. https://doi.org/10.1080/01419870.2022.2099747.

Ritholtz, Samuel, and Rebecca Buxton. "Queer Kinship and the Rights of Refugee Families." *Migration Studies* 9, no. 3 (September 2021): 1075–95.

———. "Sanctuary After Asylum: Addressing a Gap in the Political Theory of Refuge." *American Political Science Review* 117, no. 3 (2023): 1166–71.

Ritholtz, Samuel, and Miguel Mesquita. "The Transnational Force of Anti-LGBT+ Politics in Latin America." In *The Right against Rights in Latin America*, edited by Leigh A. Payne, Julia Zulver, and Simón Escoffier, 98–111. Oxford University Press, 2023.

Ritholtz, Samuel, and Margaret Renata Neil. "LGBTQ+ Parents Are Being Removed from Their Children's Birth Certificates in Italy: Here's What's Behind This Disturbing Trend." *The Conversation*, June 28, 2023. https://theconversation.com/lgbtq-parents-are-being-removed-from-their-childrens-birth-certificates-in-italy-heres-whats-behind-this-disturbing-trend-208241.

Robertson, Dylan. "Kenya Blocks LGBTQ+ Refugees from Resettling in Canada." 76Crimes, 2024. https://76crimes.com/2024/12/11/kenya-blocks-lgbtq-refugees-canada/.

Robinson, Brandon Andrew. "Heteronormativity and Homonormativity." In *The Wiley Blackwell Encyclopedia of Gender and Sexuality Studies*. Wiley, 2016, 1–3.

———. *Coming Out to the Streets: LGBTQ Youth Experiencing Homelessness*. University of California Press, 2020.

Rodriguez-Pena, Naiara. "Moving across (Im)Mobility Categories: The Importance of Values, Family and Adaptation for Migration." *Journal of Ethnic and Migration Studies* 49, no. 3 (May 2022): 1–18. https://doi.org/10.1080/1369183X.2022.2064839.

Roth, Danielle, Alexandra Blackwell, Mark Canavera, and Kathryn Falb. "Cycles of Displacement: Understanding Exclusion, Discrimination and Violence Against LGBTQI People in Humanitarian Contexts." International Rescue Committee, 2021.

Ryan, Hannah. "These Are The 'Inappropriate' Questions Asylum-Seekers Were Asked By Australia To Prove They Were Gay." *BuzzFeed*, January 8, 2019. https://www.buzzfeed.com/hannahryan/two-men-seeking-australias-protection-from-lgbt-persecution.

Saeed, Adeel. "Pakistan's Trans Community Is Especially Vulnerable to Climate Crises." *Global Health Now* (blog), September 27, 2024. https://globalhealthnow.org/2024-09/pakistans-trans-community-especially-vulnerable-climate-crises.

Sager, Alex. "Methodological Nationalism, Migration and Political Theory." *Political Studies* 64, no. 1 (October 28, 2014): 42–59. https://doi.org/10.1111/1467-9248.12167.

Sandven, Hallvard. "The Practice and Legitimacy of Border Control." *American Journal of Political Science* 68, no. 2 (August 2022). https://doi.org/10.1111/ajps.12736.

Sandven, Hallvard, and Antoinette Scherz. "Rescue Missions in the Mediterranean and the Legitimacy of the EU's Border Regime." *Res Publica*, April 1, 2022. https://doi.org/10.1007/s11158-022-09550-7.

Sangiovanni, Andrea, and Juri Viehoff. "Solidarity in Social and Political Philosophy." *The Stanford Encyclopedia of Philosophy*, 2023. https://plato.stanford.edu/entries/solidarity/.

Sari, Elif. "Lesbian Refugees in Transit: The Making of Authenticity and Legitimacy in Turkey." *Journal of Lesbian Studies* 24, no. 2 (2020): 140–58.

———. "Unsafe Present, Uncertain Futures: LGBTI Asylum in Turkey." In *Queer and Trans Migrations: Dynamics of Illegalization, Detention, and Deportation*, edited by Eithne Luibhéid and Karma R. Chávez. University of Illinois Press, 2020.

Sarup, Madan. "Home and Identity." In *Traveller's Tales: Narratives of Home and Displacement*, ed. Jon Bird, Barry Curtis, Melinda Mash, Tim Putnam, George Robertson, and Lisa Tickner. Routledge, 1994.

Scalettaris, Giulia. "Refugees and Mobility." *Forced Migration Review* 33 (2009).

Schewel, Kerilyn. "Understanding Immobility: Moving Beyond the Mobility Bias in Migration Studies." *International Migration Review* 54, no. 2 (June 2020): 328–55. https://doi.org/10.1177/0197918319831952.

Schneider, David Murray, and Raymond Thomas Smith. *Class Differences in American Kinship*. University Microfilms International, 1978.

Schulman, Sarah. *Let the Record Show: A Political History of ACT UP New York, 1987–1993*. 1st edition. Farrar, Straus and Giroux, 2021.

———. *The Fantasy and Necessity of Solidarity*. Thesis, 2025.

———. *Ties That Bind: Familial Homophobia and Its Consequences*. The New Press, 2009.

Schweiger, Gottfried. "Should States Prioritize Child Refugees?" *Ethics & Global Politics* 12, no. 2 (December 13, 2019): 46–61. https://doi.org/10.1080 /16544951.2019.1649958.

Scicchitano, Dominic. "The 'Real' Chechen Man: Conceptions of Religion, Nature, and Gender and the Persecution of Sexual Minorities in Postwar Chechnya." *Journal of Homosexuality* 68, no. 9 (July 2021): 1545–62.

Scuzarello, Esteban Octavio. "Adjudicando protección: el proceso de refugio para personas LGBTQI+ en Sudamérica," *Relaciones Internacionales* 58 (2025): 58–78.

Seawright, Jason and John Gerring, "Case Selection Techniques in Case Study Research: A Menu of Qualitative and Quantitative Options." *Political Research Quarterly* 61, no. 2 (2008): 294–308.

Sedgwick, Eve Kosofsky. *Epistemology of the Closet*. University of California Press, 2008.

———. "Queer and Now." In *The Routledge Queer Studies Reader*, edited by Donald E. Hall and Annamarie Jagose, 3–17. Routledge, 2012.

Serrano-Amaya, José Fernando. *Homophobic Violence in Armed Conflict and Political Transition*. Springer, 2017.

Serrano-Amaya, José Fernando. "La tormenta perfecta: Ideología de género y articulación de públicos." *Sexualidad, Salud y Sociedad* (Rio de Janeiro) 27 (2017): 149–171.

Shachar, Ayelet. *The Shifting Border: Legal Cartographies of Migration and Mobility*. Manchester University Press, 2020.

Shacknove, Andrew. "Who Is a Refugee?" *Ethics* 95, no. 2 (1985): 274–84.

Shakespeare, Tom. "The Social Model of Disability." In *The Disability Studies Reader*, edited by Lennard J. Davis. Psychology Press, 2006.

Shakhsari, Sima. "Killing Me Softly with Your Rights." In *Queer Necropolitics*, edited by Jin Haritaworn, Adi Kuntsman, and Silvia Posocco, 93–110. Routledge, 2014.

———. "The Queer Time of Death: Temporality, Geopolitics, and Refugee Rights." *Sexualities* 17, no. 8 (2014): 998–1015.

Shaw, Ari, and Namrata Verghese. *LGBTQI+ Refugees and Asylum Seekers: A Review of Research and Data Needs*. Williams Institute UCLA School of Law, June 2022.

Shelby, Tommie. *The Idea of Prison Abolition*. Princeton University Press, 2022.

Sheller, Mimi. "Racialized Mobility Transitions in Philadelphia: Urban Sustain-Ability and the Problem of Transport Inequality." *City and Society* 27, no. 1 (2015): 70–91.

Shire, Warsan. "Home, and: Conversation About Home (At the Deportation Centre)." *Transition* 132, no. 1 (2021): 336–42.

Shklar, Judith. "The Liberalism of Fear." In *Liberalism and the Moral Life*, edited by Nancy Rosenblum. Harvard University Press, 1989.

Siddons, Edward. "'We're Brothers, Sisters and Activists': The Greek Collective of Gay and Trans Refugees." *The Observer*, September 16, 2018. https://www.theguardian.com/world/2018/sep/16/we-are-brothers-sisters-and-activists-greek-gay-trans-collective-of-refugees.

Sjoberg, Laura. *Gendering Global Conflict: Toward a Feminist Theory of War*. Columbia University Press, 2013.

Sledge, Matt. "ICE is Erasing Rules That Protect Trans Detainees." The Intercept, March 27, 2025. https://theintercept.com/2025/03/27/ice-trans-immigrant-detainees.

Smiley, Sandra. "Out of Sight, out of Mind? Transgender People in Humanitarian Emergencies." Humanitarian Law and Policy Analysis. March 31, 2020. https://blogs.icrc.org/law-and-policy/2020/03/31/out-sight-mind-transgender-people-humanitarian-emergencies/.

Smith, Kate. "10 Transgender Women Seeking Asylum Just Won Their Immigration Cases After Months of Violence and Discrimination." CBS News, 2019. https://www.cbsnews.com/news/lgbt-rights-ten-lgbt-asylum-seekers-are-winning-theirimmigration-cases-after-months-of-violence-and-discrimination/.

Song, Sarah. *Immigration and Democracy*. Oxford University Press, 2019.

Souter, James. "Towards a Theory of Asylum as Reparation for Past Injustice." *Political Studies* 62, no. 2 (June 2014): 326–42. https://doi.org/10.1111/1467-9248.12019.

Spirlet, Thibault. "Russian LGBTQ+ Asylum Seekers Face Uphill Battle to Make Claims in EU." *The Parliament*, April 15, 2024. https://www.theparliamentmagazine.eu/news/article/russian-lgbtq-asylum-seekers-face-uphill-battle-to-make-claims-in-eu.

Spivak, Gayatri Chakravorty. "Can the Subaltern Speak?" In *Colonial Discourse and Post-Colonial Theory: A Reader*, edited by Patrick Williams and Laura Chrisman, 66–111. Routledge, 2015.

Stake, Robert. E. *The Art of Case Study Research*. Sage, 1995.

Stanley, Eric. "Near Life, Queer Death: Overkill and Ontological Capture." *Social Text* 29, no. 2 (2011): 1–19.

———. *Atmospheres of Violence*. Duke University Press, 2021.

Stanley, Eric A., Dean Spade, and Queer (In)Justice. "Queering Prison Abolition, Now?" *American Quarterly* 64, no. 1 (2012): 115–27. https://doi.org/10
.1353/aq.2012.0003.

Steele, Abbey. *Democracy and Displacement in Colombia's Civil War.* Cornell
University Press, 2017.

Stein, Barry N., and Frederick C. Cuny. "Refugee Repatriation During Conflict:
Protection and Post-Return Assistance." *Development in Practice* 4, no. 3
(1994): 173–87. https://doi.org/10.1080/096145249100077811.

Stonewall. "New Data: Rise in Hate Crime against LGBTQ+ People Continues,
Stonewall Slams UK Gov 'Inaction.'" Stonewall, October 2023. https://www
.stonewall.org.uk/news/new-data-rise-hate-crime-against-lgbtq-people
-continues-stonewall-slams-uk-gov-.

Storey, H. "What Constitutes Persecution? Towards a Working Definition."
International Journal of Refugee Law 26, no. 2 (June 1, 2014): 272–85.
https://doi.org/10.1093/ijrl/eeu017.

Stryker, Susan. *Transgender History: The Roots of Today's Revolution.* Seal
Press, 2017.

Su, Yvonne, and Samuel Ritholtz. "How LGBT Refugees from Ukraine Are
Highly Vulnerable." *The Washington Post,* April 13, 2022. https://www
.washingtonpost.com/politics/2022/04/13/lgbtq-trans-ukraine-asylum
-human-rights/.

Sussman, Aaron. "Expanding Asylum Law's Pattern-or-Practice-of-Persecution
Framework to Better Protect LGBT Refugees." *University of Pennsylvania
Journal of Law and Social Change* 16, no. 2 (2013): 111–32.

Sussner, Petra. "Addressing Heteronormativity: The Not-So-Lost Requirement
of Discretion in (Austrian) Asylum Law." *International Journal of Refugee
Law* 34, no. 1 (March 2022): 31–53. https://doi.org/10.1093/ijrl/eeac018.

Tabak, Shana, and Rachel Levitan. "LGBTI Migrants in Immigration Detention: A Global Perspective." *Harvard Journal of Law & Gender* 37, no. 1
(2014): 1–44.

Tabberer, Jamie. "Trump Administration Deports Gay Make-Up Artist to
Maximum Security Prison in El Salvador." *Attitude Magazine,* April 7, 2025.
https://www.attitude.co.uk/news/el-salvador-gay-makeup-artist-deported
-482195/.

Talbot, Anna, Anthea Vogl, and Sara Dehm. "The Gender- and Sexuality-Based
Harms of Refugee Externalization: A Role for Human Rights Due Diligence."
International Journal of Refugee Law 36, no. 1–2 (March 1, 2024): 60–76.
https://doi.org/10.1093/ijrl/eeae010.

Taylor, Diane. "Barrister Says She Became Legal Expert While in Home Office
Immigration Detention." *The Guardian,* October 22, 2022. https://www
.theguardian.com/uk-news/2022/oct/22/barrister-says-she-became-legal
-expert-while-in-home-office-immigration-detention.

Taylor, Helen. "Refugees, the State, and the Concept of Home." *Refugee Survey Quarterly* 32, no. 2 (2013): 130–52.

Thomson Reuters Foundation, "Nigerian LGBTQ Activist Granted Asylum in UK After 13-Year Legal Battle." NBC News, August 14, 2017. https://www.nbcnews.com/feature/nbc-out/nigerian-lgbtq-activist-granted-asylum-uk-after-13-year-legal-n792661.

Thoreson, Ryan. "Trump Administration Moves to Reject Transgender Identity, Rights." Human Rights Watch, 2025. https://www.hrw.org/news/2025/01/23/trump-administration-moves-reject-transgender-identity-rights.

Threadcraft, Shatema. *Intimate Justice: The Black Female Body and the Body Politic*. Oxford University Press, 2016.

———. "North American Necropolitics and Gender: On #BlackLivesMatter and Black Femicide." *South Atlantic Quarterly* 116, no. 3 (July 2017): 553–79. https://doi.org/10.1215/00382876-3961483.

Thrush, Glenn. "Under Trump, U.S. Prisons Offered Gender-Affirming Care." *The New York Times*, October 16, 2024. https://www.nytimes.com/2024/10/16/us/politics/trump-prisons-transgender-care-harris.html.

Tomaselli, Davide. "'Forced' Refugees versus 'Voluntary' Migrants: Deconstructing a Binary through SOGIESC Claims of Asylum." *International Journal of Refugee Law*, 2025.

Tomsen, Stephen. *Violence, Prejudice and Sexuality*. Routledge, 2013.

Tondo, Lorenzo. "'I Will Not Be Held Prisoner': The Trans Women Turned Back at Ukraine's Borders." *The Guardian*, March 22, 2022. https://www.theguardian.com/global-development/2022/mar/22/i-will-not-be-held-prisoner-the-trans-women-turned-back-at-ukraines-borders.

Torpey, John. *The Invention of the Passport*. Cambridge University Press, 2000.

Torres, Trixie. "Asylum Interview Sample Questions: Shoreline Immigration." Shoreline Immigration, July 18, 2022. https://shorelineimmigration.com/asylum/asylum-interview-sample-questions/.

Townsend, Mark. "EU Unable to Retrieve €150m Paid to Tunisia Despite Links to Rights Violations." *The Guardian*, October 11, 2024. https://www.theguardian.com/global-development/2024/oct/11/eu-funding-migrant-deal-tunisia-human-rights-violations-asylum-icc.

Townsend, Mark, and Diane Taylor. "'Home Office Wouldn't Believe I Was Gay: How Do You Prove It?'" *The Observer*, February 8, 2014. https://www.theguardian.com/uk-news/2014/feb/08/home-office-gay-asylum-seekers-questioning.

Tschalaer, Mengia. "Between Queer Liberalisms and Muslim Masculinities: LGBTQI+ Muslim Asylum Assessment in Germany." *Ethnic and Racial Studies* 43, no. 7 (2020): 1265–83.

———. "Black Lesbians Denied Asylum in Germany," Open Democracy, August 14, 2019. https://www.opendemocracy.net/en/beyond-trafficking-and-slavery/black-lesbians-denied-asylum-germany.

———. "Victimhood and Femininities in Black Lesbian Asylum Cases in Germany." *Journal of Ethnic and Migration Studies* 47, no. 15 (2020): 3531–48.

United Kingdom Home Office. "Asylum Interviews (Version 9.0)." 2022. https://www.gov.uk/government/publications/conducting-the-asylum-interview-process.

———. "Asylum Policy Instruction: Sexual Orientation in Asylum Claims." UK Home Office, 2016. https://assets.publishing.service.gov.uk/media/5a804b17ed915d74e622d9dc/Sexual-orientation-in-asylum-claims-v6.pdf.

———. "Family Reunion: For Refugees and Those with Humanitarian Protection Version 4.0." January 9, 2020. https://assets.publishing.service.gov.uk/government/uploads/system/uploads/attachment_data/file/856915/family-reunion-guidance-v4.0-ext.pdf.

United Kingdom Lesbian and Gay Immigration Group (UKLGIG). "Failing the Grade." Rainbow Migration. 2010. https://www.rainbowmigration.org.uk/publications/failing-the-grade/.

United Nations. "Rome Statute of the International Criminal Court, 17 July 1998, in Force on 1 July 2002, United Nations, Treaty Series, Vol. 2187, No. 38544, Depositary: Secretary-General of the United Nations, http://Treaties.Un.Org." 1998.

———. "United Nations Conference of Plenipotentiaries on the Status of Refugees and Stateless Persons." Geneva, July 25, 1951. https://www.unhcr.org/protection/travaux/40a8a7394/final-act-united-nations-conference-plenipotentiaries-status-refugees-stateless.html.

———. "Universal Declaration of Human Rights." 1948. https://www.un.org/en/universal-declaration-human-rights/.

United Nations General Assembly. "Affirmation of the Principles of International Law Recognized by the Charter of the Nürnberg Tribunal." December 11, 1946. https://www.refworld.org/docid/3b00f1ee0.html.

———. "Convention Relating to the Status of Refugees." United Nations, July 28, 1951. https://www.refworld.org/docid/3be01b964.html.

United Nations High Commission for Refugees (UNHCR). "Background Note for the Agenda Item: Family Reunification in the Context of Resettlement and Integration." UNHCR, 2001. https://www.unhcr.org/3b30baa04.pdf.

———. "Figures at a Glance, 2024," UNHCR, 2024. https://www.unhcr.org/uk/figures-glance.

———. "Global Trends: Forced Displacement in 2020." UNHCR, 2021. https://www.unhcr.org/flagship-reports/globaltrends/.

———. "Guidelines on International Protection No. 1: Gender-Related Persecution Within the Context of Article 1A(2) of the 1951 Convention and/or Its 1967 Protocol Relating to the Status of Refugees." UNHCR, 2002. https://www.refworld.org/policy/legalguidance/unhcr/2002/en/31754.

———. "Policy on Alternatives to Camps." UNHCR, 2009. https://www.unhcr
.org/uk/media/unhcr-policy-alternatives-camps.

———. "UNHCR Guidance Note on Refugee Claims Relating to Sexual Orientation and Gender Identity." United Nations High Commission for Refugees,
November 21, 2008. https://www.refworld.org/docid/48abd5660.html.

———. "UNHCR Statement on the Situation of LGBTIQ+ Refugees in Kakuma
Camp." March 25, 2021. https://www.unhcr.org/ke/19859-unhcr-statement
-on-the-situation-of-lgbtiq-refugees-in-kakuma-camp.html.

United Nations Human Rights Council Working Group on Arbitrary Detention.
"Opinion No. 14/2017 Concerning Cornelius Fonya (Cameroon). A/HRC/
WGAD/2017/14." United Nations, 2017.

———. "Opinion No. 20/2021 Concerning Douglas Tumuhimbise et al. (Uganda).
A/HRC/WGAD/2021/20." United Nations, 2021.

United Nations Working Group on Arbitrary Detention et al. Communication
to the Government of Kenya Alleging Violence, Arbitrary Detention, and
Ill-Treatment of LGBT Refugees in Kakuma Camp, Reference AL KEN
9/2018, September 21, 2018.

United Nations Independent Expert on Sexual Orientation and Gender Identity.
*Protection Against Violence and Discrimination Based on Sexual Orienta-
tion and Gender Identity in Relation to Forced Displacement*, Reference A/
HRC/59/43, April 17, 2025. https://www.ohchr.org/en/documents/thematic
-reports/ahrc5943-protection-against-violence-and-discrimination-based
-sexual.

Urbina, Ian. "The Secretive Prisons That Keep Migrants Out of Europe." *The
New Yorker*, November 28, 2021. https://www.newyorker.com/magazine
/2021/12/06/the-secretive-libyan-prisons-that-keep-migrants-out-of-europe.

US Citizenship and Immigration Services. "Obtaining Derivative Refugee/
Asylee Status for a Spouse." US Citizenship and Immigration Services, 2019.
https://my.uscis.gov/exploremyoptions/obtain_refugee_asylum_status_for
_spouse.

———. "USCIS Guidance for Adjudicating LGBTI Refugee and Asylum Claims."
2015. https://www.aila.org/library/uscis-guidance-adjudicating-lgbti
-refugee-asylum.

Valdez, Inés. "Association, Reciprocity, and Emancipation: A Transnational
Account of the Politics of Global Justice." In *Empire, Race and Global
Justice*, edited by Duncan Bell, 120–44. Cambridge University Press, 2019.

Van Hear, Nicholas. "Refugees in Diaspora." *Refuge: Canada's Journal on
Refugees* 23, no. 1 (2006): 9–15.

———. "'I Went as Far as My Money Would Take Me': Conflict, Forced Migration
and Class." In *Forced Migration and Global Processes: A View From Forced
Migration Studies*, edited by Francois Crepeau, Delphine Nakache, Michael

Collyer, Nathaniel H. Goetz, and Art Hansen, 125–58. Rowman and Little-field, 2006.

Vartabedian Cabral, Julieta. "Geografía travesti: Cuerpos, sexualidad y migraciones de travestis brasileñas (Rio de Janeiro-Barcelona)." PhD diss., Universitat de Barcelona, 2012. https://www.tdx.cat/handle/10803/95889 #page=81.

Vasanthakumar, Ashwini. "Exiles as Solidary Intermediaries." In *The Ethics of Exile: A Political Theory of Diaspora*, edited by Ashwini Vasanthakumar. Oxford University Press, 2021.

———. *The Ethics of Exile: A Political Theory of Diaspora*. Oxford University Press, 2021.

Vasquez, Tina. "Trump's Border Policy Tore Apart Many Families: Nobody Knows What Happens to Them Now." *The Guardian*, January 17, 2025. https://www.theguardian.com/us-news/ng-interactive/2025/jan/17/trump -policy-family-separation-future.

Vera Institute for Justice, "ICE is Excluding Data on Transgender People in Detention." June 30, 2025. https://www.vera.org/news/ice-is-excluding-data -on-transgender-people-in-detention.

Viteri, María-Amelia. *Desbordes*. SUNY Press, 2014. https://sunypress.edu /Books/D/Desbordes.

Vitikainen, Annamari. "LGBT Rights and Refugees: A Case for Prioritizing LGBT Status in Refugee Admissions." *Ethics & Global Politics* 13, no. 1 (January 1, 2020): 64–78. https://doi.org/10.1080/16544951.2020.1735015.

Vogel, Katrin. "The Mother, the Daughter, and the Cow: Venezuelan Transform-istas' Migration to Europe." *Mobilities* 4, no. 3 (2009): 367–87.

Vogler, Stefan, and Rocío Rosales. "Classification and Coercion: The Gendered Punishment of Transgender Women in Immigration Detention." *Social Problems* 23, no. 2 (April 2022): 454–81. https://doi.org/10.1093/socpro/spac022.

Wachter, Karin, Laurie Cook Heffron, and Jessica Dalpe. "'Back Home You Just Go Talk to the Family': The Role of Family Among Women Who Seek Help for Intimate Partner Violence Pre- and Postresettlement to the United States." *Journal of Interpersonal Violence* 36, no. 15–16 (August 2021): 7574–98. https://doi.org/10.1177/0886260519835861.

Wakefield, Lily. "Gay Asylum Seeker Flees Persecution in Morocco, Only to Endure More Homophobia When Arriving in the UK." *PinkNews*, Febru-ary 6, 2021. https://www.pinknews.co.uk/2021/02/06/morocco-gay-asylum -seeker-cardiff-wales-housing-homophobia-abderrahim-el-habachi/.

Walzer, Michael. *Spheres of Justice*. Basic Books, 1983.

Wayar, Marlene. *Travesti: Una Teoría lo suficientemente buena*. Editorial Muchas Nueces, 2018.

Wellman, Christopher Heath. "Immigration and Freedom of Association." *Ethics* 119, no. 1 (2008): 109–41. https://doi.org/10.1086/592311.

Weigel, Alicia Roth. *Inverse Cowgirl: A Memoir.* HarperOne, 2023.

Wesangula, Daniel. "On the Run from Persecution: How Kenya Became a Haven for LGBT Refugees." *The Guardian*, February 23, 2017. https://www.theguardian.com/global-development-professionals-network/2017/feb/23/on-the-run-from-persecution-how-kenya-became-a-haven-for-lgbt-refugees.

Wessels, Jana. "Sexual Orientation in Refugee Status Determination." *Refugee Studies Centre Working Paper Series* 74, 2011. https://www.refworld.org/reference/themreport/rsc/2011/en/106701.

Weston, Kath. *Families We Choose: Lesbians, Gays, Kinship.* Columbia University Press, 1997.

———. "Get Thee to a Big City: Sexual Imaginary and the Great Gay Migration." *GLQ: A Journal of Lesbian and Gay Studies* 2, no. 3 (June 1995): 253–77. https://doi.org/10.1215/10642684-2-3-253.

White House, The. "Realigning the United Statement Refugee Admissions Program." Presidential actions, January 20, 2025. https://www.whitehouse.gov/presidential-actions/2025/01/realigning-the-united-states-refugee-admissions-program/.

Wiggins, Christopher. "Gay Makeup Artist Andry Hernández Romero Describes Horrific Sexual & Physical Abuse at CECOT in El Salvador." *The Advocate*, July 26, 2025. https://www.advocate.com/news/andry-hernandez-romero-cecot-torture.

Willis, Raquel. "Six LGBTQ+ Activists on What We Should Abolish and Legalize by 2069." *Out*, June 10, 2019. https://www.out.com/out-exclusives/2019/6/10/six-lgbtq-activists-what-we-should-abolish-and-legalize-2069.

Wilson, Jade. "Why LGBTQ+ Refugees Are Stuck in Limbo in Kenya." Context, 2025. https://www.context.news/socioeconomic-inclusion/why-lgbtq-refugees-are-stuck-in-limbo-in-kenya.

Wimark, Thomas. "Housing Policy with Violent Outcomes: The Domestication of Queer Asylum Seekers in a Heteronormative Society." *Journal of Ethnic and Migration Studies* 47, no. 3 (2021): 703–22.

Women for Refugee Women. "See Us, Believe Us, Stand with Us: The Experiences of Lesbian and Bisexual Women Seeking Asylum in the UK." 2023. https://www.refugeewomen.co.uk/see-us-believe-us-stand-with-us/.

Wright, Melissa W. "Necropolitics, Narcopolitics, and Femicide: Gendered Violence on the Mexico-U.S. Border." *Signs: Journal of Women in Culture and Society* 36, no. 3 (March 2011): 707–31. https://doi.org/10.1086/657496.

Yarwood, Vanessa, Francesco Checchi, Karen Lau, and Cathy Zimmerman. "LGBTQI + Migrants: A Systematic Review and Conceptual Framework of Health, Safety and Wellbeing during Migration." *International Journal of Environmental Research and Public Health* 19, no. 2 (January 2022). https://doi.org/10.3390/ijerph19020869.

Yoshino, Kenji. "Covering." *Yale Law Journal* 111, no. 4 (2002): 769–939.

Young, Iris Marion. "House and Home: Feminist Variations on a Theme." In *Motherhood and Space: Configurations of the Maternal Through Politics, Home, and the Body*, edited by Sarah Hardy and Caroline Wiedmer, 115–47. New York: Palgrave Macmillan US, 2005.

———. *Justice and the Politics of Difference*. Princeton University Press, 1990.

Youngsook Choi. "The Meaning of Home for Transgendered People." In *Queer Presences and Absences*, edited by Yvette Taylor and Michelle Addison. Basingstoke: Palgrave Macmillan, 2013.

Zacka, Bernardo. *When the State Meets the Street*. Harvard University Press, 2018.

Zeffman, Henry and Sam Francis. "Anti-Gay Discrimination Not Qualification for Asylum, Says Suella Braverman." BBC News, September 26, 2023. https://www.bbc.co.uk/news/uk-politics-66919416.

Zelada, Carlos J. "Cuerpxs indisciplinadxs: Hacia una mirada cuir (Queer) (Cuy-r) de la regulación jurídica de las sexualidades disidentes." In *Repensando las reglas de juego: Caminos para evitar el colapso institucional y social*, edited by Ronnie Farfán, Santiago Mariani, and Cecilia O'Neill, 153–90. Fondo Editorial Universidad del Pacífico, 2018.

Index

ACHR. *See* American Convention on Human Rights
administrative segregation, 92
admission, ethics of, 71, 123–25
adoption, queer kinship and, 113–14
Advisory Opinion on Gender Identity, Equality, and Non-Discrimination of Same-Sex Couples, 110–11
Afghanistan, 64
African Rainbow Family, 84
Ahmed, case of, 95–96
Aiken, Sharry, 100–1
Aizura, Aren, 69
Alice, case of, 62, 64, 69
American Civil Liberties Union, 88
American Convention on Human Rights (ACHR), 183n25
American Enterprise Institute, 5
anecdotes, selecting, 13–14. *See also various cases*
anti-gender ideology, 2
Anti-Homosexuality Act, 98. *See also* Uganda
anti-queer and anti-trans politics, popularity of, 8
Anu, case of, 42–45, 47–52, 58, 60, 164n19
Anzaldúa, Gloria, 73–74
Apata, Aderonke, case of, 83–84

Arellano, Victoria, case of, 87–88, 92–94, 181n4
Are Prisons Obsolete? (Davis), 102
Argentina, 116
Arnold, Emily, 115–16
Asquith, Nicole, 34
assessment, 19, 126; assumption of deceit, 83–84; asylum interviews, 79–81; guidance regarding, 82–83; and "political theory of implementation," 82; searching for authenticity, 81–82. *See also* asylum seekers; interviews
asylum: ceasing processing of claims of, 87; challenges Black queer women face in receiving, 47–50; courts, 1, 59; denying, 134; LGBTIQ refugees in state of, 125–30; receiving, 23, 47, 192n13; recognizing eligibility for, 4, 162n2; sanctuary after, 130–32; seeking, 6, 47, 66, 95, 119, 126, 128, 140–41, 177n6; state of, 18–20, 41, 84, 92, 122–23; submitting applications, 182n19. *See also* asylum seekers; interviews
asylum judge, encounter with. *See* Darío, case of
asylum seekers, 4–8, 19–20, 103, 121, 134, 176n2, 177n8, 181n11; applications, 44, 182n19; in Australia, 95–96; calling for

asylum seekers (*continued*)
specialized housing for, 121; in camps and detention centers, 91–92; deporting to Rwanda, 68; "derivative asylee status," 105–6; documenting, 169; in Dutch camps, 95; experiencing harms at home, 40; extraordinary risks taken by, 64; in Germany, 164n23; guidance on interviewing, 177n6; identifying safe havens for, 132–33; interviews with, 79–84; LGBTIQ refugees in state of asylum, 125–30; overcoming immobility, 76; and queer interpretations of violence, 50–56; and queer kinship, 116–18; and "rainbow caravan," 104–5; and refugee prevention regime, 66–68; rejecting claims of, 48, 51; sanctuary after asylum, 130–32; separating from "migrant caravan," 104; stirring up fears of, 150n14; and "third country alternatives," 173n28; undermining cases of, 57–61; in United Kingdom, 129–30; and US Southern border, 191n67; writing to Australian government, 95. *See also* interviews; LGBTIQ asylum seekers
Atala Riffo and Daughters v. Chile, 110
Atshan, Sa'ed, 133–34
Atuhwera, Chriton, case of, 89–90
Australia, 4, 7, 84, 95
Australian Migration Act of 1958, 46
Ayoub, Phillip, 8

Bailey, Marlon, 115–16
bell hooks, 31–32
Ben, case of, 36–39
Benhabib, Seyla, 196n57
Bernstein, Matt, 133
Bhutan, 150n9
Bird, Gemma, 92
Black Diaspora Liberty Initiative, 181n6
Bohmer, Carol, 59
border anxiety, 52–53, 166n39. *See also* homophobia
Bosnia and Herzegovina, 28
Boyle v. UK, 110
Bradley, Megan, 29
Braverman, Suella, 5–6, 150n14
Brazil, 116
British Conservative Party. *See* Braverman, Suella; Patel, Priti; United Kingdom
British Home Office, 46. *See also* United Kingdom
Brown, Gavin, 154n58
Browne, Kath, 12, 152n38

Brunei, 150n9
Bryant, Jason, 38–39
Butler, Judith, 16, 35, 53, 113–14, 116

Calhoun, Cheshire, 37
Camminga, B, 96, 184n47, 195n49
camps, 19, 28, 117, 172n26; intragroup harm, 96–100; joint approach to camps and detention centers, 90–92; overview, 87–90, 102–03; problems of, 93–96; queer critique of, 100–02. *See also* detention; encampment
Campuzano, Giuseppe, 117
Canada, 4, 84, 195n50
Carillo, Héctor, 173n30
Carling, Jørgen, 71
Cass Identity Model, 178n13
Chávez, Karma, 187n10
children, 113–14. *See also* "chosen family"
Choi, Youngsook, 38
"chosen family," 6, 10, 20, 117, 120; development of, 119; embodying kinship relations of, 105; and queer and trans complications of home, 37–38; queer kinship, 114–15
Chossière, Florent, 155n62
cis gay male experience, idealization of, 50–51
cisheteronormativity, 15, 41, 100, 140, 144; biases, 113, 150n12; couples, 106; environment of, 120; family units, 20, 109, 111, 118–19; ideology, 22, 97, 106; ideology of "sexual brokenness," 22, 156n2; kinship, 114. *See also* family; homophobia; persecution; transphobia
cishetero women, 43–44, 128
CJEU. *See* Court of Justice of the European Union
climate change, 7, 16, 64, 78, 157n14
colectivos, los, 136–38. *See also* Venezuela
Collins, Patricia Hill, 13
Colombia, 1–3, 136–38, 177n8, 196n1
complications of home: assumed collective identity, 35–36; calls for queering of concept of home, 38–39; characteristics of familial violence, 34–35; and "chosen family," 37–38; expansion of home, 38–40; experiencing homelessness, 37; heteronormative compliance, 35; home as first site of prejudice-based violence or persecution, 33–34; home as space for identity affirmation and protection, 38. *See also* home
containment, 19–20, 126; camps and detention centers, 90–92; and intragroup harm, 96–100; joint approach to question of,

90–92; overview, 87–88, 102–103; practices of, 98, 101, 103; problems of, 93–96; queer critique of, 100–102; refugee camps, 88–90; structures of, 90, 100. *See also* camps; detention; encampment

Convention on the Rights of the Child (CRC), 107

conversion therapy, 22–23; mechanisms of, 156n2

converting, conceptualizing, 69–70. *See also* Yoshino, Kenji

Court of Justice of the European Union (CJEU), 174n41

covering, conceptualizing, 69–70. *See also* Yoshino, Kenji

Crawley, Heaven, 17, 97

CRC. *See* Convention on the Rights of the Child

Crenshaw, Kimberlé, 12–13, 153n43

criminalization, 5, 18, 41, 133, 181n11, 186n75; *de facto* criminalization, 156n7, 177n8; *de jure* criminalization, 156n7, 173n28, 177n8; fleeing contexts of, 58; and humanitarian aid, 64; and persecution at home, 23–25; state-led criminalization, 43

Cuba, 4

Cuny, Frederick, 29

Darío, case of, 1–3

Davis, Angela, 102

deceit, assumption of, 83–84. *See also* assessment; interviews

de facto criminalization, 156n7, 177n8

de facto state authorities, 45

DEI. *See* diversity, equity, and inclusion

de jure criminalization, 156n7, 177n8

De León, Jason, 67

detention, 6–7, 17, 19–20, 24, 43, 67; abolition of, 20, 102; criticizing practice of, 93–96; harms of, 93–94; ICE detention, 88, 90, 94, 102; immigration detention, 6, 20, 87–88, 93, 101–103, 133, 186n75; and intragroup harm, 96–100; joint approach to detention centers and camps, 90–92; overlapping with encampment, 90–92; problems of, 93–96; queer critique of, 100–102; US immigration detention, 180n2, 181n6, 187n10

detention centers, 7, 20, 105, 118, 172n26; and intragroup harm, 96–100; joint approach to camps and detention centers, 90–92; overview, 87–90, 102–103; problems of, 93–96; queer critique of, 100–102

Directive 2004/83/EC, 169n75

Directive 2011/95/EU, 164n17

discretion requirement, 174n41

discrimination, 3, 5, 19, 63, 150n14, 168n74, 173n28, 181n6; avoiding, 70, 94, 118; conceptualizing confluence of, 49–50, 52; consequences of immobility, 73; employment discrimination, 142; fleeing home due to, 23; humanitarian assistance and, 64; induced immobility arising from, 65; line between persecution and, 45–49; overcoming immobility, 74–75; prejudice-based violence, 52; queer interpretations of violence, 50–53; sanctuary, 121, 129; targeted discrimination, 63. *See also* asylum seekers; homophobia; LGBTIQ displaced people; LGBTIQ refugees; misogyny; persecution

displacement: cycles of, 3, 5, 10, 17, 27, 138; discussions of, 63; drivers of, 26, 41, 130, 157n14; experiences of, 140; LGBTIQ displacement, 10, 24–25, 126, 141; losing home as way of thinking about, 26–30; mass displacement, 63; process of, 27; queer and trans displacement, 5, 10, 15, 23, 50, 83, 141–42, 157n14; settlement-based solutions to, 30; situations of, 137–39, 142; theory of, 14, 139–41; understandings of, 10, 13, 28, 141. *See also* LGBTIQ displaced people

displacement journey: assessment, 79–84; conclusions, 136–44; containment, 87–103; flight, 62–78; home, 22–41; overview, 10–11; persecution, 42–61; reunion, 104–20; sanctuary, 121–35; structure of study, 17–21. *See also* assessment; containment; family; flight; home; persecution; reunion; sanctuary

diversity, equity, and inclusion (DEI), 138

Dixson, Tina Nina, 197n12

documentation, Western-centric need for, 187n9

double backlash, LGBTIQ displaced people and, 7–9, 195n47

Dummett, Michael, 124

Dustin, Moira, 44

duties of resettlement, 127

ECHR. *See* European Court of Human Rights

Edelman, Lee, 114

Egypt, 150n9

El Salvador, 6–8, 94, 104

encampment, 19, 91, 101, 126. *See also* camps

endosexism, 194n35
Eng, David, 39
Engels, Friedrich, 111
engineered regionalism, 66–68
Enloe, Cynthia, 66, 172n17
Epistemology of the Closet, The (Sedgwick), 35–36
Eritrea, 88
Eskridge, William, Jr., 114–15
Esther (queen), 35–36
Ethiopia, 88–89
European Court of Human Rights (ECHR), 95
European Union, 7, 172n20; agreements with, 67; involvement in Libyan detention centers, 93
Executive Committee (ExCom), UNHCR, 108
extrajudicial border enforcement, 170n2

failure of state-protection approach, persecution and, 46–47
Familia: Trans Queer Liberation Movement, 102
family, 20, 22–23; case for refugee family unity, 107–9; characteristics of familial violence, 34–35; defining family unit, 109–12; "family values," 113, 157n13; members of, 5, 24, 34, 49, 58, 82, 108, 115, 120, 168n74; overview, 104–6; and queer kinship, 112–18; and queer and trans complications of home, 33–40; reproducing symbolic materials of, 115–16; right to queer family reunion, 118–20. *See also* "chosen family"; flight; home; persecution; reunion
Feinberg, Leslie, 38
"feminine mystique," articulating idea of, 30–31
feminist political thought, complicating concept of home in, 30–33
feminist theory, indispensability of intersectionality for, 153n43
flight, 18–19, 48, 61, 104, 106, 125, 128; consequences of immobility, 73–74; induced immobility, 68–73; overcoming immobility, 74–77; overview, 77–78; and refugee prevention regime, 65–68; trans women fleeing from Ukraine, 62–66. *See also* home; persecution
forced migration, 13, 27, 37, 139, 141
Fortier, Anne-Marie, 39
Fortress Europe, 66
Fox, Christopher, 34
Friedan, Betty, 30–31

GATE. *See* Global Action for Trans Equality
gender identity, 4–5, 13, 150n14; assessment and, 81–83; containment and, 89; conversion therapy and, 22–24; ethics of admission, 123; flight and, 70, 73, 75, 78; LGBTIQ refugees in state of asylum, 126, 128; note on terminology, 15–16; persecution and, 43–44, 51, 53, 56–58; queer and trans complications of home, 33–40; and reunion, 115, 118
Geneva Convention, 5, 45, 50–51, 82; history of, 14–15; Refugee Convention, 43, 46, 176n2, 192n13; on the Status of Refugees, 107
Germany, 47–50, 84, 95, 164n23
Gibney, Matthew, 108–9
Global Action for Trans Equality (GATE), 151n27
Global North, 13, 19, 21, 139; assumption of ensured protection in, 122; asylum seekers entering, 7–8; border control apparatus created by, 66; and centrality of home, 29–30; and debates of ethics of admission, 125; focus on "refugee question," 63; "idealized gay experience" in, 50–51; and idea of home, 28; implementing "third country alternatives," 173n28; and intragroup harm, 97; LGBTIQ refugees in state of asylum, 125–30; Mediterranean functioning as scapegoat for, 67; and overcoming immobility, 76; queer and trans displacement from states in Global South to states in, 193n16; and refugee prevention regime, 66–68; and sanctuary, 122, 125–27, 129–31, 134; sanctuary after asylum, 130–32; and sexual imaginary, 57–58; undertheorizing, 193n16. *See also* Global South; states
global refugee regime, 3, 25, 40, 48, 105, 115, 126; and broader protection system, 118; implementing displacement justice within, 143–44; overview of, 9–15; persecution as, 56–61; presumption of mobility in, 65; treatment of sending-states, 73–74. *See also* refugee prevention regime
Global South, 7, 13, 76, 154n58; and centrality of home, 29–30; and debates of ethics of admission, 125; and engineered regionalism, 66; focus on movement from, 69; and intragroup harm, 98; LGBTIQ refugees in state of asylum, 125–30; men from, 97; and narrative of humanitarian "liberal" West, 76; painting image of people leaving, 96–97; queer and trans displacement from states in, 193n16; and queer

interpretations of violence, 55–56. *See also* Global North; states
Gómez, María Mercedes, 35, 52
González-López, Gloria, 35
Grahl-Madsen, Atle, 163n9
Guardian, The, 36, 117
Gündoğdu, Ayten, 100
Guttiérez, Jennicet, 102

Habachi, Abderrahim El, case of, 121–22, 125, 131, 192n2
Harris, Kamala, 6
Hathaway, James, 46
Hegel, G. W. F., 111
Hernández, Óscar Juárez, case of, 105–6, 110
Hernández, Vicky, case of, 163n11
heteronormative compliance, 35
heteronormative conceptions of family, 38, 109
heterosexuality, 12, 22, 52, 113–14
HJ (Iran) and HT (Cameroon) v. Secretary of State for the Home Department, 174n41
home, 18, 41, 129; complicating concept of, 30–33; conceptualizing subjectively, 29–30; critiquing "home as safety," 30–33; drivers of LGBTIQ displacement, 23–25; example of fleeing home, 22–24; as foundational site for relational account of harm, 26; identifying values of, 32–33; losing home, 26–30; queer and trans complications of, 33–40; as theoretical destination, 26; using centrality of, 29–30. *See also* family
homeplace. *See* feminist political thought, complicating concept of home in
"Home" (Shire), 27
homesickness, experiencing, 27
homonationalism, theory of, 97, 127
homophobia, 21, 55, 113, 131, 137, 142, 166n39, 169n82, 182n48; facing in state of asylum, 127; fleeing harms enforced through, 120; and interconnected forms of oppression, 133–34; and intimate familial violence, 35; locating, 98, 157n11; "naïve" account of, 24–25; prevalence in Global North, 122; regional variations in, 97–98; relational harms fueled by, 10, 122; social structure of exclusion undergirded by, 57; and solidarity, 135; and unique forms of vulnerability, 48–49. *See also* humanitarianism; transphobia
homosexuality, 12, 19, 22, 67, 89; anxiety-producing nature of, 166n39; Cass Identity Model of, 178n13; explicitness of, 48;

and intragroup harm, 97–98; and invisibility of internal displacement, 63; public rejection of, 56; and refugee regime, 4; sexuality of Black women, 60; transmission of, 34; Western expectations of, 49. *See also* homophobia
Honduras, 20, 104–6, 110, 163
Honohan, Iseult, 108, 111–12
Hope, case of, 47–49, 51–52, 58, 60
Horvath v. Secretary of State for the Home Department, 46
humanitarianism, 16, 157n14, 171n7, 197n12; aid, 11, 64; assistance, 64, 91; considerations, 108; corridors, 75, 77–78; intervention possibility, 75–76; liberal actor moral status, 76; providing temporary relief, 137; relief denial, 64
Human Rights Committee, 109
Human Rights Watch, 64, 180n2
Hungary, 128
Hutchings, Kimberley, 76
hyper-visibility, 100

IACtHR. *See* Inter-American Court of Human Rights
ICCPR. *See* International Covenant on Civil and Political Rights
ICE. *See* Immigration and Customs Enforcement
IDPs. *See* internally displaced persons
ignorance, epistemologies of, 59
Immigration and Customs Enforcement (ICE), 7–8, 88, 90, 94, 99–100, 102, 180n2. *See also* United States
immobility: calls for renewed focus on, 174n45; consequences of, 73–74; contemporary immobility, 65; induced immobility, 68–73; involuntary immobility, 174n47; overcoming, 74–77; overview, 77–78; and refugee prevention regime, 65–68; voluntary immobility, 174n47; of women, 72. *See also* induced immobility
imperialist feminisms, 176n61
induced immobility, 72–73, 175n56; disparity in movement experiences defining, 68–71; and encoded gender norms, 70–71; mobility as core concept in discussions of queer life, 68–69; questions of visibility and being "out," 69–70; and refugee prevention regime, 65–68; studying constraints on movement, 69
Inter-American Court of Human Rights (IACtHR), 110–11, 163n11

internal displacement, 63, 171n6, 171n7
internally displaced persons (IDPs), 63, 171n7
International Covenant on Civil and Political Rights (ICCPR), 107, 183n26
International Organization for Migration (IOM), 77, 138
International Rescue Committee, 67
intersectional identities, persecution created by, 47–50
intersectionality, defining, 12–13
interviews: assumption of deceit, 83–84; example, 79–81; guidance, 82–83; searching for authenticity, 81–82
intragroup harm, creating conditions for, 96–100
Invention of the Passport, The (Torpey), 183n23
involuntary immobility, 174n47
IOM. *See* International Organization for Migration
Iran, 95–96, 174n41
Istanbul Convention, 165n27
Italy, 8, 48, 189n38

Judis, case of, 62, 64, 69
Julia, case of, 96
justice, 3, 131, 137, 143; account of, 10, 12; approaching concept of, 141; considerations of, 142; criticizing detention as practice, 93; critiquing global justice literature, 130; displacement justice, 11, 14, 139–44; emphasizing importance of, 140–41; ICE detention centers as "justice free zones," 88; promotion of, 101; questions of, 135, 139; sanctuary and, 122; solidarity for 133–34; universities and, 138

Kagarura, Gilbert, case of, 89
Kakuma (refugee camp), 88–89, 95–98, 182n17, 186n76
Kenya, 117; LGBTIQ asylum seekers from, 64; refugee camps in, 88–90, 95. *See also* Kakuma (refugee camp)
Khader, Serene, 176n61
Kilbride, Erin, 168n69, 168n71
kinship, queer articulations of: "chosen family," 114–15; commonalities, 116; complexities, 116–17; deconstructing cis-heteronormative assumptions, 112; fraught relationship between queer and trans people and family, 112; observations in LGBTIQ refugee support networks, 117–18; reproducing symbolic materials of

family, 115–16; role of child, 113–14; seeking asylum together, 118; specificity loss, 114; state recognition, 113
Kyiv, Ukraine, 63, 71–72, 75. *See also* flight; Ukraine

Land of Open Graves, The (De León), 67
Latin America: court decisions in, 110–11; LGBTIQ organizations in, 132; queer and trans people in, 116–17
LBQ women, 14, 18, 44, 153n48, 168n69; assessment of, 82–83; persecution of, 56–61. *See also* LGBTIQ displaced people; LGBTIQ refugees
Lenard, Patti Tamara, 127
lesbian, bisexual, and queer (LBQ). *See* LBQ women
lesbian, gay, bisexual, trans, intersex, and queer (LGBTIQ). *See* LGBTIQ asylum seekers; LGBTIQ displaced people; LGBTIQ refugees
lesbian refugees, persecution of, 56–61
lesbian women, 44, 51, 57–60, 168n74. *See also* LBQ women
LGBTIQ asylum seekers, 4–6, 64, 117, 121, 181n11, 186n76, 187n10; in Dutch camps, 95; identifying safe havens for, 132–33; interviewing, 82–83; judgment of, 51; in "migrant caravan," 104–5; research on, 48; responding to needs of, 164n23; vulnerabilities faced by, 76
LGBTIQ displaced people, 18, 25, 88, 195n47; assessment, 79–84; in camp settings, 95; changing world of, 4–6; complications of home, 33–40; conclusions, 136–44; containment, 87–103; current world of LGBTIQ asylum seekers and refugees, 4–5; defining experiences, 5; defining "queer and trans," 15; developing insight from experiences, 11–12; flight, 62–78; harm driving, 10, 157n14; highlighting experiences of different sets of people, 14; home, 22–41; note on terminology, 15–17; persecution, 42–61; recognition of, 3–4; relational forms of harm following, 78, 106; reunion, 104–20; sanctuary, 121–35; sitting at intersection of double backlash, 7–9; structure of studying, 17–21
LGBTIQ refugees, 4–5, 14, 18, 88, 104, 106, 122, 134, 139, 141, 142–43, 150n11, 182n17, 185n55, 191n70; arguing for better inclusion of, 197n12; being immobilized, 19, 185n51; in camps, 95; concerns about

treatments of, 68; creating alternative protection systems, 105, 107, 109, 117–18; and ethics of admission, 123–25; experiences of, 8, 11; facing double burden, 84; and induced immobility, 70; and intragroup harm, 96–99; literature, 19; overcoming immobility, 75–76; persecution as socially situated phenomenon, 56–61; qualifying for asylum, 10; queer critique of containment, 98; responding to induced mobility, 65; and right to queer family reunion, 118–20; sanctuary after asylum, 130–33; in state of asylum, 125–30; term, 16–17
Libya, 67
Liinason, Mia, 58
Llewellyn, Cheryl, 57
Long, Katy, 28–29
Lorde, Audre, 38
Lubkemann, Stephen, 71
Luibhéid, Eithne, 57, 178n13, 187n10

Macedo, Stephen, 108
Madonna, 116
Maha, case of, 117
Mahtab, case of, 130–31, 191n70
Malawi, 168n73
Malkki, Liisa, 26–27, 30
Manne, Kate, 24, 158n15, 158n17
Marckx v. Belgium, 110
marginalization, suffering induced by, 12
Martin, Biddy, 31
Mbembe, Achille, 54
McNamarah, Chan Tov, 97
Meili, Stephen, 150n14, 162n2
Meloni, Giorgia, 8, 189n38
Micro Rainbow, 129
"migrant caravan," news coverage of, 104–5
migration: double backlash and, 7; forced migration, 13, 27, 37, 139, 141; global migration regime, 126; imperfections within global migration governance, 11–12; limiting flows of, 19, 186n75; management of, 67–68, 73; migration literature, 16–17; plans for, 68, 71, 75; queer migration, 39; studying, 71
Miller, David, 124
misogyny, 24, 48, 72, 75, 122, 133, 158n15, 158n17
mobility, queer life and, 68–69. See also immobility; induced immobility
Mohanty, Chandra, 31
Monterrosa, Laura, case of, 94

Moore, Hester, 169n82
Morocco, 119
Mustafa Doymus v. Secretary of State for the Home Department, 46

Nairobi, 169n82, 182n17
Nash, Catherine, 12, 152n38
National Asylum Support Service, 121
National Center for Lesbian Rights (NCLR), 58–59, 168n74
natural environment, immobilizing people using, 67. See also immobility; induced immobility
Nayak, Meghana, 49, 126
NCLR. See National Center for Lesbian Rights
necropolitics, 54
Netherlands, The, 3–4
New Zealand, 4
NGOs. See nongovernmental organizations
Nigeria, 22–26, 42–43, 51–52, 83, 164n19, 170n2. See also Anu, case of; Victor, case of
nongovernmental organizations (NGOs), 5, 23, 100, 129, 151n27
No Pride in Detention, campaign, 133
Nuremberg Principles, 162n8
Nussbaum, Martha, 108

Office of the United Nations High Commissioner for Refugees, 28. See also United Nations High Commissioner for Refugees
Organization for Refuge, Asylum and Migration (ORAM), 7, 87
Organization Intersex Europe, 153n48
Owen, David, 124
Owens, Patricia, 182n22

Pakistan, 64
Palestine, 133–34, 195n55
Papua New Guinea, 95–96
parallel legal regimes, 181n11
Parekh, Serena, 71, 123–24
Paris is Burning (film), 116
passing, 69–70, 73, 173n38. See also Yoshino, Kenji
Patel, Priti, 68, 172n27
patriarchy, 54–55; cisheteronormative patriarchy, 61; misogyny as policing arm of, 24–25; Third World patriarchy, 60. See also misogyny
persecution: applications of, 18; characterization of, 46; classification of, 162n8; concept of, 18, 41, 44–45, 47, 56, 61, 82; conceptualization of, 46, 53, 61; criterion

persecution (*continued*)
of, 46; definition of, 44–45; demonstrating well-founded fear of, 43–44; experience of, 43–44, 49, 82; failure of state-protection approach, 46–47; fear of, 2, 6, 43–45, 58, 82; fleeing from, 104, 125; forms of, 23, 44, 48, 51, 59, 61, 103, 127, 129, 141, 169n75, 169n82, 170n84; "ordinary meaning" approaches to, 45–46; presentation of, 50; queer interpretations of violence, 50–56; and queer subjects, 45–50; recognizing, 42–45, 170n84; site of, 26, 43, 90; as socially situated phenomenon, 56–61. *See also* flight; home

Peru, 116

Poland, 128

political right, 8

Portillo, Darwin, case of, 105–6, 110

Pose (series), 116

postadmission, 122–23, 125–28

prejudice-based violence, 18, 33–34, 47, 49, 52–53, 60

"Prevention Through Deterrence," policy, 67

prioritization, discussions of, 74, 101–102, 175n55

prisons, "crime control" function of, 186n73

private harms, 23

Puar, Jasbir, 97, 127

public harms, 23

Purim, Torah story of, 35–36

Putin, Vladimir, 8. *See also* Russia

queer and trans displaced people. *See* LGBTIQ displaced people

queer and trans refugees. *See* LGBTIQ refugees

queer family reunion, right to, 118–20

queering: and concept of family, 113; and concept of home, 38–39; drawing on analytical approach of, 12–13; and intersectional feminist and decolonial analysis, 14–15; and legal regimes, 150n12; method of, 14–15

Queer In(justice), 102

queer non-futurity, 189n44

queer search, 9, 13, 17, 40, 120, 135, 138–39, 141–42

queer solidarity, 133–34

queer subjects, persecution and: broad ways of thinking about persecution, 45–47; legal definition of "refugee," 45

queer utopianism, 40

Rahman, Momin, 13

"rainbow caravan," 20, 104–5, 117–18. *See also* "migrant caravan," news coverage of

Rainbow Railroad, 19, 23, 66, 74, 76–77, 89, 101, 150n11

Rao, Rahul, 12, 98, 157n11

Red Cross, 75

Red Regional por la Movilidad Humana LGBTIQ+, 19, 76

refuge, queer search for: assessment, 79–84; conclusions, 136–44; containment, 87–103; flight, 62–78; home, 22–41; introduction, 1–15; persecution, 42–61; reunion, 104–20; sanctuary, 121–35; structure of study, 17–21. *See also* asylum seekers; displacement journey; LGBTIQ displaced people; LGBTIQ refugees

refugee: defining by loss of home, 26–30; demonstrating well-founded fear of persecution, 43–44; and ethics of admission, 123–25; family reunification, 107–9; final destination of, 28; legal definition of, 45; lesbian refugees, 56–61; LGBTIQ refugees in state of asylum, 125–30; production of, 30; and queer interpretations of violence, 50–56; question of refugee women, 95; and right to queer family reunion, 118–20; sanctuary after asylum, 130–32; standard model of "political refugee," 61; status determination process of, 79–84, 176n2. *See also* asylum seekers; LGBTIQ displaced people; LGBTIQ refugees

Refugee Convention, 43–44, 46, 176n2, 192n13. *See also* Geneva Convention

refugee family unity, case for, 107–9

refugee-led organizations (RLOs), 197n12

refugee prevention regime, 19, 65–68

refugee protection regime, 11, 17, 23, 65. *See also* global refugee regime

refugee status determination (RSD), 19, 105, 126, 177n8

Regional Network for LGBTIQ+ Human Mobility. See *Red Regional por la Movilidad Humana LGBTIQ+*

relational harms, 10, 78, 106, 122, 124, 131; confronting, 120; considering relational solutions, 103, 134–35; containment and, 20, 90; driving displacement, 41; persistence of, 20–21; and queer interpretations of violence, 56; and traditional modes of family reunion, 119; transcending borders, 125

repression. *See* states: state repression

return, term, 29. *See also* home
reunification (of families), promoting, 107–9
reunion, 20; case for refugee family unity,
107–9; defining family unit, 109–12; over-
view, 104–7; and queer kinship, 112–18;
right to queer family reunion, 118–20. *See
also* sanctuary
Riffo, Atala, case of, 110
RLOs. *See* refugee-led organizations
Rome Statute of the International Criminal
Court, 162n8
Romero, Andry José, case of, 6–7
Roth, Steven, 7
RSD. *See* refugee status determination
RuPaul's Drag Race, 116
Russia, 129, 150n9; divisive rhetoric against
LGBTIQ populations in, 157n13; protect-
ing "traditional values" in, 8. *See also*
Ukraine
Rwanda, 68, 88, 173n28

sanctuary, 20–21; after asylum, 130–32; and
ethics of admission, 123–25; finding sanctuary in solidarity, 132–34; LGBTIQ refugees in state of asylum, 125–30; overview,
121–23
San Pedro Service Processing Center. *See*
Arellano, Victoria, case of; United States
Sari, Elif, 115, 169n81
Sarup, Madam, 29
Schulman, Sarah, 135
Sebastián, case of, 136–38, 142, 196n1
Second World War, 5
sedentary bias, overcoming, 28–29
Sedgwick, Eve Kosofsky, 12, 35–36, 112, 113
segregation, 20, 94, 99–100, 102, 105
settlement, resolving refugee status with,
28–30
sexual acts, criminalizing, 168n73
sexual imaginary, impact of, 57–58
sexualities, fluid nature of, 154n58
Sexual Orientation and Gender Identity
Claims of Asylum Project (SOGICA),
178n11
Shakhsari, Sima, 130
Shelby, Tommie, 186n73
Shire, Warsan, 27
Shuman, Amy, 59
Silverman, Stephanie J., 100–101
socially conservative left, rise of, 8–9
socially situated phenomenon, persecution as,
56–61

SOGICA. *See* Sexual Orientation and Gender
Identity Claims of Asylum Project
solidarity: communities of, 10, 138; debates
regarding, 133–35; finding sanctuary in,
132–34; networks of, 64, 123; practicing,
132–33; queer solidarity, 133–34; representations of, 115. *See also* queer solidarity; reunion; sanctuary
Somalia, 88
Song, Sarah, 111
South Africa, 4, 55, 117, 195n49
South Sudan, 88
Spade, Dean, 102
Stanley, Eric, 54, 57, 100, 102
states, 9, 17, 19, 21, 50, 139–40, 144, 193n16;
accepting LGBTIQ refugees, 4–5; camps
and detention centers, 91–92, 103, 172n26;
case for refugee family unity, 107–9; and
centrality of home, 29–30; and consequences of immobility, 73–77; criminalizing same-sex relations, 168n73; in current
international order, 82; defining family
unit, 109–12; failure of state-protection
approach, 46; in Global North, 7, 63,
66–67, 125, 134, 172n27; and homesickness, 27; host states, 118–19, 127, 177n8;
intragroup harm and, 97, 99; necropolitics
and, 54; obliging, 188n25; and problems of
containment, 93–96; question of social
environment in, 25; recognizing "safe"
countries, 177n8; recommendations for,
192; and refugee prevention regime,
66–68; sanctuary and, 122, 124–25,
127–28, 130, 132–34; state repression,
23–25, 41; and "third country alternatives,"
173n28; universal needs recognized by,
118. *See also* Global North; Global South;
United Kingdom; United States
Steele, Abbey, 155n64
Stein, Barry, 29
Stoeckl, Kristina, 8
Stone Butch Blues (Feinberg), 38
Syria, 75, 160n53

Tayeb, Fatima El-, 126–27, 184n48
Taylor, Helen, 28
terminology, note on, 15–17
Terrorism Confinement Center. *See* El
Salvador
"third country alternatives," implementing,
173n28
Threadcraft, Shatema, 54

Toboso-Alfonso, Fidel, case of, 4
Torpey, John, 183n23
transphobia, 131, 133, 169n82, 184n48; defin-
    ing experiences of LGBTIQ displaced
    people, 5; facing in state of asylum, 127;
    familial transphobia, 34; fleeing harms
    enforced through, 120; flight and, 63, 72,
    75; "naïve" account of, 24–25; persecution
    as socially situated phenomenon, 57;
    regional variations in, 97–98; relational
    harms fueled by, 10, 122; and solidarity,
    135; targets of, 51; transmission of, 34. See
    also homophobia; persecution; violence
Trump administration, 6, 94, 138, 180n2,
    191n67
Trump, Donald, 94, 132
Tschalaer, Mengia, 47–49, 57, 60, 165n27,
    169n76
Tunisia, 172n20
Türkiye, 67, 172n21

Uganda, 47–50, 52, 88, 96, 98, 157n11
Ukraine, 8, 62–66, 75, 128
UNHCR. See United Nations High Commis-
    sioner for Refugees
United Kingdom, 4–5, 7, 9, 21, 36; Abderrahim
    El Habachi fleeing to, 121–22; accepting
    claims of couples, 120; asylum interviews
    in, 84; child refugees receiving status in,
    109; "cracking down" on human trafficking
    and smuggling, 68; detention centers in,
    91; fleeing from Nigeria to, 22–26, 129;
    homelessness in, 37; House of Lords defin-
    ing "persecution," 45–46; No Pride in
    Detention campaign, 133; refugee preven-
    tion regime in, 66; Rwanda and, 68; seek-
    ing asylum in, 66; transphobic movement
    in, 36; traveling to, 42; Yarl's Wood in, 42,
    91. See also Global North; states
United Nations, 111; Conference of Plenipo-
    tentiaries, 107–8; Independent Expert on
    Sexual Orientation and Gender Identity,
    8, 192n2; Office of the United Nations
    High Commissioner for Refugees, 28;
    Working Group on Arbitrary Detention,
    103, 157n10, 186n75–76
United Nations High Commissioner for Refu-
    gees (UNHCR), 77, 176n2, 177n6; defining
    family unit, 109; Executive Committee,
    108; on gender-related persecution,
    162n3; and Kakuma refugee camp
    dilemma, 88–89, 98–99; pursuing alter-
    natives to camps, 103

United States, 7, 20, 31–32; Andry José
    Hernández Romero in, 6–7; asylum inter-
    views in, 84; Black Lives Matter move-
    ment in, 54; brutality against queer and
    trans subjects in, 54–55; and containment,
    87–90; courtroom scene in, 1–3; ending
    right to seek asylum or resettlement in, 6;
    gender-based asylum in, 49, 57; homeless-
    ness in, 37; legal spouses in, 110; LGBTIQ
    vulnerability narrative in, 126; "migrant
    caravan" coverage, 104–6; and problems
    of containment, 93–95; queer kinship in,
    115–18; "rainbow caravan" reaching, 105;
    recognizing asylum eligibility, 4; and refu-
    gee prevention regime, 67; right to queer
    family reunion in, 119; surveillance of
    Black citizens in, 69; Underground Rail-
    road in, 76; undermined bulwarks of, 138.
    See also Global North; states
Universal Declaration of Human Rights, 107
universities, 138, 196n3

Valdez, Inéz, 130
Vallianatos, Gregory, 95
Venezuela, 116, 136–38
Victor, case of, 22–26, 131
violence: acts of, 1, 22, 35, 43, 47, 52–53, 99,
    165n27; domestic violence, 58, 60, 128,
    169n75; ever-present a bettor of, 24;
    forms of, 49, 55, 58, 82, 87, 125, 169n75;
    gender-based violence, 44, 54, 162n3,
    169n75; generalized violence, 104, 125;
    homophobic violence, 1, 47, 49; interpre-
    tations of, 50–56; intrafamilial violence,
    18, 26, 39, 41, 47; intragroup harm,
    96–100; against LGBTIQ people, 18, 55,
    99, 177n8; necropolitical element of anti-
    LGBTIQ violence, 54–55; normalization
    of, 50; persecution as socially situated
    phenomenon, 56–61; prejudice-based
    violence, 18, 33–34, 47, 49, 52–53, 60;
    "private" forms of, 49; queer interpreta-
    tions of, 50–56; sexual violence, 60, 83,
    168n69, 177n6; structural violence, 55. See
    also homophobia; transphobia
Vitikainen, Annamari, 125
Vogel, Katrin, 116
"Vogue" (song), 116
voluntary immobility, 174n47
"voluntary" migrants, 153n44
vulnerability, 2–3, 13, 137, 157n14; asylum
    seekers and, 76; Blackness and, 31; and
    considerations of justice, 139;

containment creating, 20, 98, 100–01, 103; creating new forms of, 92; and disclosing LGBTIQ identities, 94; documenting, 89; exacerbating, 64, 125–26; inherent vulnerability, 17, 97; intersectional identities producing, 48; LGBTIQ refugees as "innately" vulnerable, 17; rights abuses and, 168n69; women and, 17, 58

Walzer, Michael, 123–24
Western visibility paradigm, 58
Weston, Kath, 39, 68, 113, 115
women: Black women, 31–32, 54, 60, 153n43; cishetero women, 43–44, 128; complicating concept of home in feminist political thought, 30–33; confinement of, 31; experiences of, 58, 97, 153n43; family controlling behavior of, 58; and induced immobility, 68–73; and intragroup harm, 97; LBQ women, 14, 18, 44, 56–61, 82–83, 153n48; lesbian women, 44, 51, 57–60, 168n74; locating ideological hatred of, 24; migrant women, 172n20; queer women, 45, 47, 49, 51, 55, 57–59, 141, 168n69; and refugee prevention regime, 66–68; refugee women, 17, 97; trans women, 19–20, 63, 65, 72, 78, 88, 94, 100, 105, 128, 181n6; understanding through neocolonial frame, 97; violence against, 54; white women, 31. See also LBQ women; LGBTIQ displaced people
womenandchildren, 66, 172n17
Women for Refugee Women, 162n1

Yarl's Wood, 42, 91
Yogyakarta Principles, 15
Yoshino, Kenji, 70
Young, Iris Marion, 32–33, 35, 38, 52–53, 166n39

Zacka, Bernardo, 82
Zambia, 89
Zami: A New Spelling of My Name (Lorde), 38
Zelada, Carlos, 150n12
Zelensky, Volodymyr, 62. See also Ukraine
Zi, case of, 63, 69, 72, 75

Founded in 1893,
UNIVERSITY OF CALIFORNIA PRESS
publishes bold, progressive books and journals
on topics in the arts, humanities, social sciences,
and natural sciences—with a focus on social
justice issues—that inspire thought and action
among readers worldwide.

The UC PRESS FOUNDATION
raises funds to uphold the press's vital role
as an independent, nonprofit publisher, and
receives philanthropic support from a wide
range of individuals and institutions—and from
committed readers like you. To learn more, visit
ucpress.edu/supportus.